The Tyranny of the Two-Party System

POWER, CONFLICT, AND DEMOCRACY
AMERICAN POLITICS INTO THE TWENTY-FIRST CENTURY
ROBERT Y. SHAPIRO, EDITOR

POWER, CONFLICT, AND DEMOCRACY:
AMERICAN POLITICS INTO THE TWENTY-FIRST CENTURY
ROBERT Y. SHAPIRO, EDITOR

This series focuses on how the will of the people and the public interest are promoted, encouraged, or thwarted. It aims to question not only the direction American politics will take as it enters the twenty-first century but also the direction American politics has already taken.

The series addresses the role of interest groups and social and political movements; openness in American politics; important developments in institutions such as the executive, legislative, and judicial branches at all levels of government as well as the bureaucracies thus created; the changing behavior of politicians and political parties; the role of public opinion; and the functioning of mass media. Because problems drive politics, the series also examines important policy issues in both domestic and foreign affairs.

The series welcomes all theoretical perspectives, methodologies, and types of evidence that answer important questions about trends in American politics.

The Tyranny of the Two-Party System

LISA JANE DISCH

COLUMBIA UNIVERSITY PRESS NEW YORK

Columbia University Press
Publishers Since 1893
New York Chichester, West Sussex

Library of Congress Cataloging-in-Publication Data

Disch, Lisa Jane.
The tyranny of the two-party system / Lisa Jane Disch.
p. cm.—(Power, conflict, and democracy)
Includes bibliographical references and index.
ISBN 0-231-11034-0 (cloth: alk. paper)
—ISBN 0-231-11035-9 (pbk.: alk. paper)
1. Political parties—United States. I. Title. II. Series.
JK2265 .D565 2002
324.273—dc21
2002022542

Casebound editions of Columbia University Press books are printed
on permanent and durable acid-free paper.
Printed in the United States of America
c 10 9 8 7 6 5 4 3 2 1
p 10 9 8 7 6 5 4 3 2 1

For Steven Gerencser

Contents

Preface

When I began researching this book I hoped it would participate in renewing and reviving a lost democratic strategy by explaining its simple but esoteric practice. The strategy, called fusion, occurs when a third party combines forces with a dominant party or other smaller parties to run a single candidate on multiple party lines in the general election. Its significance is that it defies the foremost commonplace of our winner-take-all system, that a vote cast for a third party candidate is a vote wasted. Unbeknownst to most contemporary voters, third political parties used fusion in nineteenth-century United States to put dissenting views into the public arena and to survive over time, even though they could not have captured popular majorities. Fusion made possible then something that many citizens wish were possible today: to cast a protest vote that counts and that will not throw the election to the establishment candidate they least prefer.

This book makes two central arguments. The first is that the two-party system as we know it shortchanges democracy because it "wastes" the votes and silences the voices of dissenters. The second is that the two-party system, as we know it, is an interloper. There is no constitutional warrant for two-party duopoly, nor do winner-take-all elections necessarily set third parties up to fail. These are political constraints on the value of our votes. They were imposed, in part, by antifusion statutes that Republican-dominated legislatures enacted at the turn of the century to put third political parties out of business.

I would never have heard of fusion had it not been for the Twin Cities Area New Party (TCANP), the Minnesota affiliate of the national New Party. The New Party began organizing in 1992 as a progressive alternative to a Democratic Party that was moving rapidly rightward in search of both money and votes. The New Party distinguished itself from other third-party efforts by focusing first and foremost on winning elections, not on elaborating an ideology. In practice this meant that the party was willing to lend its forces to Democrats wherever a stand-alone third party candidacy would "spoil" the race for a progressive in the major party. Making fusion legal again was critical to the New Party's pragmatism because it would mean that the party could join major-party candidacies on a ballot line of its own. In 1994

TCANP launched a legal and legislative campaign to lift Minnesota's antifusion laws, a campaign that (if all went well) would challenge the constitutionality of antifusion statutes nationwide.

This book is, in part, a product of that campaign. I was an active member of TCANP for the duration of the effort to resurrect fusion. I helped canvass neighborhoods to gather signatures for the fusion nominating petitions, worked on public education materials, and learned how to write press releases and Op-Ed submissions. For just over a year, most of these ended up in party file drawers, as the local media could not be persuaded that this effort was newsworthy.

In winter 1996 an appellate court ruling changed all that by declaring Minnesota's antifusion statutes unconstitutional. The state was obliged to rewrite its law for the November election. Over night, members of TCANP became amateur historians—and lobbyists. We instructed legislators on the past benefits of fusion and attempted to persuade them to bring it back without restrictions. We did the same with journalists. I learned something from this effort that I had previously known only in theory: the very words *two-party system* stood in the way of change.

Legislators cited the "two-party system" by way of explaining why third parties are a waste of state resources. Journalists cited the "two-party system" by way of explaining what is newsworthy. It was not simply that they allowed the "two-party system" to define the parameters of democratic elections and front-page news. They also invested it with legitimacy, as if it were inherently democratic.

In April 1997 the U.S. Supreme Court intervened, overturning the appellate decision. Its ruling impressed me even more with the power that is vested in words. For the majority held that as the "traditional two-party system" had "contributed enormously to sound and effective" government, state legislatures had a justifiable interest in enacting electoral regulations (including antifusion statutes) that "favor" it. Its ruling invented constitutional warrant for one of the most powerful myths of American political culture: that the two-party system is traditional and that it is the secret to the longevity of this democracy.

The Supreme Court ruling forced me to reconsider this project. I had first proposed it, before the ruling came down, anticipating a different outcome. I expected to write a timely book, one that would explain to citizens, legislators, and scholars how fusion had been practiced in the past so that they could best adapt it to the present. As such, the book was shaping up to be a work of "reform political science," harkening back to a scholarly ideal that guided the discipline from its outset at the turn of the century.

Reform political scientists regarded themselves as democratic activists with a professional mandate to produce academic knowledge that could be put to practical use. They imagined that "political science would enter democratic politics not just as an academic field but as part of an entirely new tradition of political thinking and of counsel to the democratic state."[1] They were particularly concerned to open up democracy by reforms to voting and elections.

Admittedly, the affinities of this work to that earlier ideal were somewhat embarrassing. To begin with, those very reformers had laid the groundwork legislatures seized upon to outlaw fusion. This alone suggested a certain caution in the domain of strategy. In addition, reform political science is an anachronism. It came to an end in the 1950s, when the social sciences undertook to model themselves after a natural science conception of objectivity. It was further discredited in the 1960s, when leftists took democracy to the streets, leaving parties, voting, and elections behind as fixtures of the establishment. Although it did not trouble me to violate the canons of objectivity, to put myself on the side of political parties seemed to violate a politics I identified with even though I am too young to have practiced it.

The Supreme Court ruling came as a disappointment and a relief. Although it was a political setback, it restored me to the comfortable posture of critic to the state rather than its counselor. There was no longer a pressing need to explain fusion so that citizens could put it to use; nonetheless, writing the book felt even more urgent. For over the course of the project, I came to believe that a study that would lay bare the myths that keep the two-party system in business could have an even greater impact on the way we imagine and practice democracy than a handbook for relegalizing fusion would have done.

The story of the politics of fusion, past and present, brings to light the tyranny of the two-party system. It shows how dissenting voices are organized out of electoral politics, and provides new motivation for voting experiments to stimulate participation and make this democracy responsive to a broader range of citizens.

Acknowledgments

This project started with a phone call on a summer evening from a union member and activist named Eric Jensen. His mission: to recruit canvassers for the newly forming Twin Cities Area New Party (TCANP). Steven took the call, committing us to what would stretch into more than two years of leg work in third-party politics and more than five years of research and writing to produce this book. As the time line shows, the writing pulled me away from the activism. I regret that. One thing I learned from the experience, however, was that the rhythms of politics differ from those of scholarly production. If I were to write the book, I could not sustain the interruptions, last-minute meetings, and frantic strategy sessions that the activism seemed to demand. From participating in those sessions, however, I gained insight that no amount of research could have yielded.

I am indebted to the many people who took part in building TCANP and waging the struggle for fusion. Although there are too many to mention each one, I am especially grateful to Cara Letofsky, who helped me to respect organizing as a craft and inculcated me in aspects of its practice. Sunday Alabi set the standard for the citizen-activist. I learned alongside my University of Minnesota colleagues M. J. Maynes and Barbara Laslett just how rewarding and how hazardous it can be for scholars to practice politics. Working for TCANP took place on the streets and in the state capital as well. Joe Mansky of the Minnesota Secretary of State's Office generously shared his knowledge of ballot and election law. State Senator John Marty, who did not support fusion's relegalization, took the movement seriously and made reasoned arguments against it. State Senators Sandra Pappas and Ellen Anderson, together with State Representative Karen Clark lent legitimacy to TCANP by accepting its fusion nominations. State Representative Andy Dawkins set an inspiring example for what a politician can be by his principled commitment to democratic innovation, his eloquence on its behalf, and his willingness to burn leisure time to make it happen.

One challenge to writing a book that crosses specialties within an academic field is imagining how it will be received by scholars with whom one does not ordinarily converse. I had a wealth of resources to meet this challenge, thanks to my American politics colleagues in the Department of Political Science at the University of Minnesota who gave me the benefit of their knowledge, not to mention the benefit of the doubt. Larry Jacobs made this a book. He urged me to write it, set me off into the wilderness of party scholarship with a rough map and a great compass, and helped me prune an argument out of an overgrown first draft. Virginia Gray and Bill Flanigan leant me books and bibliographies. August Nimtz first suggested to me that the subversive potential of the *Timmons* case lay in its revealing how the Supreme Court reproduces institutions like two-partyism. Also crucial to realizing this project were opportunities to present it to colleagues and graduate students beyond the University of Minnesota. I thank John Aldrich, Kim Curtis, Jeffrey Isaac, Jim Stimson, and Michael and Catherine Zuckert for inviting me to give colloquia at their departments. I did my first year of concentrated research on this project in South Bend, Indiana, where I was warmly welcomed into the political science community of Indiana University South Bend by John Lewis and where I benefited from the prompt and efficient work of the interlibrary loan staff at Schurz Library.

Many colleagues took the time to read this manuscript and provide written comments. I thank John Aldrich, Douglas Amy, Ike Balbus, Benjamin Barber, Susan Bickford, Bruce Braun, Emily Hauptmann, Bob Grady, Jim Johnson, Jeffrey Isaac, Jason Kassel, Greg MacAvoy, Jeani O'Brien, Jennifer Pierce, Fred Solop, Paul Soper, Les Thiele, and Catherine Zuckert. I am indebted to Andrew Seligsohn, who found the elusive argument of chapter 5. I thank Martina Anderson, whose labor on the endnotes and references shaved two months off the production time of this book. Greg MacAvoy persuaded me that party scholars would actually enjoy reading a discourse analysis of their writings. Susan Bickford lent clarity and focus to the argument at times when I struggled to formulate it. Sam Chambers gave me the gift of reading three drafts of this manuscript, filling the margins with praise, sound rephrasings, and observations that read my mind—even where I had not yet managed to put thoughts to paper. Sam's enthusiastic annotations guided my many revisions of this project and helped to keep doubt at bay. Finally, I thank Benjamin R. Barber, who continues to mentor me as a writer and thinker, fifteen years out of graduate school. Although I talk back to him in these pages as always, I trust he will regard them as a tribute to the example he sets as a scholar and public intellectual.

That Jesse Ventura was elected governor of Minnesota in 1998 drew public attention to third political parties and opened opportunities for me to formulate the arguments of this work to interested citizens. For these opportunities I thank Ethele Krawetz and the members of the St. Paul College Club, the editors of *Minnesota Law and Politics*, and especially Katherine Lanpher, host of *Midmorning* at Minnesota Public Radio, whose listeners brought this project alive.

The University of Minnesota supported my writing with a year's sabbatical, which was funded by the College of Liberal Arts and a Bush Supplementary Sabbatical Grant. I thank Dean Steven J. Rosenstone for endorsing my proposal to the Bush review committee. An undivided summer's work was made possible by a works-in-progress grant from the Minnesota Humanities Commission in cooperation with the National Endowment for the Humanities and the Minnesota State Legislature.

At Columbia University Press I am fortunate to have had the patience, good humor, and excellent advice of editor John Michel and series editor Robert J. Shapiro. John has buoyed me with his jokes about Minnesota's weather as well as its political idiosyncracies; royalties permitting, I hope to send him a Jesse Ventura action figure doll. It has been a pleasure working with Susan Pensak, who made copyediting a creative process and whose precision sharpened my prose.

This is the first time in my academic career that I have written a book whose details I could share with my parents, Ed and Elaine Disch. They raised me to be engaged in politics, taking me on my first political marches during the struggle for integration in the sixties and to my first presidential convention in Chicago, 1968. As lifelong Democrats, they may not agree with much in this book, but they will surely recognize the spirit that animates it.

Steven Gerencser has done everything for this project, short of actually putting words to paper. We joked throughout that he should really have been the one to undertake it, with his mind for the details of politics—especially state politics—his propensity to argue with the radio, and the joy it gives him to talk about politics. I dedicate this book to him for sharing all that with me, for convincing me that I could do it—and so much more.

The Tyranny of the Two-Party System

Introduction
The Tyranny of the Two-Party System

On November 3, 1998, Minnesota's voters handed the nation a big surprise. They turned out in near record-breaking numbers to elect Reform Party candidate Jesse Ventura to the state's highest executive office. Although Minnesotans made front-page news the morning after, it was not for electing their first third-party governor in over half a century. The *New York Times* ran a full-color photo of Jesse "the Body" that said it all: Minnesota's governor-elect is Bozo the clown on steroids.

How could the mild-mannered folk of Lake Wobegon elect a head-butting sport celebrity to lead their state? National and local news analysts cast it as a failure of civic judgment. The *New York Times* charged that Minnesotans were "faked out by an underplayed ad campaign" into believing that a Ventura vote made them "part of a small, independent-minded community making a creative choice."[1] The *Minneapolis Star Tribune* apologized for the election as a "reawakening of a cantankerous populism that has always had a home in Minnesota."[2] One editor at the *St. Paul Pioneer Press* denounced the result as "a triumph for political showmanship, anti-intellectualism and the trivialization of the electoral process."[3]

Jesse Ventura is a political anomaly. This is not because he is six feet, four inches. It is not because he once made a lemon-yellow feather boa the accessory of choice for his pink tuxedo. It is not even because his campaign ads featured him as a twelve-inch plastic action figure and as Rodin's "thinker" (wearing gym shorts). The anomaly is that he trounced two well-respected establishment candidates as an alternative party challenger—and did so without spending a fortune on his campaign, resorting to attack ads, or targeting any single disaffected demographic.[4] Jesse Ventura was every inch the Minnesota phenomenon the pundits made him out to be. But this was due neither to the state's "populist" political culture nor to its hick susceptibility to Ventura's star appeal. The state's election and campaign finance law made it uniquely possible for Ventura's supporters to defy the most prominent of our "copybook maxims about democracy."[5] Ventura invoked this maxim on election night when, finding the one place where the vernacular of action heroes meets that of political scientists, he boasted, "Well guess what? Those 'wasted votes' wasted them."[6]

More surprising than the prospect of Jesse "the Body" as governor was the fact that Minnesota ballot, registration, and election law made his election possible: Ventura subsidized his challenger candidacy with the resources of the very establishment he sought to overturn. Although Newt Gingrich attempted to claim him as a Republican, and others simply called him an independent, the fact is that Jesse Ventura ran as a *party* candidate. He ran on the ballot line of the Reform party, which had achieved major party status in Minnesota by garnering 5 percent of the vote with a 1994 United States senate candidacy. This was significant because of the benefits that major party status carries with it in Minnesota.

When a third party qualifies as a major party, it typically earns a guaranteed ballot line, which is access to compete on a playing field that—while open—nonetheless remains strikingly unequal. Established major parties enjoy credibility with citizens, mass media, and contributors, which ensures they will capture the lion's share of resources, publicity, and votes. In Minnesota major party status brings access to events and resources that offset these disadvantages. Major party candidates enjoy the right to participate in televised debates, town meetings, and other organized opinion forums on public radio and at the state fair. These occasions are significant not only for the exposure but for the engagement: they force establishment candidates to go head-to-head with third-party challengers.

Major party candidates also participate in the state's comprehensive campaign finance program. To major party candidates who agree to accept spending limits and who demonstrate popular support (by raising a sum—variable by office—in fifty-dollar donations) this program provides two forms of subsidy. The first of these is block grant money, which is allocated differentially by office but shared *equally* between the candidates for any given office, regardless whether theirs is a challenger or an established major party. The second of these, which exists in no other state, is the small donation rebate program, which provides in-cash rebates to individuals for small donations. Contribute fifty dollars to the candidate or (qualified) party of your choice and look for a reimbursement check from the state in approximately six weeks. This program recognizes that today's high-technology elections have made political contributions as much or more important a form of political participation as the ballot. It is unique in providing candidates an incentive to mobilize money as they would (ideally) mobilize votes: from a broad base.

The last feature of Minnesota's party system that played out to Ventura's advantage was election-day registration, a reform that the state adopted in

1976 to revive flagging voter turn out rates. Just over 15 percent of the electorate took advantage of the provision in 1998. There is good reason to assume that many of these were Ventura voters. Preelection polling picked up a surge for Ventura in the last week of October; this lured many disaffected and first-time voters to the polls.[7] In most states that surge would have come too late for those voters to register; in Minnesota election-day registration made it a quantifiable promise that a Ventura vote might not be wasted.

Although the significance to Ventura's victory of these regulatory openings can hardly be exaggerated, they were largely overlooked by the media—local and nationwide. Deadline pressure had something to do with this oversight, to be sure. But it is also consistent with patterns of coverage that discredit third-party candidates. It was far less disruptive to frame Ventura's election as a *celebrity* challenge to the two-party system than as a *regulatory* one. To emphasize the institutional innovations that helped make it possible would be to disclose what Theodore Lowi has called "one of the best-kept secrets in American politics . . . that the two-party system has long been brain dead—kept alive by support systems like state electoral laws that protect the established parties from rivals and by Federal subsidies and so-called campaign reform. [It] would collapse in an instant if the tubes were pulled and the IV's were cut."[8]

Certainly, Minnesota had not pulled the plug on the two-party system. Nonetheless, it had removed some of the prerogatives that protect the two-party status quo in most other states. The analysts who wrote off Ventura's election as an effect of "wrestler chic," a harbinger of the untutored voting habits of "Generation X," or as a resurgence of Minnesota "populism" did their readers a disservice.[9] By exaggerating the idiosyncracies of Minnesota's political culture, and glossing over the regulatory innovations that render Minnesota a relatively hospitable ground for third-party movements, they stepped up the life support to the two-party establishment.

Ventura's achievement "wastes" the wasted vote maxim more profoundly than even *he* was inclined to boast because it calls two of our most trusted political axioms into question. The first of these holds the two-party system to be immutable, a "fixed point of the political universe" whose constancy "is mathematical and conclusive."[10] The second, which follows from the first, holds a third-party vote to be "wasted" by the very logic of single-member district/plurality rule. So self-evident are these truths that they compel even those of us who are dissatisfied with the two-party system to cast a vote within its terms—if we vote at all. This produces what V. O. Key has called the "ancient dilemma" of third-party sympathizers.[11] It prevents us from voting our convictions because, as much as we may say that the trouble with the major parties is that there is not a "dime's worth of difference between them," we continue to perceive enough of a difference that we cannot bring ourselves to cast a third-party vote, if doing so might throw the election to the establishment candidate we least prefer.

Ventura's victory challenged the axiomatic status of these truths and pointed to an escape from the dilemma to which they lead. By prevailing in a state where participatory reforms have (unintentionally) created a hospitable environment for third-party efforts, he showed that it is not the "logic" of winner-take-all elections that dooms third-party candidacies to failure but rather the *politics* of the two-party system. Ventura's victory disclosed this politics. It revealed the extent to which "the two-party system" is just another a "regulatory system," one "made possible and constituted through laws," administrative practices, and voter expectations.[12] Like any institution, it is no "fixed point" against which everything else must be calibrated; it is a legislative contrivance that is shifting, contestable, and must be repeatedly shored up for its limitations to appear necessary and its maxims to remain imperative. And shore it up we do: every time we invoke "the two-party system" as a rationale for the way we vote, every time we accept "bipartisan" as a synonym for political impartiality, and every time we succumb without protest to the "logic" that deems a third-party vote to be a vote wasted.

The Doctrine of the Two-Party System

It is no exaggeration to say that the two-party system is the focal point of an American civil religion. As historian John D. Hicks observed in his 1933 presidential address to the Mississippi Valley Historical Association, "There is something peculiarly sacred about it":

> It is like the decalogue, or the practice of monogamy, or the right of the Supreme Court to declare a law of Congress unconstitutional. Right-minded citizens never question the wisdom of such a division of political forces. They see in the two parties a sort of guarantee of good government.[13]

As academics will, Hicks went on to demystify this sacred object. He began by attacking its originary status, observing that although a "good many intelligent voters would be surprised to learn" it, "the two party system was not ordained by the Constitution, [nor was] a division into political parties . . . even desired by some of those who first guided the nation's destinies."[14] He went on to attack its status as simple fact, noting "that the United States has never possessed for any considerable period of time the two party system in its pure and undefiled form."[15] On the contrary, he reminded his listeners that "at least for the last hundred years one formidable third party has succeeded another with bewildering rapidity." And in a third and final challenge to the preeminence of the established parties, he asserted that these "third parties have . . . played perhaps quite as important a role as either of the major parties in making the nation what it is today."[16] To the "chronic supporter of third party tickets," Hicks had these words of comfort: the third-party voter "need not worry . . . when he is told, as he surely will be told, that he is 'throwing his vote away' " . . . [because] "his kind of vote is after all probably the most powerful vote that has ever been cast."[17]

Hicks' words, which would probably be as striking to many voters today as they were when he delivered them, enumerate the tenets of what I term the two-party "doctrine."[18] This doctrine, which contributes immeasurably to rebuffing challenges to the two-party system, consists of three distinct premises. These premises—that the two-party system is original, immutable, and indispensable to democratic progress—can be found in any American government textbook and any election-year newscast.

Scholars have called the two-party system the "most obvious characteristic" of the United States political system,[19] its "most conspicuous and perhaps . . . most important fact,"[20] and "one of the oldest political institutions in the history of democracy."[21] This is the tenet of originality. As Hicks suggests, it represents the two-party system as having been inscribed into our electoral system at its origin by the mandate for single-member district, plurality rule voting.

The second tenet, immutability, holds the two-party system to be a "bedrock" of democracy that is itself unmoved by partisan contest.[22] At once a foundation of United States politics and a force that transcends it, the two-party system is held to ensure third-party failure as a matter of course rather than politics. This tenet combines with the first to assure us that the condition that prevails today—that third parties do not stand a chance in our winner-take-all system—has never been otherwise. Immune to politics, it is timeless and unchanging.

Democratic progress is at once the central tenet of this doctrine and its most counterintuitive element. It falls to this tenet to reconcile the distinctive characteristics of the United States political party—that it lacks a unifying ideology and is far too bureaucratic to be run by its members—with such basic democratic principles as accountability and participation that it seems by its very structure to defy. E. E. Schattschneider explained it best when he argued that our political parties bring us democracy not because we *join* them but because we can *exit* them effectively.

Arguing against critics who denounced United States parties for their lack of accountability to their members, Schattschneider countered that they neither could nor should be member centered. Indeed, he rejected the very notion of "party membership" as a dangerous fiction because it set up expectations that no democracy could meet in the contemporary world. The party as Schattschneider defined it was no principled community, committed to expressing the core ideals of its membership.[23] Instead, he defined a political party as "an organized attempt to get . . . control of the government."[24] Whereas this effort can be "*supported* by partisan voters," it is in no sense joined by them.[25]

How, then, is popular sovereignty possible? Some would answer that popular sovereignty is *not* possible within the United States political system. In fact, the strength of this system is that it asks no more of the citizenry than that they choose their governors from among competing elites.[26] Schattschneider seems to echo this view when he insists that

> the sovereignty of the voter consists in his freedom of choice just as the sovereignty of the consumer in the economic system consists in his freedom to trade in a competitive market. That is enough; little can be added to it by inventing an imaginary membership in a fictitious party association. Democracy is not to be found *in* the parties but *between* the parties.[27]

But Schattschneider sought to go beyond the competitive elites model of democracy by retaining some meaningful conception of mass popular sovereignty; he defined this, however, not in participatory terms but in terms of the capacity for exit. Schattschneider emphasized that voter sovereignty has meaning wherever an opposition vote has a realistic chance to displace the party in power. United States citizens hold their leaders accountable by threatening not to vote for them next time. This threat works because of the two-party system which, because it accords the second major party a "monopoly of the opposition," maximizes the leverage of an opposition vote.[28]

Schattschneider's argument, first published in 1942, was exemplary of a time when scholars believed they had good reason to prefer United States democracy over all others. Scholars proclaimed two-partyism to be "an essential mechanism of democracy" that, by contrast to the multiple-party systems of Europe, presented a simple binary option that "focuses the issues, sharpens the differences between contending sides, [and] eliminates confusing cross-currents of opinion."[29] Well into the cold war the conviction persisted that "where two parties contend, the electorate can choose between readily understood, either-or options of personnel or policy."[30] That either/or choice is said to assure popular sovereignty because it fosters clarity and stability. The same principle surfaced even as recently as the 2000 presidential campaign when the *New York Times* castigated Ralph Nader for embarking on a "misguided crusade" that would "distract voters from the clear-cut choice represented by the major party candidates." The *Times* urged Nader to withdraw from the race so that the public could "see the major party candidates compete on an uncluttered playing field."[31]

Herein lies the central tension of the two-party doctrine. It identifies popular sovereignty with choice, and then limits choice to one party or the other. If there is any truth to Schattschneider's analogy between elections and markets, America's faith in the two-party system begs the following question: Why do voters accept as the ultimate in political freedom a binary option they would surely protest as consumers? Douglas Amy has put it this way: "Just as it would be ludicrous to have stores that provided only two styles of shoes or two kinds of vegetables, it is no less absurd to have a party system that provides only two choices to represent the great variety of opinions in the United States."[32]

This is the tyranny of the two-party system, the construct that persuades United States citizens to accept two-party contests as a *condition* of electoral democracy. I emphasize this term *condition* to play on its twofold meaning as that which is stipulated as requisite to an agreement or process and that which is suffered as an affliction. Scholars, citizens, and even Supreme Court justices have stipulated two-party competition as a condition of a stable mass democracy; it consolidates an amorphous popular will into a public mandate. Even as it facilitates choice, however, the two-party system constricts options to frame the terms of that mandate as a simple antithesis: *This* one? Or *that* one? We accept this oversimplification as ours to suffer—a condition that afflicts voting in a single-member plurality system.

That we accede to this limit on electoral expression has nothing to do with overt coercion. The tyranny of the two-party system is effected by a system of meaning that associates third-party candidates with lost causes, political extremism, and authoritarian populism while promoting established party candidates as the responsible and effective choice. It is also a complex of rules governing ballot access and design, voter registration, and campaign finance that virtually ensures that mounting a challenger candidacy—whether from outside the party or from within it—is a losing cause. It is, finally, an ideology that heralds two-party protectionism as the very measure of political competitiveness.

THE TWO-PARTY SYSTEM AS SYSTEM OF MEANING

Most third parties wither for lack of media attention. Those who make the news might wish they had not, for they are depicted, like Ralph Nader, as a threat to an orderly electoral process, or, like Jesse Ventura, as a lunatic fringe lacking the experience, the principles, and the political government to govern responsibly. As for those who vote for them, they open themselves to ridicule, as when the New York Times dismissed Ventura's supporters for having been "faked out" into believing they had made an independent, creative choice.

Certainly there is some truth to these representations. No third-party candidate has a realistic shot at winning the United States presidency as this electoral system is currently constituted. Consequently, voters who cast third-party ballots believing that they are voting for change are deceived. Mind you, the same could be said for some voters who faithfully cast their ballots with the major parties. Do not African American and left liberal voters make dupes of themselves every time they cede their votes to a Democratic Party that is moving steadily rightward on poverty, crime, and labor (to name just a few key issues)? Why should it be "rational" to cast a major-party vote for a candidate who has no intention of representing you, whereas to cast a third-party vote for a candidate who has no chance of winning is deemed "wasted"? *This* is the tyranny of the two-party system, a tyranny of systematically managed perception.

THE TWO-PARTY SYSTEM AS COMPLEX OF RULES

In the spring 2000 Republican presidential primary, Senator John McCain had to sue his way past New York State's byzantine ballot access rules just to get into the contest. State law requires candidates to qualify their delegates for the ballot by gathering signatures in each of New York's thirty-one congressional districts.[33] This is a laborious undertaking for any candidate, but it is made considerably easier for the party's anointed contender: he or she commands party foot soldiers to do the canvassing and is represented on the ballot by high-profile delegates whose own name recognition draws votes at the polls. In the end McCain was not listed on the ballot statewide. This spared George W. Bush a head-to-head contest with his chief opponent. Party's choice foreclosed people's choice.

This is the tyranny of the two-party system, and it is noteworthy because McCain confronted as a major-party challenger the regulatory barriers that block third-party candidacies nationwide as a matter of routine. Most states regulate ballot access and design, voter registration, and campaign finance so that challenger candidates must exhaust their finances and their volunteer time just getting to the starting line. These regulatory obstacles virtually ensure that insurgent candidacies—third party efforts and, sometimes, even challengers from within the ranks of the establishment—will burn out. More insidiously, they ensure that insurgent efforts will come increasingly to mimic the mainstream, running candidates of wealth and/or celebrity to break into the contest at whatever cost to principle.

The two-party system as ideology

It is said that competition between two parties is both inevitable and beneficial to United States democracy. It is inevitable because, simply put, no third-party candidate can run to win. This is the "law" of single-member plurality systems, which have a seemingly timeless and inexorable tendency to whittle the field of parties down to two.[34] Why two? Although political scientists admit to being better at describing this tendency than at explaining it, most agree that the tendency toward party duopoly has something to do with the privileged position of the second major party in a two-party system. This party's "monopoly" on political opposition gives it an incalculable advantage over a defeated third party.[35] As a nationwide organization with automatic ballot status in all fifty states, its candidates may lose from time to time, or even repeatedly, but the party will endure.

There are at least three reasons why this arrangement is held to benefit democracy. First, two-party competition produces major parties that are "grand coalitions."[36] Unlike their fractious counterparts in proportional representation systems, United States parties conciliate conflict and temper ideological extremes. We trust them "to speak for the nation as a whole—or at least for a substantial majority—and not merely for a small part of it."[37] Second, the choice between only two parties clarifies the vote and produces unambiguous electoral outcomes: Yes or No? Continuity or Change?[38] Third, alternating control of government between one party or the other provides for smooth transitions and "responsible" opposition.[39] A "two-party nation," James Q. Wilson averred shortly before the 2000 presidential election, "makes it easier for the president to govern and easier for the voter to choose."[40] Like so many things American, the two-party system brings us moderation, simplicity, and stability.

Understood as a system of meaning, a complex of rules, and an ideology, the two-party system forms a *common sense* that accords to major-party dominance and third-party failure the status of "what is obviously the case or in the nature of things."[41] It also heralds as the very measure of political competitiveness a duopolistic arrangement that provides the established parties with the political equivalent of a trade embargo.[42] Our political system prices a third-party vote out of the market and ensures that we spend our votes on the two established parties—if we vote at all. The genius of this arrangement is that, unlike a trade embargo, which is explicitly stated and therefore recognizable as an act of power, the two-party system issues no edicts and imposes no injunctions. It is a power-laden and partisan construct that manages to render its own force invisible because it seems to follow from the nature of things.

In other words, the power of the two-party system is the power of "discourse."[43] This is not to say that it exists "only" in words but rather that two-party competition in the United States is no simple fact or object of study. It is the effect of "rules, manners, power relationships, and memories"[44] that mask their power whenever two-partyism is taken for granted as an empirical object (a "system") that follows from the framework of single-member plurality elections.

In the preface to his classic study of populism, historian Lawrence Goodwyn brilliantly argued that industrial democracies have a special need for common sense, which they rely on to reconcile the competing priorities of capitalism and democracy. As *democracies* they must universalize political freedoms; as *industrial societies* they must ensure that an enfranchised and economically exploited population will not turn its freedoms against the economic order. In this context common sense is the most effective form of insurance, because it achieves "domestic tranquillity" without excessive recourse to the police or the military. Common sense produces an enfranchised but inactive citizenry by persuading "the population . . . to define all conceivable political activity within the limits of existing custom."[45] Under these conditions "protest will pose no ultimate threat because the protesters will necessarily conceive of their options as being so limited that even should they be successful, the resulting 'reforms' will not alter significantly the inherited modes of power and privilege."[46]

I take from Goodwyn an important insight about the manufacture of consent to the vast disparities in wealth and power that characterize modern industrial societies. Mass populations assent to these disparities *not* simply because they are won over by bootstrap ideologies and bought off with material prosperity. Capitalist cultural myths must be paired with an equally powerful political mythology about the futility of radical opposition. This is hegemony (although Goodwyn did not call it that); it is cultural warfare waged *not* by indoctrination but by means of institutionalized social and political practices that affect what comes to be taken for granted as fact.[47] Such processes need not put forward an explicit message (like the Horatio Alger story). It is enough to erode the "democratic aspirations" of the populace so citizens "conclude that past American egalitarians such as the Populists were 'foolish' to have had such large democratic hopes."[48]

Important as it is to recognize forms of power that work not by violence but by eliciting consent, it is equally important to recognize that no common sense is ever complete. On the contrary, as it must be perpetually reproduced, it is repeatedly open to failure. It is also open to an analysis that strips culturally dominant constructs of their apparent stability by setting them into the context of the historical battles from which they emerged. I have argued that the election of Jesse Ventura, understood in terms of the regulatory innovations that helped make it possible, opens a fissure in our two-party common sense. It prompts us to conceive of two-party competition as the effect not of a "system" but of historically specific electoral regulations that can be politically challenged. As such, it prompts us to imagine new ways beyond the "ancient dilemma" of third-party voting.

Against the Tyranny of the Two-Party System

This book aims to dislodge "the two-party system" from its privileged place in American thinking about democracy. This is no small task, for as citizens we come to understand the most basic features of politics through this ubiquitous catchphrase. Casually attributed to the United States in everyday conversation, media analysis, American government textbooks, and even specialized studies of electoral politics, the two-party system is typically represented as original, immutable, and a measure of progress toward democracy that should be a model for the world.

In 1999, for example, a failed referendum against proportional representation in Italy and an election in Turkey (for their "sixth government since 1995") prompted the *Wall Street Journal* to warn both governments that they "probably won't be around much longer" because of the "political instability" and "parliamentary stagnation" of proportional regimes.[49] By contrast, the *New York Times* found cause for celebration in the 1997 parliamentary elections in Poland, which showed signs of consolidating its multiparty system into a two-party pattern. The *Times* judged the former Soviet satellite to be "fast approaching *adulthood*" and applauded its voters for "learning about the *realities* of political parties," settling into "politics as usual."[50] Even the United States Supreme Court holds "the traditional two-party system" to be so important to democratic accountability, consensus building, and political stability that "the Constitution permits" states to craft their election laws to "favor" this arrangement.[51]

I undertake to challenge this common sense by telling a history of "the two-party system" from an alternative vantage point that is afforded by electoral "fusion." Also known as "cross-endorsement" or "multiple-party nomination," fusion is a nominating strategy third political parties commonly used in the nineteenth-century to sustain themselves within the winner-take-all system. In a fusion candidacy two or more parties combined forces to run a single candidate on multiple party lines in the general election. Fusion is not an endorsement. It is a multiple-party nomination in which typically a dominant-party candidate ran on the lines of an established party and a third party. The votes were first tallied separately so that each party to the alliance had a precise accounting of its contribution to the outcome, then they were added together to determine the candidate's total share of the balloting.[52]

All but lost to voters and parties today, the strategy was used throughout the nineteenth century, but most notoriously by the People's Party, to make organized opposition manifest at the polls. The fusion tally demonstrated exactly how much the candidate's support derived from dissident constituencies and showed exactly how many votes the candidate stood to lose by failing to remain accountable to that constituency after the election. By amplifying dissenting voices *within* the consensus-building imperatives of winner-take-all elections, fusion provided what one nineteenth-century proponent described as a "mechanism for achieving proportional representation" by other means.[53]

As a protest vote that could be counted, fusion opened strategic possibilities for third parties that no longer exist today. They could "spoil" races, as they do now by siphoning votes from the established candidate nearest them on the ideological spectrum. But they could also *combine forces* with the weaker of the two established parties to run a single candidate on multiple party lines, thereby fortifying and consolidating the opposition rather than splitting it. Fusion was a unique means for dissenting groups to mount political opposition through the electoral process. By making it possible to vote on a third-party line *without* throwing one's ballot away, fusion helped guarantee "that dissenters' votes could be more than symbolic protest, that their leaders could gain office, and that their demands might be heard."[54] Moreover, a well-organized third party that timed its convention right could do more than lend its ballot line to a candidate anointed by the establishment; it could influence that party's nominations, even its policy choices. Fusion turns the conventional wisdom about the fate of third parties in a winner-take-all system on its head. As Howard A. Scarrow has noted, the separate ballot line renders the "single-member-district-plurality system of election . . . positively beneficial to a minor party; it is only because there is only one winner under this system that a major party may be willing to pay the price demanded."[55]

Today, few voters will have heard of fusion, except in New York, where it remains legal and is commonly practiced.[56] Republican legislatures outlawed the strategy beginning in the mid-1890s as part of a package of electoral reforms aimed to weed corruption out of the electoral process. The reforms, which included adopting the secret ballot, implementing personal registration and ballot access laws, and moving to direct popular election of senators and presidential electors, installed unprecedented obstacles to third-party participation in elections. Combined with the changes that accompanied industrialization, urbanization, and state building, the reforms brought the vibrant third-party activity of the 1900s virtually to an end—except in states where fusion remained legal. Though it was practiced in only half as many states, Scarrow has calculated that fusion "reached an all-time high" between 1910 and 1919, when it served as an electoral vehicle for "progressivisim and other expressions of political ferment."[57]

Technical and esoteric as it sounds now, many nineteenth-century dissidents regarded fusion as the only thing standing between them and the tyranny of the two-party system. This book takes up fusion politics as an uncommon vantage point from which to provide a historical perspective on and a philosophical critique of that regime. It differs from existing scholarly works on third parties and democracy because it neither catalogues third-party movements nor analyzes what causes them to emerge and to fail. Its core argument is not about third parties but *against* the tyranny of the two-party system. I contend that the story of fusion, its practice and the struggle to prohibit it, reveals that third-party failure is not endemic to winner-take-all voting. On the contrary, it is an effect of institutional obstacles and ideological fictions that have rebuffed third-party challenges for most of the twentieth century. This is the politics of the two-party system, an arrangement that may rather limit democracy than foster it.

Fusion made a brief return in the 1990s thanks to a United States Supreme Court case, *Timmons v. Twin Cities Area New Party*,[58] that challenged anti-fusion statutes on the grounds that they severely burden third parties' right of association as defined by the First and Fourteenth Amendments. If the Supreme Court had agreed, as many legal experts expected it would, the case would have made fusion legal again nationwide. Instead, in April 1997, the justices ruled six to three to uphold the fusion bans.[59] The majority reasoned that "the traditional two-party system" has figured so centrally in "sound and effective government" that states should enjoy the prerogative to protect it whatever the cost to third political parties.[60] The decision, breathtaking for its endorsement of the two-party doctrine, perpetuated the tyranny of the two-party system in the most obvious way. It represented third political parties as interlopers on the terrain of United States democracy and dismissed fusion as a parasitic strategy for parties that cannot command votes as they ought to—on the strength of their own organizing.

Contrary to that ruling, and to commonsense notions of electoral democracy, I maintain that third political parties were in their heyday an institutionalized vehicle for organized political opposition. When states quashed that vehicle, in part by way of restrictive legislation (including laws against fusion), they raised the cost of political dissent. They also narrowed the democratic aspirations of the voting public.

I do not suggest that voters today are mistaken to shun most third parties as "sure losers" or to dismiss them as "spoilers," extremists, and opportunists that lack the qualifications to govern well. I contend, however, that the place of the third party in the late nineteenth-century electoral system was different in some important respects. Genuine organizations that built from the grass roots, mobilized dissident citizens, and groomed candidates to represent them, these parties were a significant force for political change. Fusion, which helped them to defy the "wasted vote" maxim, and thereby to dispel the "ancient dilemma" of third-party voting, accounts for part of the difference between third parties then and third parties now. Today's voter has lost the fusion strategy together with the legacy of what third parties can contribute to democratic politics: an institutionalized pathway for organized opposition that is not majority opposition. The two-party system, understood at once as an institutional arrangement and powerful cultural logic, stands in the way of reclaiming that legacy.

The Map of the Argument

Chapter 1 examines the two-party doctrine at work at two sites: the grassroots struggle to relegalize fusion in Minnesota and the *Timmons* ruling. I begin by relating the details of the Minnesota effort. I then demonstrate how *Timmons* validated each of the tenets of the two-party doctrine, thereby reaffirming as natural and necessary a legislative contrivance that in fact *regulates* organized opposition out of the electoral process. I judge this decision to be a blow against democracy. I say this less out of a certainty that democracy needs fusion today than out of the conviction that the two-party doctrine inures us against the pathologies of democracy. Our belief in the necessity of the two-party system and in the inevitability of such dynamics as the "wasted vote" maxim helps to render citizen apathy and nonparticipation innocuous. It predisposes us to mistake for systematic properties of winner-take-all voting what are effects of the political struggles that carried this electoral system into the twentieth century.

Chapter 2 takes a close look at these struggles. I date major party duopoly to the turn of the century. I contend that ballot, voter registration, and election law consolidated the two-party system as we know it: a closed system that precludes meaningful third-party competition. This will be a controversial thesis. For one thing, prominent party scholars cite the mid-nineteenth century as the birth of "modern political parties" and the two-party system.[61] I do not dispute that this decade marked the development of the political party as a mass-based national organization. It is true that, from then onward, two parties had emerged as dominant. They monopolized control of the Congress and the presidency, ran slates of candidates in every state, and contested offices at every level of the federal system. And both had developed the tripartite structure—party organization, party in office, party in the electorate—that distinguished the mass parties of representative democracy from the party caucuses of the early decades of the republic. Alongside these important continuities, however, there was one significant discontinuity: the dominant parties did *not* lock out their third-party competitors. I emphasize this discontinuity, and detail the struggle to ban fusion, in order to underscore that both the two-party system and the tenets of its doctrine are twentieth-century common sense.

Chapter 3 analyzes the relationship between party discipline and the discipline of political science. Coupling historical argument with discourse analysis, I trace the lineage of the two-party system through twentieth-century American government and political party textbooks. I do not imagine that party scholars invented the two-party system, nor do I charge them with having crafted their work to inculcate its doctrine. On the contrary, the puzzle of this chapter is that party scholars continue to deploy this term even though most of them deny that the two-party system is real in any straightforward empirical sense.

Chapter 4 situates this puzzle in the context of American exceptionalism, the "national ideology" to which Dorothy Ross has argued that "American social science owes its distinctive character."[62] My argument is not that exceptionalism has determined political scientists' statements about two-party democracy. Instead, party scholarship was one terrain on which contending republican and liberal versions of exceptionalism did battle. Scholars treated the "two-party system" as a measure of the nation's progress toward democracy. It also afforded them a working definition of democracy that could be operationalized by a positive social science. In short, despite its dubious empirical validity, the two-party system provided a moral orientation for popular government and an organizing framework for academic political inquiry.

Chapter 5 makes an intervention into the citizenship debates that have emerged in answer to the purported crisis of American public life. I criticize theorists of democracy who, in their eagerness to imagine more fulfilling forms of public participation, have indulged what E. E. Schattschneider called a "blind spot" for political parties. Enlisting Schattschneider as an unrecognized theorist of democracy, I propose a strategic understanding of democracy—one that focuses more on the features of the "conflict system" than on the character of citizens—to which third parties could be central as an institutional mechanism for organized opposition. I argue that a principal obstacle toward realizing such a vision of democracy are third parties themselves. The contemporary third party is nothing like those of the nineteenth century, which Progressive-era scholars praised for correcting the majoritarian tendencies of two-partyism.

Chapter 6 closes the book with an analysis of election 2000 as an object lesson in the tyranny of the two-party system. I advance suggestions for reform, including an argument for fusion. I argue that, paired with cumulative voting, that strategy provides a means not simply to opening the electoral system up to more parties but to revitalizing the oppositional third-party tradition of the nineteenth century.

CHAPTER 1

The Politics of Electoral Fusion, 1994–1997

At a sparsely attended press conference in St. Paul, Minnesota on July 18, 1994, a third party and an incumbent state legislator made a historic announcement. They proposed to file the state's first fusion candidacy in nearly a century. The proposed alliance would have joined the Twin Cities Area New Party (TCANP) to the Democrat-Farmer-Labor (DFL) Party behind the candidacy of Representative Andy Dawkins. TCANP was the Minneapolis–St. Paul chapter of the national New Party.

What was the New Party? Founded in 1992, the New Party aspired to be a political home for progressives who saw no room for themselves in Bill Clinton's Democratic Party.[1] A coalition of labor, community groups, and disaffected progressives, the New Party had built, by 1994, chapters in eleven states, with a dues-paying membership of approximately ten thousand. The Minnesota chapter had been in existence for just under two years and counted fewer than three hundred members when the fusion initiative began.

Dawkins did not need the support of TCANP to be reelected. An incumbent who had served in the legislature since 1987, Dawkins was so popular with his constituents that they would probably have returned him to the House whether he knocked on their doors to remind them or not. Why would he agree to lend his name—and his credibility—to this tiny party and its esoteric cause? The New Party earned its stripes with Dawkins by supporting his unsuccessful run for St. Paul mayor in 1993, a campaign in which leading members of the Democratic Party came out in favor of the *Republican* candidate, Norm Coleman. That experience, combined with the challenge of representing a district largely composed of working-class whites, African Americans, and Hmong immigrants—constituencies that were increasingly ill-served by a Democrat-Farmer-Labor Party that had turned outward toward the suburbs—persuaded Dawkins of the "big tent" parties' fundamental injustice. To Dawkins, a charismatic "small-*d*" democrat who had made his career out of championing unfashionable issues such as urban renewal, or block grants for low-income home ownership, and would even sport a ponytail for the duration of the 1996 legislative session in protest against a regressive tax scheme, fusion seemed almost tame.

The strategy appealed to him as a means to give relatively disempowered interests more leverage within the major party coalition. It would allow diverse groups in the party electorate to subcaucus, withdrawing first to their own corners to gather strength and only then uniting under the common umbrella. The promise of an autonomous ballot line might also be an organizing tool to increase turn out among people who no longer identified with the DFL but were unwilling to break with it (as that would further advantage the Republicans). Dawkins was in search of an alternative that would not further disenfranchise his district within the two-party system and willing to take a chance that fusion might be that alternative. Together, the maverick legislator and the fledgling party took on the party establishment in the Minnesota legislature and initiated a legal battle that went all the way to the Supreme Court.

We rarely hear the stories of these kinds of grassroots actions. The third-party activists who sought to relegalize fusion reopened a century-old debate about the rights of third parties and the limitations of two-party competition. This was a peculiarly contemporary fight for democracy, not a struggle to win the vote but, in the words of E. E. Schattschneider, a contest "over theories of organization, over the right to organize and the rights of political organizations, in other words, about the kinds of things that *make the vote valuable.*"[2] Although less dramatic than the sit-ins and street protests of an earlier era, contests of this kind are no less vital to the ongoing effort to democratize the United States electoral system than those celebrated struggles. The story of Dawkins and the effort to make fusion legal again is a tale worth telling because it is in the details of such obscure efforts that battles for democracy are fought and—in this case—lost.

Fusion in the Streets

In Minnesota it takes five hundred signatures to nominate an independent or third-party candidate for state legislature. The filing period begins in late June, after the major parties hold their conventions, and extends for about two weeks. Five hundred signatures is a relatively modest ballot access threshold; nonetheless, it posed a challenge for a small party. As every organizer knows, it takes about seven hundred signatures to ensure five hundred *valid* ones, and an experienced canvasser can not gather much more than ten signatures in an hour. Nominating petitions can go more slowly than that because they must be signed by eligible voters in the candidate's district, which rules out signature gathering in shopping centers and other high-traffic areas.

New Party volunteers, many of them first-time canvassers, found themselves going door-to-door, trying to talk their way into apartment buildings to win support for an obscure and esoteric practice. Just finding the words to sell "fusion" at the doors was difficult enough (given the association with nuclear power). The language of the petition made it even more so. The secretary of state's office required that the petition include language committing the signatories to declare that they would not cast a vote in the primary for any office for which they had signed a nominating petition. Although technically unenforceable, the language had a chilling effect on some would-be supporters. How could they know whether TCANP was working *for* Dawkins or was subtly trying to disenfranchise his voting base in order to make way for a primary challenge? The nascent party would never have made its signature quota without reinforcements from the Association of Community Organizations for Reform Now (ACORN), a community organization that was well-established in Dawkins's district for helping low-income residents secure mortgages, find employment, and enforce housing codes on absentee landlords. ACORN lent foot soldiers to the nominating effort together with much-needed tactical advice regarding how to persuade people to sign.

On filing day in July, Dawkins proceeded to the Office of the Secretary of State accompanied by TCANP representatives and ACORN organizers who (truth be told) crossed their fingers that they had met the signature threshold. He filed over fifty petitions, dog-eared and pulpy from being passed hand to hand in the humid Minnesota summer. As expected, Dawkins was informed that according to a Minnesota statute enacted in 1901, "no individual who seeks nomination for any partisan . . . office at a primary shall be nominated for this same office by nominating petition."[3] Unless he was willing to give up his DFL endorsement and withdraw from that primary, the TCANP nomination could not proceed. When Dawkins declared his intent to run as the candidate of *both* parties, the secretary of state's office refused the petitions, and the signatures were never validated.

Weeks later, TCANP filed suit in Federal District Court in St. Paul, challenging Minnesota's antifusion law as an unconstitutional burden on third parties' First and Fourteenth Amendment rights of association.[4] Although the district court quickly ruled to uphold Minnesota's antifusion law,[5] early in 1996 that decision would be reversed on appeal by the Ninth Circuit Court in St. Louis, Missouri. The state appealed the circuit court ruling in turn, which kicked the case to the United States Supreme Court. Oral argument was scheduled for fall 1996. All told, Dawkins's TCANP candidacy (certifiable or not) would generate almost three years of litigation and a pronouncement by the nation's highest court.

Fusion in the Legislature

As the case worked its way through the courts, TCANP launched a second line of attack. At the start of the 1995 legislative session the party introduced a new democracy act, a bill that proposed to lift the ban on fusion as part of a broader "good citizenship" initiative. The proposal included the establishment of campaign juries, provision of free air time on public broadcast stations to balloted candidates, weekend voting, and the enfranchisement of sixteen year olds for school board elections as measures to stimulate active and informed voter participation. Representative Dawkins agreed to sponsor the bill, thereby demonstrating that state law could prevent him from *running* as a DFL–New Party candidate but not from *legislating* like one.[6] The bill made little headway. Although it received a hearing in the House Elections Committee, it never reached the floor but was instead relegated to "summer study," where the leadership probably hoped it would evaporate in the prairie heat.

Why should sitting legislators have done otherwise? It is a constitutional prerogative of state legislatures to regulate the time, place, and manner of voting. And state legislatures are controlled by members of the dominant parties. Any successful politician develops a reflex for weighing substantive proposals against the odds of reelection. No doubt most politicians know only slightly more about the law than the average citizen; thus, except in the most obvious instances (such as redistricting), they may not have an intuitive feel for how a given structural change will affect their prospects. Even if they cannot always calculate it, however, they are well aware that there is a politics to what political scientists call electoral "frameworks." Legislative aides, legal counsel, and long-term civil servants are their tutors in this regard. They are the specialists on whom politicians rely to brief them on the current state of the law and to assess the *strategic* implications of structural change.

Minnesota legislators had little need to consult their advisers to recognize that the new democracy act, at least in its fusion plank, proposed to do away with one of the protections that sustains major party duopoly. What could possibly persuade them to entertain it? Powerful arguments could be made *in a context where the two-party doctrine did not sanctify major party duopoly as a democratic design*. But wherever that doctrine holds sway, where journalists pay homage to its tenets as much by the stories they refuse to tell as by those they publish, where academics pay lip service to the two-party system, and where voters take it for granted, the very culture of common sense silences those arguments. Good reasons would not persuade dominant-party legislators to relinquish the privileges that two-party duopoly affords them. As for the press, democracy's "watchdogs," the two-party doctrine robs most well-conceived arguments of the force they would need to persuade journalists to take up the cause.

On January 5, 1996, the Eighth Circuit Court of Appeals forced a sea change when it struck down Minnesota's antifusion statutes on the grounds that they "severely burden the New Party's associational rights and [that they] could be more narrowly tailored (with a consent requirement) to advance Minnesota's interests."[7] The ruling struck at the heart of the two-party doctrine, arguing that "Minnesota's interest in maintaining a stable political system simply does not give the state license to frustrate consensual political alliances." The court continued, tearing down the "ancient dilemma" of third-party voters by depicting it as a "no-win choice" imposed by "statutes [that] force . . . New Party members . . . either [to] cast their votes for candidates with no realistic chance of winning, defect from their party and vote for a major party candidate who does, or decline to vote at all."[8] The appeals court made it clear that antifusion statutes are a democratic affront: they interfere not only with the rights of third parties but with those of voters as well. It recognized the potential of fusion to provide voters with "more specific information about the candidate's views," bring political alliances out into the open, and even "invigorate [the electoral system] by fostering more competition, participation, and representation in American politics."[9]

The appellate ruling was a breakthrough for TCANP. Not only would the party get a hearing for a crucial component of its new democracy act but the practice would be legal for the upcoming election. Plans were laid to pursue nominations of two state senators and two state legislators (including Dawkins).[10] This would require gathering three thousand valid signatures, a goal that was now well within the reach of TCANP's organizational capacities. Although it was still a relatively small party, it had developed in crucial ways since its first attempt at fusion. With funds from the national New Party, TCANP had hired a full-time organizer who had almost doubled the party's membership. It had also put a living wage initiative on the ballot in St. Paul, which had given its members new expertise in signature gathering. Now two years old, experienced at canvassing and galvanized by the court victory, the small party was poised to strike.

Few legislators were ready for them. Most were unaware of what Dawkins had been up to, uninformed about the Eighth Circuit verdict, and unprepared to reconsider a law they barely knew existed. Few legislators had any idea what fusion was; consequently they failed to appreciate what it would mean to have it practiced in the 1996 election, a scant eleven months in the future. Even elections committee members whom TCANP had lobbied during the previous year were confounded by the ruling or persisted in the misconception that it remained up to them to decide *whether* fusion should be legal (as opposed to *how* it would be regulated). As they came to terms with what had occurred, key decision makers, especially in the Minnesota House, grew defensive and resentful; as they saw it, an inconsequential party had enlisted an unrepresentative institution to meddle in the domain of state prerogative.

Many had a knee-jerk reaction against fusion. They saw it as a kind of electoral affirmative action that gave third parties access to the ballot *and to public campaign monies* on votes they had not properly earned but had merely siphoned off an established-party candidate. The state's relatively low ballot access thresholds and its provisions for election-day voter registration already gave insurgents a vital assist: why make it even easier for them? Regardless what a panel of judges had said about the Constitution, it was obvious to them that they would never vote as a body to relegalize a practice that would make it easier for third parties to compete against them.

Much as they might have preferred to ignore the ruling altogether, the fact that fusion *was* legal and *would* be practiced forced their hand.[11] Doing nothing would have left the arena open for nonconsensual fusions: any group organized enough to gather the requisite signatures could have nominated an incumbent legislator for the 1996 election, *with or without* that legislator's permission. Such nominations could be used to sabotage a reelection campaign, by appending embarrassing or outlandish "party" lines to the establishment party standard. Although few legislators imagined that "sabotage" fusions would be likely, they were genuinely concerned that fusion would encourage the formation of "sham" parties.

Legislators' concerns about potential sham parties took two different forms. The first reflected their distrust of each other. They feared that politicians would use the petition process to file their political action committees as third parties, thereby listing themselves on the ballot with a separate party line for every hot button issue that might plausibly bring them extra votes. Fusion would literally turn the ballot into a billboard. The second came from legislators who, like Senate Elections Committee chair John Marty, generally favored participatory reforms but resisted fusion as a naive democratic ideal that would have illiberal consequences in practice.[12] As Marty saw it, fusion was an obscure strategy that would be difficult to explain to voters and be especially unlikely to work as an organizing tool with marginal voters. It could well serve grassroots organizing, but the groups who would make the best use of it would not be on the left. On the contrary, Marty saw it as a back-door passageway for religious interests to tap into public monies through the state's comprehensive program of campaign finance. Sham parties from the religious right would be much more dangerous than the billboard parties that others envisioned. They would intensify tensions within the DFL (whose rural and urban factions divide over the issue of reproductive rights) and potentially redirect public monies in ways that compromise the separation of church and state.

In late March the legislature produced a statute that made fusion legal again but thwarted the spirit of the ruling. It made fusion candidacies technically legal, so long as they occurred between *recognized* political parties with written consent from both party chairs. Whereas the consent provision was not controversial (the language of the appellate court invited it), it was in the definition of "minor political party" that the new law closed ranks against third-party challengers. Crafted defensively to combat sham parties, the statute was produced with as little debate as possible. The DFL leadership did everything it could to foreclose discussion on the floor of the legislature, which of course minimized the coverage it could receive in Twin Cities newspapers and Minnesota's public broadcast stations.[13] The effect was insidious. The leadership squandered a perfect opportunity to educate the public about the new voting option and thereby made one of the legislators' most powerful objections against fusion—that it was obscure and potentially disenfranchising—a self-fulfilling prophecy.

The legislators who drafted the new fusion law confronted the following challenge: they needed to keep sham parties off the ballot without rendering existing law more burdensome to third parties. Already accused of unconstitutionally frustrating "consensual political alliances," if they acted to devise a remedy that imposed new *obstacles* to third-party ballot access, they risked offending the court (if the New Party were to sue again or the Supreme Court agree to hear the state's appeal) and touching off a controversy the media might take seriously. How to resolve this dilemma? The solution came out of the House Ways and Means Committee: create a new definition of minor party that would be of no consequence *except* in the event of a fusion alliance.

When Minnesota lawmakers looked to the statute books in winter 1996, they were surprised to discover no definition of a minor party. There were access thresholds for putting an alternative candidate on the ballot, but these did not constitute a definition. In effect, a group did not actually have to *be* a party to have a ballot line in the general election; it need only gather the requisite signatures to file a nominating petition. The trouble was that fusion nominations clearly put something more at stake than access: to attach a ballot line to an established candidate lent an upstart group credibility and promised significantly greater returns at the polls. Legislators wanted some way to distinguish between fusion-worthy suitors and single-issue imposters. Whereas it would be most expedient to raise access thresholds, this was precisely what they could not risk without appearing obstructionist. Stipulating that potential fusion partners would have to be recognized by the state as qualified minor parties gave them an indirect way to do just that.

The new law managed to hold fusion parties to a higher standard without singling them out for special burdens.[14] While meeting the letter of the law, it was, in spirit, exactly the kind of protectionism to which the appellate court objected—and that I have characterized as exemplary of a tyrannical two-party system. And it probably would have been defensible in principle, if a case could be made for the importance of preventing "sham parties" from using fusion to gain public attention for single-issue causes, or turning the ballot into a billboard. Minnesota legislators did not stop there, however. They paired the new definition with a further stipulation, and an omission, that put the third party in a patently obstructionist double bind.

This was the omission: legislators would not redesign the ballot to accommodate fusion candidacies, for fear that any such accommodation would confuse voters and cause spoiled ballots.[15] Refusing either to list the candidate's name more than once or to provide a means for voters to designate which *party* they supported, they made it impossible to do a separate count of votes cast on the third-party line. The ballot would *list* multiple parties in the case of a fusion nomination; the victory would be credited to just one of them, presumably the largest and most established.[16] That legislators would be so bold as to write a fusion *law* that made no provision for a fusion *ballot* was astonishing. Trivial as it may seem, this omission altogether gutted fusion, which, as the appellate court had made clear, is meaningless without some way of counting the distinct contributions of the parties: "Minor party voters [send] an important message" when "a minor party and a major party nominate the same candidate and the candidate is elected because of the votes cast on the minor party line."[17] By its refusal to redesign the ballot to accommodate an arrow or box that would convey to which party a fusion vote should be assigned, Minnesota had failed to provide any vehicle for that message.

The law compounded the effects of this simple omission by stipulating that the votes cast in a fusion candidacy would not count toward qualifying a third party for either major or minor party status, and certainly not toward qualifying for public campaign finance. To put it simply, if there were benefits to be derived from the fusion candidacy, they would go exclusively to the established party. Moreover, third political parties would suffer for choosing fusion over an independent candidacy. Because the state's position on ballot design left challenger parties no way to claim votes that were *rightfully* theirs, the law effectively forced a fusing party to reestablish itself as a "minor party" with *every* election cycle. This made a fusion candidacy, which the appeals court had recognized as an important means for a third party "to establish itself as a durable, influential player in the political arena," a setback to any minor party that practiced it.[18] With no way to determine what percentage of the vote had been cast on the third-party line, the party would lose its status as a minor party after each election in which it ran a fusion candidacy (unless it managed to meet the 1 percent requirement by means of a stand-alone candidate for statewide office); at the next election cycle the party would either have to run a "spoiler" candidate or exhaust its membership with a yearly petition drive.[19]

The new statute made fusion legal again in name only. In fact, it subverted what the appellate court recognized as fusion's principal benefits to parties. It either imposed unprecedented access thresholds on third parties that chose to exercise their First Amendment right to fuse or else obliged such parties to run "spoiler" candidates to gain access to that right—and then proposed to strip it from them every time they used it.[20] Rather than give citizens a way out of the "no-win choice" to cast a "wasted" vote, a "spoiler" vote, or no vote at all, the new law displaced this dilemma onto the challenger parties. So unfavorable were its terms to the newly defined "minor parties" that the legislature resorted to a most unusual strategy of defending them, by appending a "purpose" section to the front of the law.

A purpose section is an address to the court that clarifies the intent of the legislature on a potentially contentious point. Although such sections are rare—and not usually welcomed by the courts—lawmakers sometimes resort to them where they anticipate further litigation. In this instance the purpose section served to call attention to precisely what the statute itself had failed provide—means for a separate count of the votes cast for a fusion candidate on the minor party line, either by providing multiple listings of candidates or separate listings of parties. The first of these it dismissed principally on the grounds of voter confusion, stating that to "permit the candidate's name to appear on the ballot more than once . . . might give the candidate an unfair advantage and might cause some voters to become confused about how to cast their votes, to vote improperly, and to have their votes not counted." As to the second, the legislators asserted:

> This act does not permit the voter to cast a vote for the candidate's party, because the function of an election in the United States is to

> *choose an individual to hold public office*, not to choose a political party to control the office and because to do so might likewise cause some voters to become confused.[21]

With just a few words Minnesota lawmakers executed a strikingly self-defeating move. They asserted that citizens vote not for parties but for candidates. To a statute that was so concerned about the integrity of parties that it took care to differentiate between bona fide parties and sham parties, they appended a purpose section that appeared to deny the electoral role of parties altogether.

In so doing they went well beyond clarifying the "purpose" of the statute to make a pronouncement on the broader "purpose" of United States elections. And in that pronouncement they destabilized the very basis on which states claim the right to prohibit fusion: that it is two-party competition that brings us accountability and responsible opposition, thereby securing our democracy. By emphasizing the extent to which candidates in today's electoral system act independently of political parties, the purpose section revealed Theodore Lowi's "best-kept secret," that "the two-party system" survives not because it is so integral to the process of government but because it is so well protected by legislative dictate. To put it simply, a statute designed to *protect* the two-party system ended up by eroding the two-party doctrine instead.[22]

Fusion in the Courts: *Timmons v. Twin Cities Area New Party*

If New Party activists found it difficult to get a public hearing for fusion on either the floor of the legislature or in the local media, the situation was quite different in the legal community. Prominent law journals featured articles on fusion before and during the Minnesota campaign. Few expected Minnesota's statute to withstand judicial scrutiny for, even though the Constitution accords states "considerable latitude in regulating elections," the Supreme Court's recent rulings have emphasized that they may not *selectively* discriminate against third-party and independent candidates so as to accord the major parties a political monopoly on electoral office.[23] Since the candidacies of George Wallace and John Anderson, the Court has enjoined state legislatures to eliminate some of the more burdensome aspects of their ballot laws, including disproportionate filing fees, unduly strict regulation of party switching by voters, and impossibly early filing deadlines for minor party and independent candidacies.[24] It has maintained, however, that there is no clear rule of law to guide its determination of when state action is permissible and when it infringes on the rights of parties and voters.[25]

Prominent law review articles have argued that antifusion laws "constitute a significant and disproportionate violation" to the associational rights of third parties that no state interest could be sufficiently compelling to justify.[26] Another defended fusion as an aspect of voters' rights "to associate and to exercise the franchise."[27] As the presence of a party label on the ballot is a "critical voting cue" that "prompt[s] party supporters to vote for the party's endorsed candidate," antifusion statutes "disproportionately burden the members of minor parties by precluding voting cues that are available to the members of other parties." Consequently, the ballot becomes a "a government-subsidized forum" that accords selective benefits to "major parties" it withholds from "minor parties."[28]

These arguments are interesting because they depart so dramatically from the legislative vantage point on fusion. Legislators viewed fusion parties as sham competitors trying to cheat their way onto the ballot and understood fusion as a benefit that "bona fide" parties may withhold. Legal scholars emphasize just how precarious is the established parties' own claim to authenticity and legitimacy as parties because they have secured their own ballot status by designing a system to weight the competition in their favor. From this vantage point it could be argued that fusion is a democratic right tyrannically denied by parties who fear that they could not prevail in a fair competition.

In *Timmons v. Twin Cities Area New Party,* the U.S. Supreme Court ruled six to three to sustain the states' right to ban fusion. It ruling signed onto the two-party doctrine and chose to view the electoral process from the dominant-party vantage point. Taking as given the historical connection between two-party competition and democracy, it held that states are entitled to conclude that political stability is "best served through a healthy two-party system" and that "the Constitution permits" them to enact such regulations as "may, in practice, favor the traditional two-party system."[29] There were two aspects to the judgment. The Court had to consider the third-party claim that antifusion statutes unjustifiably burdened their rights of association and weigh that claim against the state's assertion that antifusion laws served a significant public purpose.

As to the rights claim, the Court accepted the established parties' position that fusion was not a constitutional right but rather a "benefit" that states have no more obligation to provide than they do to "move to proportional representation elections or public financing of campaigns," other reforms that would also better a third party's odds of victory.[30] Moreover, it reasoned that antifusion legislation posed no undue burden on alternative parties' rights of association because it only prohibited their nominating a candidate who had already accepted nomination by another party. Should a challenger party persist in nominating such a candidate, the Court contended that antifusion legislation left it "free to try to convince" its choice to give up the major-party endorsement. The candidate would be free, in turn, to make the change unless "if forced to choose, [he or she] prefer[s] that other party."[31]

It is noteworthy that the majority represents the electoral arena as a marketplace where alternative parties and dominant parties compete on equal terms for the allegiances of candidates and voters. This is one effect of the two-party doctrine, in particular of the tenet of originality, which represents two-party competition as a natural formation rather than a legislative contrivance. Certainly, antifusion legislation does not leave candidates "free" to "prefer" the alternative ballot line. Antifusion statutes are themselves protections of two-party competition that force a preference for the party establishment. No party scholar would claim that alternative parties "start out on equal footing with the Democrats and Republicans" any more than an economist would suggest that the neighborhood hardware store competes equally with the Walmart conglomerate.[32] To begin with, the establishment parties offer their nominees a line on the ballot as a matter of course, whereas alternative parties must mount a labor-intensive petition drive before they can even get to the starting line. Moreover, campaign finance law that subsidizes establishment party hopefuls from the primary through the general election makes no provision whatsoever for an alternative candidate's ballot qualification drive. Just to get to the starting line, then, the third party navigates a ballot access labyrinth (from which the establishment parties have exempted themselves), and does so *without* public campaign subsidies that amount to a "major party protection act."[33]

No doubt a well-funded third party can buy its way past some of these obstacles. But the establishment parties also enjoy prerogatives that money can not buy, such as credibility with the mass media and legitimacy with the voters. From the citizens' perspective there are high costs to a third-party vote. It involves repudiating "much of what they have learned and grown to accept as appropriate political behavior, [enduring] ridicule and harassment from neighbors and friends, [paying] steep costs to gather information on more obscure candidates, and [accepting] that their candidate has no hope of winning."[34] Confronted with a choice between a major-party nomination and a third-party candidacy, there can be little doubt that the prerogatives of major party affiliation would be more "convincing" to the candidate who seriously wanted to be elected, just as the major party line is more convincing to the voter who wants to influence electoral outcomes.

Fusion, which effectively lowers the tariff against alternative party organizing, is a means to offset these protections. For the Court to deem it a third-party "benefit" that states can extend or withhold at will lends a veneer of legitimacy to the naked self-interest of the dominant parties. It also misrepresents the origins of party competition in the United States, which started out as an unregulated domain of multiple-party competition in which fusion was practiced because there were no statutes to prohibit it. Fusion did not become illegal until the turn of the century, when dominant-party legislatures passed antifusion legislation under the cover of good government reforms. By signing onto the construction of fusion as a third-party benefit that states may either grant or deny as they will, the Court establishes as a fundamental right a political prerogative that major-party legislatures granted themselves over a century ago, and it mistakes that right's beneficiary. For it is not fusion but antifusion laws that constitute a "benefit": they enable established parties to insulate the electoral arena against third-party competition. To treat that benefit as given effects a reversal that assimilates antifusion law—which is essentially protectionist—into the marketplace fiction of the two-party system as a competitive arena. Fusion—which flourished in an *unregulated* electoral market—is miscast in turn as a kind of electoral affirmative action for alternative political parties.

Having addressed the rights claim, the majority turned to consider whether antifusion statutes served a significant state purpose. In answering this question, the Court again took the vantage point of the dominant parties. The specter of sham parties, together with the two-party doctrine, figured as centrally in their reasoning as it did in the machinations of the Minnesota legislature. Accepting Minnesota's claim that states have a "valid interest" in restricting ballot access to "bonafide" third parties, an interest in "protecting the integrity, fairness, and efficiency of their ballots and election processes," and a "strong interest in the stability of their political systems," the Court affirmed antifusion law as a reasonable way to satisfy these concerns.[35] The Court imagined that parties would proliferate in a fusion-friendly system. Conjuring what Justice Stevens aptly described as a "parade of horribles," it prophesied elections where the candidate of the "newly formed 'No New Taxes,' 'Conserve Our Environment,' and 'Stop Crime Now' parties" would face off against an opponent running for 'The Fiscal Responsibility,' 'Healthy Planet' and 'Safe Streets' parties."[36] Given easy access to the ballot, these imposter parties would compromise the ballot by using it as "a billboard for political advertising" and confusing voters.[37] In the eyes of the Court, as in the eyes of the establishment parties, fusion was cheating: it allowed third parties to "bootstrap [their] way to major party status" by "capitaliz[ing] on the popularity" of the established party's candidate and siphoning off its votes. States are surely permitted to prevent such havoc. Thus the Court contended that they may have recourse to antifusion legislation to secure "the perceived benefits of a stable two-party system."[38]

Notice the rhetorical shift between the first and second parts of the decision. What the majority characterizes as "horribles" here could just as well be deemed the fruits of an open electoral marketplace. But the Court has abandoned the market idiom, where competition ensures fairness, in favor of a republican ethos that gives precedence to the worth of the competitors and the stability of the system. The majority depicts the ballot as covenanted ground, and the party line as a prize to be reserved for what they term bonafide organizations: parties that achieve access on the strength of their own membership and their own candidates. Thus sanctifying the ballot, the court pretends that the established parties actually earned their place on it. In fact, they *authored* their ballot lines into the very laws that brought the ballot into being.

This shift in rhetoric subtly but significantly alters the case against fusion. In this republican idiom the Court manages to cast fusion as a practice that seeks not simply to compete against but to compromise the two-party system. The fusion ban is no longer dismissed as an insignificant burden on alternative parties that are "free to convince" their nominees of choice. Instead, it holds those statutes to be justified precisely because they stave off the chaotic profusion of third parties. Antifusion statutes have turned from an unwarranted benefit to an *avowed* obstacle that serves states' legitimate interest in preserving two-party competition.

The decision is an exemplary double bind, created by mutually contradictory claims.[39] On the one hand, the Court maintained that antifusion statutes interfere very little with interparty competition for ballot access. On the other hand, it held them to be justified because they restrict ballot access to the point of "favoring" the two-party system. Herein lies the bind. By holding that antifusion legislation is so insignificant a barrier to third-party competition that it does not warrant close scrutiny but at the same time denouncing fusion itself as so much of a threat to the integrity of the electoral process that states are entitled to prohibit it, the Court puts third parties in a situation of contradictory constraints. To argue against the first of these premises—that fusion is inconsequential—is to confirm the second, which holds the threat of fusion to be severe. Yet to speak of reasoning with the Court is to mistake the very structure of double binds, which, as David

Halperin has observed, do not yield to rational refutation. They "operate strategically *by means of* logical contradictions" to force a single conclusion.[40] In this case the conclusion is that the two-party system—whether we understand it as the default setting of American electoral politics or as the calculated effect of a restrictive covenant—is necessary to democratic politics. We alter it at the risk of fragmentation and political instability. To accept this conclusion is to reaffirm the distinction between bona fide parties and imposters that was so central to the Minnesota statute and so foundational to the two-party system.

Why should the two-party system enjoy protected status? The Court treated it as self-evident that two-partyism has served democracy since "the time of Andrew Jackson," when it first halted the "destabilizing effects of party splintering and excessive factionalism."[41] Because we owe the establishment of "sound and effective government" to "the emergence of a strong and stable two-party system," states may enact such regulations as "may . . . favor the traditional two-party system."[42] With these pronouncements, the Court revealed itself to be guided not by constitutional doctrine but by a popular common sense.

This was evident to the dissenting Justices, who wondered why the majority saw fit to rule on the two-party system at all. Justice Stevens noted that the Court's emphasis was peculiar, as "Minnesota did not argue in its briefs that the preservation of the two party system supported the fusion ban, and indeed, when pressed at oral argument on the matter, the State expressly rejected this rationale."[43] Similarly, Justice Souter observed "that the State does not assert the interest in preserving 'the traditional two-party system' on which the majority repeatedly relies in upholding Minnesota's statutes."[44] Indeed, the majority did return repeatedly to the "two-party system," to the point where the phrase becomes a mantra. In the decisive paragraph where the Court attempts to forge the link between antifusion legislation and political stability, "two-party system" appears no less than six times and is partnered with explicitly celebratory adjectives such as "traditional," "healthy," "stable," and "strong." So excessive is this unsolicited testimonial to the two-party doctrine that it prompts Justice Stevens to wonder whether an "interest in preserving the two-party system" were not the "true basis" for the majority's holding.[45]

By its preoccupation with the two-party system, the majority put words to what typically goes without saying. In so doing, it proved to undermine the very mythology it went out of its way to affirm. For if the two-party system were so foundational to U.S. democracy as the ruling maintains, why shore it up with laws that "favor" it? If two-party competition were spontaneous and inevitable, an effect of single-member districting, why enact regulations to protect it? Unwittingly, the Court revealed the two-party system to be a social and political contrivance, no immutable foundation but a fragile construct that must be revered and protected if it is to be sustained.

The *Timmons* decision was an undramatic ruling on an esoteric electoral tactic. It might have been the last word in a quixotic struggle that would live on only in a law review footnote, except for one thing. It lays bare the tremendous effort that goes into sustaining two-partyism. The Court embraced as "traditional" an arrangement that it wrote into the Constitution by the power of its own pronouncement. It accorded the states a foundational right to protect a "system" that, by its own account of history, *succeeded* the founding by nearly half a century. Paradoxically, its investment in the two-party system dramatized that this arrangement is not a given but, like any social institution, a configuration of relationships that originated in conflict and must be renewed and reaffirmed to remain meaningful and legitimate.

The Court managed to subscribe to the two-party doctrine and to betray it at the same time: its decision disclosed the political and cultural work that goes into maintaining a feature of electoral parties that United States citizens have learned to think of as a simple fact. A demonstration of the regulations that provide life support to the two-party system *together with* the arguments that serve to redeem it, the ruling provided an opening onto the *politics* of the two-party system.

For the most part, we do not see the work that goes into sustaining this institution. The Supreme Court's ruling made it visible and in so doing opened up a new avenue of inquiry. The two-party system has long been a focal point for political scientists who have explained how it works, speculated on why it may be desirable, and, more recently, analyzed the obstacles that it poses to the viability of third parties. The *Timmons* ruling directs the attention of alternative party scholars away from the obstacles that challengers must surmount in order to break into the two-party system to focus, instead, on the means by which it is maintained as—in the words of E. E. Schattschneider—"one of the fixed points of the [American] political universe."[46] Chapter 2 pursues just such an inquiry by examining the political struggle from which two-partyism originated.

CHAPTER 2

The Politics of the Two-Party System

Most twentieth-century United States citizens accept third-party failure as a matter of course. We accept that the two-party system as *we* know it has always been, regardless whether it is the arrangement we would most prefer. We so much assume that a winner-take-all system necessarily produces two-party duopoly that, rather than question the institutions that produce them, we take the "dilemmas" of third-party voting onto ourselves.

What passes virtually unquestioned today provoked outrage just one century ago, when laws prohibiting fusion were first proposed. In Michigan, where third parties depended on the strategy for their only victories, one Populist vigorously protested that antifusion legislation "practically disfranchises every citizen who does not happen to be a member of the party in power." Without fusion he predicted that dissenters would be "compelled to either lose their vote (as that expression is usually understood)" or "else [to] unite in one organization." To this Michigan Populist the reform would have an appalling consequence: "There could *only be two parties at one time.*"[1]

The sentiments of this turn-of-the-century Michigan Populist are a potent challenge to the popular mythology that sustains the tyranny of the two-party system, for he neither accepts two-party duopoly as necessary nor relishes it as a democratic boon. If it is possible today for the two-party system to pass both as an American democratic tradition and as the default setting of the United States electoral system, it is because we have lost the history that made this worldview possible. This chapter tells some of that lost history, using it to argue that the two-party system as *we* know it dates not to the mid-nineteenth century but to the late 1890s. Not foreordained by the winner-take-all system, electoral duopoly is a legislative contrivance: an effect of ballot and party reforms that were introduced as part of the good government initiative that occurred at the turn of the century. These reforms were not an unqualified democratic advance. Despite curtailing corrupt party practices, which had their own chilling effects on democratic representation, these reforms installed bureaucratic restrictions that suppress political participation in altogether innocuous ways. As such, they dealt electoral democracy a setback that is most insidious because it no longer seems political.

The Two-Party System: *American Tradition or "Cancer" on the Republic?

E. E. Schattschneider once called political parties "orphans of political philosophy."[2] This is surely true, as the activities of contemporary political parties rarely live up to the deliberative and participatory ideals that many canonical and contemporary theorists set for democracy. Nonetheless, we would do well to amend Schattschneider's insight to recognize that these orphans of political philosophy are also bastard offspring of the American founding. Their history flaunts the two-party doctrine because they are far from original features of the nation's politics.

On the contrary, Europeans practiced politics on this continent for nearly two hundred years before political parties first emerged. There were no parties during the colonial period, despite "the vitality of representative institutions in all of the colonies."[3] The revolution was accomplished without them. The Constitution accorded them no place in the new republic. And the framers would hardly have welcomed their development. As one early party authority put it,

> Assuredly nothing would have been more incomprehensible and astonishing to the framers of the constitution than to have been informed that a political jurisdiction would be established, unknown to the constitution and without warrant of law, whose determinations would be recognized as entitled to delineate the policy of the administration and bind the proceedings of Congress.[4]

Federalist no. 10 testifies to the validity of this judgment. In it Madison famously sketched the architecture for a system that was to frustrate "communication and concert" of the people, to insulate representatives against the vagaries of public opinion, and to disperse popular majorities—a design that would forestall virtually every party function.[5] Contrary to the *Timmons* case, ours is not a two-party tradition. It is not a *party* tradition at all. For most of the eighteenth century Americans regarded party spirit as "a gangrene, a cancer, which patriotic statesmen should combine to eradicate."[6]

Party activity first emerged in the 1790s, when the Jeffersonian Republicans organized against the Federalists. Although some scholars like to imagine that this contest "marked the first full opportunity for the electorate to choose between two established, competing parties and their nominees," this is simple anachronism.[7] These early partisans had no thought of making party competition a permanent feature of government. They still equated parties with factions and aspired to eradicate them by the "gentle means of conciliation and absorption."[8] More important, these parties were not popularly based. Instead, they were associations of sitting legislators who neither mobilized public constituencies nor made any pretense of being accountable to them.[9]

From the Colonial period through the founding, and from the Constitution to the early decades of the republic, "the idea of basing government on party seemed like selecting poison as a diet."[10] It required more than two decades of insurgent organizing to force a change of regimen. The first popularly based parties emerged between 1800 and 1820 as vehicles for state-level opposition *against* the tradition of the founding. The states took issue with two key constitutional protections against popular rule. First, they sought to extend the suffrage to nonpropertied adult white males. Second, they campaigned for the right to select presidential electors either indirectly or directly by popular vote as opposed to legislative appointment. By their participation in these struggles the first political parties remade the very architecture of American republicanism. Flaunting the founders' concerns over majority tyranny, they made popular consent the basis of political legitimacy, defined the vote as its means of expression, and thereby installed themselves at the keystone of representative democracy. Transformed from outlaw organizations into legitimate mediators between the people and its government, the political parties became bona fide institutions with lines of authority, rules of procedure, and functionally differentiated tasks.[11]

If the political party is an American tradition, it is only in the manner of democracy itself: as an innovation *contrary* to the design of the Constitution. The parties may well deserve to be heralded as democratic "entrepreneurs."[12] Insofar as they do, however, it is for a transformation that puts them *at odds* with tradition, not in consonance with it.

Party Competition and the "Tradition" of Two-Partyism

What of the distinctive American pattern of two-party competition? Has it been with us from the first, as a necessary consequence of winner-take-all voting and plurality rule? Do the so-called major parties have a greater title to legitimacy than "minor" parties do?

Many United States party scholars cite the late 1830s or early 1840s for the advent of "the two-party system as we would recognize it today."[13] By that period there was regular competition between two nationally organized parties that could be counted on to take the presidency and to trade off control of Congress. The alternation of power between two popularly based parties, both national in scope, originates the "two-party pattern" of today. Although not incorrect, this is a reading of history that selects for continuity with the institutional forms of the past; as such, it overrides some striking discontinuities.

When party organizing first emerged, third parties were there. Almost "as native to the American political landscape as party conventions, smoke-filled rooms, and flowery campaign oratory," they played an active and influential role in elections for most of the nineteenth century.[14] Especially prominent at the state level, third parties took majorities in several legislatures. In the 1850s the Know-Nothings held control of Massachusetts, Rhode Island, New Hampshire, Connecticut, Maryland, and Kentucky.[15] They maintained a presence at the national level as well. Between 1840 and 1860 third parties ran candidates in every presidential contest, regularly capturing 5 percent or more of the popular vote.[16]

In 1860 the unthinkable occurred: the Republican party—a third party only six years earlier—won the presidency. Certainly it cannot be denied that passage of the Kansas-Nebraska Act in 1854 contributed significantly to its jump from minor to major party status.[17] By dividing the Whig Party against itself, this act opened a space for a new party and saved the Republicans from the nearly impossible task of beating out an established party at the ballot box. Nonetheless, third-party organizing also contributed significantly to the new party's rapid rise to power. The Liberty and Free Soil Parties had spent sixteen years cultivating a popular base of abolitionist opposition that became the foundation for the Republicans. Without it that party would have had neither the organized political capacity nor the moral force to take the presidency.[18]

Third-party activity intensified in the post–Civil War period. Between 1880 and 1896 "third party candidates accounted for over six percent of the vote in presidential elections and over ten percent of the vote in gubernatorial and congressional elections."[19] Their power differed regionally, with third parties in the North holding the balance of power "in over one-third of all elections."[20] They were stronger in the Western states, where they commanded numbers sufficient to swing the outcome in "almost one-half of all elections."[21] Elections were so closely contested in states like North Carolina, Wisconsin, Michigan, and Minnesota that "even small third parties often held the balance of power."[22]

Of the many nineteenth-century political parties, the legacy of the People's Party has been most inspiring to contemporary third-party sympathizers. This party, which C. Vann Woodward credits as the "largest and most powerful" nineteenth-century attempt at "structural reform of the American economic and political system," emerged out of the National Farmers' Alliance and Industrial Union.[23] In 1890 Alliancemen running as People's Party candidates scored remarkable victories. They won fifty-two seats in the House and three in the Senate, took three gubernatorial races, and achieved majorities in seven state legislatures.[24] Two years later they had displaced the Democrats as the second major party in South Dakota, Kansas, Nebraska, and Oregon; the Democrats survived in Wyoming, but only by fusing on the Populist slate.[25]

That third parties participated meaningfully in elections, even displacing the second "major" party in a significant bloc of states, is a good reason to hesitate before dating today's two-party system to the 1830s. Yet even though this third party legacy is widely known, it is rarely permitted to challenge the common sense that treats two-party duopoly as the default setting for United States elections. This is a puzzle: how does this common sense persist in the fact of uncontested historical evidence to the contrary? The trouble is that this evidence is interpreted through a twentieth-century lens that makes it easy to discount third-party achievements.

Third parties enjoyed their greatest successes in state and local politics. That few succeeded as national parties, none captured the presidency, and they achieved scant representation in Congress would be good reason in *contemporary terms* to discount their legacy. In the nineteenth century, however, state and local politics far outshone national contests both as spectacle and as site of power. Although the parties were national organizations, they were relatively decentralized and "locally based: local people organized rallies, printed ballots, worked to gain the votes of their friends and neighbors."[26] State- and local-level organizations mattered to citizens, then, because they mattered to the parties, which depended on them for citizen mobilization.

They also mattered because state and local government wielded power. Absent today's federal bureaucracy, local government in particular had an impact on everyday life that is hard to imagine today: "Questions of zoning, of where to build streetcar lines and parks, battles over street lighting and gas services, debates about liquor sales, public school curricula, and Sunday observances—these were at the heart of local politics" in an industrializing, urbanizing nation.[27] To the voters of the nineteenth century third parties competed, and did so successfully, at the center of the political system. It is the twentieth-century predilection for all things national that diminishes their accomplishments.

Twentieth-century citizens also have difficulty taking third parties seriously because, as third-party scholar J. David Gillespie has observed, the very definition of political "party" that circulates in contemporary textbooks has "an American major party in mind."[28] In other words, third political parties simply are *not* parties by the definition that prevails today. This is not to say that scholars agree upon how the concept of party should be defined. Some conceptions are normative and doctrinal, depicting the party as a group of like-minded people who regard politics as a way to promote their values. Others are purely instrumental, as in Anthony Downs's spare definition: "Parties formulate policies in order to win elections, rather than win elections in order to formulate policies."[29] Still others deny that parties are as cohesive as either the doctrinal or instrumental models would have it. They define the party as something like an interest group. It is "an alliance of substructures or subcoalitions" that does not seek to unify its components around a common principle "but 'bargains' with these subgroups, enters into a coalition agreement with them 'for purposes of the (political) game,' and thus develops a 'joint preference ordering' of organizational objectives."[30]

However widely they vary, the definitions of political party identify two things that render it unique among the interest groups and other associations it resembles. First is its "concentration on the contesting of elections" and second is the fact that only the party can attach its label to a candidate on the ballot and command voter loyalty on the strength of its imprimatur.[31] It is in this emphasis on electoral competition and access to the ballot that we see the imprint of the contemporary major party. That third parties are *not* parties by this definition, textbooks leave no room to doubt. Sorauf and Beck have called them "only nominally electoral organizations."[32] E. E. Schattschneider denies that third parties are parties even in name. He writes that it is so rare for a "minor" party to build the electoral capacity of a major party that it "differs from the major party *or the real party* more fundamentally than in size, merely. That is, the minor party is not a smaller edition of a real party; it is not a party at all."[33]

That our very concept of political party takes the contemporary major party as its referent cannot but affect our reception of the nineteenth-century third-party legacy. The logic goes something like this. If third parties are not proper parties as we define them today, then their history has no bearing on that of parties more generally. We may safely imagine the two-party system as we know it to be a constant because however third parties once functioned, they operated outside its parameters. When we follow this logic, however, we make the mistake of extrapolating the characteristics of parties, the two-party system, *and* third parties from the shape they have taken in twentieth-century United States.

To be sure, *today's* third political parties do seem to belong to an altogether different species than their major party counterparts. They do not contest elections to win. They neither build party organizations nor hold conventions nor mount comprehensive slates of candidates. If their ballot line commands voters, it is rarely out of party loyalty or conviction; rather, it draws protest votes for the outsider candidacy of a celebrity, wealthy, eccentric, or fugitive establishment politician. The point is that nineteenth-century third parties bore little resemblance to their contemporary counterparts. Back then, third parties were proper parties. They held nominating conventions, ran complete slates of candidates, built broad-based support at the grass roots, and persisted for more than one electoral cycle. Most significant, they had a strikingly different relationship to the dominant parties because these parties, too, differed from those of the present. In the nineteenth century the "major" parties were not *majority* parties as they are today. From about 1870 onward neither the Democratic nor Republican Party "consistently attracted a majority of the voters."[34] Instead, they depended on third parties to deliver the winning margin.[35] Contemporary electoral politics may have emboldened Schattschneider to claim that third parties are not parties even in name. The nineteenth-century electoral system would have forced him to admit that these parties *did* share the name with their more established counterparts—and a good deal more. They shared candidates, voters, and victories.

What explains the differences between nineteenth- and twentieth-century third political parties? The fierce partisanship of the electorate had something to do with it. For voters who had their party loyalties forged by the Civil War, party was a religion both symbolically—because of the lives sacrificed in that conflict—and literally, as party leaders rhetorically joined party identification to ethnic and religious identity.[36] Party switching between the *dominant* parties was rare; this made third parties an important pressure valve. A third-party vote allowed citizens to send a chastening message to an incumbent without having to defect from one established party to the other.

Electoral rules also account for these differences; fusion, in particular, opened up options for parties and voters that do not exist today. When fusion was legal, citizens could cast a protest vote without "wasting" a ballot or contributing indirectly to the victory of their least favorite establishment party candidate. The fusion ballot signified organized dissent from within the ranks of the dominant party. The elimination of fusion candidacies contributed to the decline of institutionalized third parties "and with them the more complex party system they helped to sustain."[37]

To understand the difference fusion made, it is necessary to know something about how citizens cast ballots in the nineteenth century. Voting was done by party ticket rather than by the Australian "official" or "common" ballot that we use today, which lists the nominees of all the parties on a single ballot that is published by the state and marked in secret. Under the party ticket system, states did not produce ballots or regulate them as they do now. Instead, each party printed its own ballot, usually on distinctively colored paper, and each ballot listed only that party's slate of candidates. There were no access restrictions under this system; elections were open to any party that could afford to print a ticket and pay operatives to distribute it at the polls. As each ballot was effectively a straight party ticket, this system precluded split ticket voting. It also obviated the need to mark, punch, or alter the ballot in any way to signify voter intent. Voters simply accepted a ticket (or were bribed or intimidated into doing so) and deposited it into the ballot box in full view of onlookers.

The party ticket system made fusion candidacies easy to execute because fusing organizations merely listed the same slate on their separate party tickets, with or without the consent of the fused party. In a Populist-Democratic fusion, for example, the members of both parties would have cast identical (or nearly identical) ballots, but—this detail was crucial—these ballots were printed and distributed by different parties. Consequently, fusion candidacies sometimes took place without the knowledge of the voters (who could not see, because the party tickets were separate, which candidates were running for a rival party). The discrete tickets assured the third party an "autonomous identity during the balloting"[38] while enabling its members to cast a protest vote that could count.

It is difficult to know how many fusion candidacies occurred, or how many victories resulted from fusion alliances, because official reports of state and federal elections often credited fusion victories to a single sponsor, usually the dominant-party partner to the alliance.[39] Even when fusion candidacies were recorded, there is no way to tell how they came about. Did one of the dominant parties sign onto a third-party slate? Or was the third party an unwilling partner to the effort by a dominant party to capitalize on its constituency? It was not unheard of for dominant parties to impose a fusion on a nonconsenting third party by appropriating their slate for its own ticket. These involuntary fusions were a particular concern in the West and South where third parties were popular enough to displace the second major party.

Despite the patchiness of the historical record, it is possible to make some claims about the practice of fusion and its importance to third parties. Fusion candidacies were widespread from about 1850 to 1900. In 1870 there were 250 such candidacies in congressional and gubernatorial races in more than twenty states.[40] This was neither a local phenomenon nor a short-lived, purely state-level practice, as some have contended. In 1890 210 fusions occurred in thirty states.[41] In addition to congressional and gubernatorial races, they occurred in presidential elections as well as in state legislative and local contests. Although there were only three presidential fusion candidacies of any significance, fusion was used in governor's races at least fifty-one times across twenty-four states.[42] In the 1850s the Free Soil Party allied with both the Whigs and the Republicans to elect governors in Iowa, New York, and Wisconsin.[43] In the 1870s and 1880s Greenback-Democrat alliances produced fusion governors (who were credited to the Democrats) in Maine, Massachusetts and Michigan. Similarly, in the 1890s, Populist-Democrat fusions elected governors in the Midwest and West. Only in Kansas were Populist-Democrat gubernatorial victories credited to the Populists, in the cases of Governors Lewelling (1892) and Leedy (1896).[44]

What made electoral fusion so attractive during this period? To begin with, closely contested elections made it strategically significant for both dominant and third parties. Votes cast on the third-party line could sometimes win elections, often "spoil" them, and—thanks to fusion—secure the win for a dominant-party candidate. This made fusion candidacies much more than a parasitic benefit for third parties who sought to attach themselves to establishment nominees. Dominant-party candidates actively sought out alliances with third parties. Wherever these parties commanded significant popular support, a fusion candidacy was often as critical to the survival of the dominant party as it was to the challenger. In the 1890s the Kansas Democratic Party fused on the Populist ballot, accepting the third party's nominees wholesale so as not to lose its position as the second major party.[45] Even in Michigan and Wisconsin, where the People's Party polled considerably less than it did in Kansas (under 5 percent of the vote), its separate party line still held "the balance of power in the closely contested electorate; when delivered to Democratic candidates through fusion . . . it sufficed to bring about the only Republican losses on the state ticket."[46] These elections taught Democrats a simple message: fuse or lose.

In the nineteenth century, third parties and "major" parties not only resembled each other structurally; they actually depended on each other. As a result, voters from the mid- to the late-nineteenth century did not regard a third-party ballot as a wasted ballot: it was a force that enabled dissenters to swing the "balance of power."[47] Dissenters wielded power, in part, because elections then were more closely contested than they are today. But they could not have done it without recourse to fusion, a nominating strategy that is no longer available.

The point of this history is that as much as we may think that two-party duopoly is the default setting of this electoral system, it is not. Because of the oddities of the nineteenth century ballot, fusion candidacies were the given—they had to be legislated out of existence. This belies the notion that single-member districts/plurality elections are sufficient in themselves to "condemn [third parties] to a position of unimportance," as prominent party scholars have maintained.[48] Whereas our first-past-the-post arrangement has certainly limited the capacities of third parties, it does not lock them out of the electoral arena as a matter of course.

The Deinstitutionalization of Third-Party Opposition

The electoral successes of the nineteenth-century third parties, together with their distinctive organizational form, came to an end at the turn of the century. I take their decline, together with the legislation that helped precipitate it, as reason to argue that the two-party system as we know it is a late-nineteenth-century invention. It is an effect of reforms that both cleaned up the electoral process and transformed the American state. Against this contention it could be argued that the decline of third parties was part of a weakening of political parties more generally. Although there would be some truth to this objection, it must be recognized that this period of reform did not affect all political parties equally. Even though the party generally lost ground as an institution, the dominant parties were fortified in specific ways.

The late Populist through the Progressive era was a "watershed" for American political development. As Stephen Skowronek has argued, it was a period of state building that transformed a "fragmented institutional structure" whose integrity derived from the "routines" of courts and parties into a more centralized government by "national administrative apparatus."[49] This transformation was achieved at great cost to political parties.

Party politics in the nineteenth century was a potent site of powers, some literal, others symbolic. Parties were self-governing. They orchestrated elections, controlled the production and distribution of ballots, and managed voter access to the polls. They also governed the lives and livelihoods of their constituents by providing social services and distributing patronage. But political parties not only governed wards and neighborhoods, they also invested the local with a sense of *place*. Through such forms of civic entertainment as neighborhood rallies, marching companies, and campaign clubs the parties created local identity and imbued local politics with military intensity.[50]

That politics back then was a thoroughly masculine domain contributed in no small measure to its appeal. Much like sport today, it was erotically charged. Campaigns and elections were a site for rituals of cooperation and competition through which "males [acted] to enhance the status of males."[51] To put it simply: politics *paid*. It paid in cash, in jobs, and in what might be termed the "wages" of manhood, those occasional affirmations of heroic potency that are no less urgent than these more tangible public goods.[52]

Turn-of-the-century reform curtailed these manifold powers. Patronage and electoral reform was in every respect an assault on party prerogatives. Professionalizing the civil service, enacting voter registration and ballot access requirements, adopting the Australian ballot, deciding nominations by direct primary, providing for initiative, referendum, and recall, and amending the Constitution to provide for direct election of United States senators made elections something to regulate and put the state in charge of doing so. State building further attenuated party power, first, by transposing social welfare from a constituent service into an administrative task and, second, by relocating political power away from local governments where "political parties had been strongest" to the national bureaucracy.[53] Writing immediately in the wake of this transformation, Herbert Croly observed that "by popularizing the mechanism of partisan government the state has thrust a sword into the vitals of its former master."[54] In a similar vein, contemporary historian Paula Baker argues that state building effected the "domestication of politics," not only stripping the parties of their patronage but also taming their intensity by converting high-stakes competition into administrative routine.[55]

State building also demoted elections from a direct pathway to power to just one among many arenas of contest. In the new administrative order "legislatures, administrative agencies, and public opinion were established as competing foci of American politics."[56] This new pluralism no longer "presumed a highly mobilized democratic polity."[57] Instead, it fostered interest-based forms of political organizing that were addressed not to the mass electorate but to bureaucratic elites.[58] No longer crucial, the muscular local party organizations that had formerly spurred voters to the polls began to atrophy. Mass electoral participation declined, in turn. Some have attributed this decline to reforms that, while implemented to discourage "corrupt voters," proved incidentally to "[price] out of the system those who simply did not have the motivation to take such action [register to vote]."[59] This interpretation rests on far too voluntarist a theory of mobilization. State-building produced a new administrative order that neither depended upon "labor-intensive electioneering practices" nor subsidized them; consequently, as Mark

Kornbluh has argued, it is not that participation simply declined but, rather, that state expansion precipitated "the *demobilization* of the mass electorate."[60]

The election of 1896 only exacerbated these institutional and legal changes. A realignment of the balance of power between the dominant parties, 1896 transformed the highly competitive party system of the late nineteenth century into a sectional order that gave Republicans a one-party stronghold in the North and West and granted conservative Democrats dominion over the South.[61] Both parties enjoyed such wide margins of victory within their sectors that party opposition *of all kinds* was suppressed. With neither party facing a credible threat of exit, party organization deteriorated. The result, intones Walter Dean Burnham, was that "democracy . . . was effectively placed out of commission—at least as far as two-party competition was concerned—in more than half the states."[62]

The turn of the century was a watershed for American political development. It was also the End of American Party Politics. Never again would party politics be so compelling to voters, nor so central to government. The political implications of this change have been hotly debated. Burnham has denounced this period for transforming the most "thoroughly democratized" political system "of any in the world" into an antiparty, antipopulist, corporate business "oligarchy."[63] Jerrold G. Rusk welcomed it for putting an end to stuffing the ballot box, intimidating voters, and mobilizing citizens by their prejudices, and marking the beginning for a "new pluralist politics in which groups learned to bargain, compromise, and get along with one another."[64] No longer would voters' participation in politics be motivated by an uncompromising intensity, for the new pluralist politics was accompanied by a switch to an "advertising campaign style" in which the "mass drilling of people to vote their party identification" would give way to "politicians attempt[ing] to educate the people on the issues."[65]

Notice that this debate puts the fate of democracy either in the hands of "two-party competition" (Burnham) or in the dawn of pluralism (Rusk). Third political parties fall out of the picture altogether. To write them back in is to discover a qualification to the end-of-parties thesis. Administrative expansion was not a zero-sum game for the dominant parties. Whereas reform curtailed dominant-party prerogatives, especially over the ballot and patronage, it also lent them an institutional legitimacy they had previously lacked. Parties began the century as private associations and political insurgents; they finished it as "public utilities" accepted by law to provide a valued political function, and even enjoying a kind of monopoly on its provision.[66] They came to enjoy this status primarily with the advent of the Australian ballot, a regulatory innovation that the parties received as a mixed blessing—even though they had fought for its adoption. As Peter H. Argersinger has noted, ballot reform brought political parties within the compass of the state by generating an unprecedented field of regulation, "for by providing official ballots at public expense in place of party ballots privately distributed, the Australian system gave the state the authority and responsibility for regulating nominations, campaign procedures, and other party activities."[67]

Certainly, the new ballot enabled the state to exercise unprecedented control over formerly party functions. But it also brought unforseen benefits to the *dominant* parties. First, political parties enjoyed new integrity as "the new rules strengthened central party organizations." Mark Kornbluh explains that even as it weakened them relative to interest groups and bureaucracies, reform meant that "the major parties no longer had to contend with [the] intra party rivalries" that had cropped up under party ticket voting. The Australian ballot system, which required that a single ballot be provided by the state, thereby "produced a single 'official' party candidate for each office," an outcome that could not be guaranteed "when the parties themselves printed the ballot."[68]

Second, the new ballot occasioned new opportunities to fix the competition. Argersinger notes, "those who controlled the state thus gained the power to structure the system in their own behalf, to frustrate or weaken their opponents, in a manner that would have astounded their predecessors and that was not only effective but by definition legal."[69] Whereas the dominant parties exploited this opening to gain the upper hand on each other, they also joined forces to shut third parties out of the electoral arena. Ballot access was a *bipartisan* benefit that the dominant parties used to frustrate their third-party opponents.

As I have noted, there were no formal access restrictions under the party ticket system. Elections were open to all parties that could afford to print and distribute a ticket. To act as a party was to *qualify* as one. The Australian ballot made party fitness a matter for the states to decide. Predictably, major party–dominated legislatures settled that question in their own favor. They granted themselves *automatic* ballot status, while requiring new and "minor" parties to *prove* their qualifications by petition. Ballot access requirements are a double burden to alternative parties; already less well financed, they must deplete their scarce resources just getting to the starting line.

The point is that if electoral reform did weaken the parties' power over campaigns, elections, and patronage, it proved to have unforseen compensatory benefits for the dominant parties. Where third parties were concerned, ballot law—especially ballot access regulation and antifusion statutes—imposed all the constraints but canceled out the compensations. Scholars who bemoan (or celebrate) the decline of parties generally overlook the fact that this transformation did not affect all parties in the same way. The dominant parties were merely displaced from the center of the governing apparatus. By contrast, third political parties were thoroughly deinstitutionalized.

To appreciate the significance of this change, it is necessary to remember that nineteenth-century voters did not chart their political universe in terms of the differences between one party and the other. Before the Civil War abolitionists were not looking to the Whigs to promote their cause but organizing the Liberty and Free Soil Parties. Discontented southerners did not vote Democratic but formed the Constitutional Union and Southern Democratic Parties. From the 1870s to the 1890s, dissidents in the largely Republican West were backing Alliancemen, the Greenbackers, and, ultimately, the People's Party. Turn-of-the-century reform brought an end to what Peter H. Argersinger calls a "major characteristic of late-nineteenth-century politics—the importance and even existence of significant third parties."[70] Even as it sapped mass party organization, this period served to fortify the dominant parties by imposing unprecedented and virtually insurmountable obstacles to third-party competition. In short order this transformation served to lock third parties out of the electoral arena, thereby consolidating the two-party system as *we* know it: an electoral duopoly.

Antifusion Law as Turn-of-the-Century Power Play

The two-party system is a century-old institution. Even as it passes for a necessary and original feature of United States democracy, it is no inheritance of the founding but an effect of political struggles over ballots, voting, and elections. The politics of turn-of-the-century reform has been much debated by historians, political scientists, and sociologists who, as the Burnham-Rusk debate exemplifies, have tended to cast it either as oligarchic conspiracy or public-spirited pluralism. The trouble is that reform was effected by procedural transformation whose partisan consequences are difficult to grasp in such terms. The debate has assumed that power is property to be fought for and possessed—either hoarded (the oligarchy) or shared (pluralism)—by particular social groupings.

It is not always the case that where there is power there will be specifiable group interests, or even manifest struggle. Instead, as James Ferguson has remarked in a different context, "the outcomes of planned social interventions can end up coming together into powerful constellations of control that were never intended and in some cases never recognized, but are all the more effective for being 'subjectless.' "[71] The turn-of-the-century transformation of the electoral process was a planned social intervention that produced such a constellation of control, without being planned in advance. It did mark, as Lawrence Goodwyn has contended, "the political consolidation of industrial culture."[72] As a "political" consolidation, however, it was effected by exploiting the mechanisms of a democratic political process. There was no conspiracy; as a "reconstruction of the *institutional* order of electoral politics" that profoundly altered the conditions of party competition, it may be best understood as a *power play*.[73]

In hockey a power play is an opportunity that is opened up to shift the momentum of the game when a player, charged with a penalty, is removed to the penalty box.[74] The penalty leaves the teams unevenly matched for a specified period (or until there is a score). Whereas the shorthanded team tries to "kill" the penalty, the advantaged team does its best to exploit its superior numbers. If this were all there was to it, the power play would be all power and no play—a contest where only numbers matter and one side has a simple numerical advantage. For the duration of the penalty, however, the shorthanded team has one offsetting privilege. It is exempt from a rule that ordinarily governs play: it may "ice" the puck (shoot it across the center line to the other end of the rink) and thereby kill time to reduce the chance that the other team will capitalize on its one-man advantage.

The beauty of the power play is that it is a game within the game, occasioned by a penalty that transforms the structure and strategies of regular play. It can be termed "subjectless" because, even though the players have everything to do with the power play—they must adapt their strategies to take advantage of it—the power play is not theirs to initiate. The team with the edge in numbers battles for primacy over an opponent that enjoys a slight edge because they can ice the puck.[75] The penalty initiates a hard-fought contest. More so than in football or basketball—where a penalty stops play, compensation is assessed off the clock, and the offended team gains an advantage that is *theirs to lose* (free yardage in football or a free throw in basketball)—a penalty puts the advantage up for grabs in hockey: the teams *play it out*. The power play, then, is a structural opportunity for a momentum shift in which *strategy* continues to matter.[76]

The analogy between hockey and politics is useful in this context because it offers a way to think about power as a matter of strategy and tactics rather than as a calculable property of a group or class. It also dramatizes the difference between a set-up, where the outcome of a contest is fixed in advance, and a structural transformation that puts relations of power in play. Finally, it serves as a potent reminder of the *politics* of the two-party system. No simple consequence of single-member districting and plurality rule, this arrangement is a political creation—but not a political conspiracy. During this turn-of-the-century period, as Peter H. Argersinger has maintained, electoral procedure was "contested terrain in [a] political war of maneuver: While the Populists fought to remove structural limits, major parties counter-attacked to restrict and disrupt third parties, the Populists in particular."[77] What is distinctive about a war of maneuver is that the antagonists are not necessarily fixed (by class, for example, or by gender) and the strategies unfold not by design but as opportunities present themselves.

What occasioned this transformation? It was the instability of the nineteenth-century American state, which at once *fostered* social protest and *frustrated* radical social reform. Stephen Skowronek has argued that the United States government of the nineteenth century was no centralized state but, rather, an "ingenious framework" that derived integrity and coherence from the "routines" of courts and parties.[78] Whereas parties professionalized contests for public office and helped to standardize governmental procedure, the court acted as a "surrogate" administration and provided "the chief source of economic surveillance" in the "public interest."[79] This "ingenious framework" began to break down in the decades following Reconstruction, when there emerged an "impasse" in the relations between the governing apparatus and the emerging industrial economy.[80]

This impasse resulted, on the one hand, from increasing popular suspicion of a governmental apparatus run by party machines. This was matched, on the other hand, by rising citizen protest against unregulated markets in land and agricultural commodities, against deflationary credit policies, and against arbitrary and extortionist railroad charges. It was a distinctive feature of late nineteenth-century politics that agrarian and socialist critics of industrial capitalism made democratic elections a powerful weapon of protest. Difficult as it is to imagine today, when the leading political parties are powered by corporate wealth, radical insurgencies in the 1880s and 1890s found organized expression at the ballot box through third-party candidacies. Their ventures yielded sufficient votes for Gilded Age elites to fear that social dissidents would use "popular electoral mobilization" to stage a revolution against capital entirely by the democratic process.[81] If the electoral process was open to radical opposition, the "radically deconcentrated" apparatus of courts and parties frustrated wholesale structural reform because it had been organized to provide a "regional focus for governmental action."[82]

Skowronek contends that the deficiencies of this apparatus forged a Populist-elite coalition for reform.[83] Regardless whether their objective was to challenge corporate monopolies or to coordinate commerce in "an interdependent industrial society," all the parties to this coalition needed to chasten the party machines and required a national administrative apparatus to execute change.[84] State building offered a "bureaucratic remedy" to which a range of competing interests could be joined because it held out "a dual potential for promoting the further development of the private economy and providing new rights and guarantees to the average citizen."[85] As such, Skowronek argues that it appealed "to all who were fearful of socialists and agrarian radicals but were, at the same time, uncomfortable with making stark choices between support for industrial capitalism and support for democracy."[86] Because electoral procedure was at once a foundation of party power and its most prominent pathology, it would be a prime target for reform—with the ballot at the bull's eye.

It is not difficult to see why electoral reformers would target party ticket voting. Printed and distributed by parties, that ticket was a virtual currency of corruption. Unhindered by voter registration, ballot access requirements, or effective controls on patronage, parties were free to buy votes, sell influence, and populate government offices with their powerful supporters.[87] Bad as it was, however, it would be too easy to dismiss party ticket voting as simply corrupt and to applaud ballot reform as a good government initiative. The party ticket was no simple instrument of corruption, any more than the official ballot was a straightforward mechanism of reform. Party ticket voting emerged not by intent to subvert a democratic process but, on the contrary, to supply a mechanism for popular election where the design of the founders necessarily failed. The party ticket effected a juncture between the mass public and its representatives that the Constitution aimed to inhibit. That document left the conduct of elections to the states. It made no provision for ballots because its authors never imagined that elections would be decided by popular vote. For republican government—which was to be deliberate, dispassionate, and once removed from the people—to proceed by popular will would have seemed like an oxymoron. The party ticket is characteristic of the regime of courts and parties: it is an instance where parties stepped in to standardize procedure for a vital governmental function whose omission was a legacy of the antiparty republic.

The shift from the party ticket system to the Australian ballot, though arcane, was the flashpoint at which the ostensibly nonpartisan projects of state building and good government reform intersected with the popular struggle to challenge monopoly capitalism. Because party power depended on controlling the electoral process, transferring that prerogative to state governments augmented administrative capacity at the *direct expense* of party organization. Weakening party organization proved a boon—anticipated or wholly unexpected, depending on who tells the story—for those who wished to quell agrarian and working-class insurgency: the new procedures turned out to be a disproportionate burden on rural, lower-income, and less-educated voters. Voter registration in particular imposed "informal barriers [that] tended to exclude those who were less educated and less self-confident, and in any case were often administered so as to secure that effect."[88] At the same time as registration made it more onerous for such citizens to participate, thereby raising the cost to parties of mobilizing the vote, civil service reform dissipated the resources that "local party organizations, especially in the big cities, [had used] to enlist working- and lower-class voters."[89] Ballot access restrictions that imposed disproportionate burdens on third political parties compounded these effects by depriving agrarian radicals of their principal vehicle for electoral insurgency.

Ballot access is one provision that contemporary party scholars have studied as a strategy in a war of maneuver by looking for patterns in the ways that states imposed restrictions on third-party electoral participation.[90] Regulation of ballot access, then, was no simple consequence of ballot reform but a highly politicized tactic in a war of maneuver.

It is odd that most scholars have overlooked the place of antifusion legislation in this war, for antifusion law was no less a burden on third-party organizing than were ballot access restrictions. Moreover, it was specifically targeted at states where Republican majorities were threatened by Democrat-Populist fusions.[91] Peter H. Argersinger has deemed antifusion legislation "the most widespread attempt to use election machinery for partisan purposes" to occur during the 1890s.[92] He contends that the statutes "involved a *conscious* effort to shape the political arena by disrupting opposition parties, revising traditional campaign and voting practices, and ensuring Republican hegemony—all under the mild cover of procedural reform."[93] By contrast to ballot access thresholds, which were designed to frustrate third parties, the dominant parties did not set out to stamp out fusion; only later did they recognize that the new ballot format afforded them an opportunity to do so. This lag time makes antifusion law the perfect illustration of a power play, a structural opportunity to shift the balance of power that cannot be planned in advance.

Ballot reform brought fusion under attack because the Australian format, on which the candidates of all qualified parties would be listed in common, raised a question that never needed to come up under the party ticket system: How would states list a jointly sponsored candidacy on the common ballot? Republican-dominated legislatures answered this question in a way that eliminated the threat of potent Democrat-Populist fusions. They contrived to pass statutes that either prohibited the practice in name or proscribed it indirectly by prohibiting multiple listings of a single candidate. What makes this story interesting is that whereas Republican legislatures pushed for antifusion legislation to thwart the Democrats, it proved over time to benefit both "major" parties equally. It contributed to creating a duopolistic two-party system that would accord its second-place major party a "monopoly" on political opposition.[94]

Although it seems mundane, the question of ballot listing was crucial to determining whether fusion would survive the new ballot format: the common ballot made it clear for the first time that a fusion vote was (at least indirectly) a vote for the candidate of a rival party. This was not the case under the party ticket system, where parties issued separate ballots and voters cast—and so, saw—only one. Under that system a lifelong Republican who had joined the Populist cause in the West (and who would never have considered casting a Democratic ballot) could vote for the Democratic slate "without explicitly acknowledging [the] shared behavior or its significance."[95] Many voters must have cast ballots without knowing who was running for rival parties; consequently, they may have supported fusion candidacies without even knowing it. The common ballot would put an end to the fiction of autonomy. It made the fusion partnership visible and hence troubling to citizens in a way that it had never been before.

Given the intense partisanship of the nineteenth century electorate, the shift to the Australian ballot might have been enough to kill the practice of fusion. But rather than let it die on its own, Republican legislators took steps to choke it off. They prohibited a candidate's name from appearing more than once on the ballot, or with more than one ballot line, thereby denying separate ballot lines to the various fusing parties. The restriction meant that a voter could support a fusion alliance only if he were willing to cast his vote on an alien party's line.[96]

As Argersinger tells it, antifusion statutes were an especially pointed illustration of the way that ballot reform became a dominant party–third party battleground. The story begins in Oregon in 1892, where Republican legislators first discovered the power that ballot reform had given them to manipulate electoral outcomes.[97] Republicans enacted the first antifusion provision by passing a statute that prohibited a candidate's name from appearing more than once on the ballot. The new law still permitted parties to fuse, but it denied them separate listings—and this made all the difference. If the Australian or common ballot format made fusion alliances plain to see, because voters could finally compare the slates of the competing parties, the prohibition against double-listing put it in the starkest terms: voting for a fusion candidate necessitated voting on a rival party line.

It is not surprising that the law was immediately contested; it is surprising, however, that the protests came not from the Populists but from the national *Democratic* party, which had planned a partial fusion with the People's Party in the presidential race.[98] This first test of postreform fusion proved to be particularly interesting. Due to an ambiguity in the new law, the Democrats managed to go ahead with the fusion, and to have their fusion candidate (a Populist presidential elector named Pierce) listed twice on the ballot—in Democratically controlled counties only.[99] In those counties the Australian format came as close as possible to replicating the party ticket system. By listing each party's candidates in separate columns, and listing Pierce under both the Democrat and the Populist column, the ballot design represented fusion candidates as discrete choices, thereby making it possible to cast a fusion vote *without* crossing over into the column of a rival party. By contrast, in Republican-controlled counties Pierce's name appeared only in the Populist column, where he was listed with a dual party affiliation as a Populist-Democrat.

If the adoption of the Australian ballot raised the question whether fusion would survive the shift to the common ballot format, the Oregon vote—with its two ballots—provided a test of that question. As Argersinger observes, it was also a demonstration of the "effect of ballot format in shaping electoral outcomes and disrupting fusion coalitions."[100] On the Democratic-designed ballots, where both Populists and Democrats could vote for Pierce without crossing party lines, Pierce received near unanimous support from Populist voters and 92 percent of the Democratic vote. On the Republican-designed ballots, where Pierce was listed in the Populist column but identified as a Populist-Democrat, 9 percent of the Populists defected. The defections were even higher among Democrats. This is not surprising because the ballot design made it plain that they were voting for a Populist elector (because it *listed* Pierce in the Populist column while *labeling* him a Populist-Democrat). In the end Republicans won a majority of the electoral votes; the combined forces of the Populists and Democrats would have defeated them.

Events unfolded similarly in Minnesota, Wisconsin, and Michigan. Republican legislators discovered that the new ballot format made it possible for them to outlaw fusion indirectly, through seemingly innocuous prescriptions regarding ballot design. This strategy was, as Argersinger has argued, an exemplary maneuver: the prohibition of double-listing was an "institutional change . . . purposely designed to exploit the observed behavioral patterns in the political culture" that had *explicit* partisan effects without being overtly partisan.[101] The Republicans who initiated these changes acted not on "some abstract or disinterested impulse toward 'reform' " but in the knowledge that the intensely partisan voters of the time would not support fusion candidates if it meant casting a ballot on what they would have seen as a rival party line.[102] Whereas under these circumstances Democrat-Populist fusions would certainly depress vote totals, separate Democratic and Populist candidacies would split the opposition. Either way, Republican victory was guaranteed.[103]

Under the new regulations parties could still make alliances, but now the members of the unlisted sponsor or sponsors would have to cross party lines to cast a ballot. Consequently, even a successful fusion would be a short-term victory for the unlisted party or parties. Because whatever votes they had drawn could not be counted, fusing parties would lose their right to a place on the ballot and have to petition for access next time around. In order to back a winner, as one contemporary judge described it, the third party would have to " 'surrender your existence as a party and lose your right of representation upon the official ballot in the future.' "[104] The new laws forced third parties to run candidates with no chance of winning simply to defend their ballot lines. By denying those ballot lines any possibility of effecting electoral outcomes, the laws emptied fusion of meaning. Faced with the no-win circumstance of casting a ballot for a candidate who was sure to lose or voting "as members of another party," many third-party supporters chose not to vote at all.[105]

After 1896 state-level Populist parties collapsed. Populist activists, and many of the historians who have told their stories, have blamed this collapse on fusion—not on antifusion statutes but on the *practice of fusion itself.* This charge makes a significant counterargument to the premise of this chapter that antifusion law helped legislate fusion out of existence. To answer that charge requires a few details about what made fusion so controversial in its time.

Many scholars maintain that fusion divided the Populists against themselves. No sooner had the party become an electoral force than its members divided, with "fusionists" pitting themselves against the misleadingly named "midroaders" who were adamantly opposed to its practice. On the one hand, the midroaders argued that fusion made the People's Party a party like any other: "Cooperation with either [major party] would mean the . . . adoption of the sordid practices of voter manipulation for offices and spoils that Populists believed they had abandoned [when they cast off] their former partisan allegiances."[106] Indeed, interpreted in the worst possible light, fusion was a particularly egregious form of horse trading, one that involved a bartering not of votes (as on the floor of the legislature) but of actual *voters* by lending the party's line and constituency to a rival party candidate. Often concluded without the knowledge of the rank and file (and concealed from them by party ticket voting), fusion betrayed "the original Populist demands that the people should participate directly in political decisions."[107]

The midroaders not only opposed fusion on principle but for selling out the party's practical goals as well. All too often fusion victories proved to secure short-term electoral success at the cost of broad social transformation. Because the People's Party did not have a critical mass in the legislature, its victorious candidates found themselves without the means to impose the party's "will or principles on their campaign allies."[108] The Populists found themselves used on election day and betrayed immediately thereafter. Sometimes they even betrayed themselves, capitulating when "Democratic participants in the coalition expected patronage as their reward" and selling out their own rank and file.[109] Argersinger quotes one "despondent Populist" who observed in 1897, "We were successful at the polls but defeated in the legislative halls."[110] One year earlier the ill-fated Populist nomination of William Jennings Bryan evoked even stronger sentiments. Ignatius Donnelly put it this way: "The Democracy [i.e., the Democratic party] raped our convention while our own leaders held the struggling victim."[111] North Carolina Populist Tom Watson was even more adamant.[112] Following the election, he protested, "Our party, as a party does not exist any more. Fusion has well nigh killed it."[113]

Most subsequent historians have embraced this view. They have made fusion a litmus test of Populist radicalism and an exemplar of the tension between movement integrity and party politics that strains any radical group that pursues electoral power in the struggle for social change.[114] I think it is a mistake to cast the question in such stark terms. Fusion is a strategy. Its existence helped third political parties to survive in a winner-take-all electoral arena and thereby made the electoral process more sensitive than it is today to social and ideological change. As Mark Kornbluh has noted, eliminating this strategy not only "undermined the existence of minor parties and deprived the major parties of a key strategic option," it also "limited the *responsiveness* of the party system to changing political circumstances."[115] To pose fusion as something to be either "for" or "against" is to posit a pure space of choice beyond the structural and commonsense constraints of this single-member plurality system.[116] Given that, at present, third parties in the United States have no choice but to compete against the established parties on disadvantageous terms, the more fruitful question is,

Under what conditions does fusion offset those disadvantages, and when does it exacerbate them?

This question will be difficult to consider if we romanticize third parties, expecting them to be a principled, unified, and ideologically pure alternative to their establishment counterparts. On the contrary, it is precisely the strength of the nineteenth-century third parties that they resembled the dominant political parties of *that* century, factions and all. That said, third political parties need to be realistic about what fusion can bring them. Fusion will not establish a party over night (over election night, to be precise). In the nineteenth century fusions occurred most frequently under conditions when the third party had a competitive advantage in the electoral process because it had displaced the second major party, or because it could command the wining margin in a closely contested election. It was a strategy for party *building* but not for party *starting*. Fusion can provide an organized third party with a ballot line and a reasonable assurance of a percentage of the vote. For that percentage to carry with it any possibility of a voice in the democratic process, the party must be large enough and sufficiently disciplined to pose the threat of exit. It must be able to impress upon the partner party what it stands to lose should those votes go elsewhere—either to the rival establishment party or to a third party "spoiler" next time.[117] Fusion votes on a third-party ballot line will be *empty* votes unless the party already has a well-developed grassroots organization. But even a strong third party must be strategic about the races in which it chooses to fuse. It can expect a return on the ballot line only where it selects close contests, or contests for state-level office where its votes can likely provide the margin of victory. In presidential politics, fusion is almost always a self-defeating strategy because even if the votes cast on the third-party ballot line are decisive, the scale of the office is far too great to imagine that the third party would wield significant influence over policy making.

Although it was a controversial strategy, fusion enabled nineteenth-century third parties to survive as parties—to have a place on the ballot, to influence electoral outcomes, to put dissenting views into the public arena—even though they could not have beaten out either of the two dominant parties. Antifusion laws did more than stop the practice of multiple-party nomination. They made this electoral system less responsive to organized opposition and "increasingly inflexible" in the face of ideological shifts.[118] This helped create the no-win situation that plagues today's third-party voter. And it redefined our electoral common sense so that voters take that no-win situation for granted as an inherent pitfall (or even a virtue) of a "two-party system."

Nowadays it may seem quite obvious why candidates ought not run on more than one ballot line at a time; in the nineteenth century it was equally obvious why they *should* do so. Fusion flourished in the nineteenth century not because it was permitted but because it was possible and not prohibited. It was, in other words, the default setting of an electoral system where citizens voted by party ticket. Antifusion legislation changed this default setting. As Argersinger has remarked, with the successful passage of the first antifusion provision in 1893 "the law became so widely adopted in other states—and so useful politically to the dominant party—that its provisions came to be seen *as logically necessary and unexceptionable.* But in the 1890s the law was a source of great controversy and its implementation *fundamentally* changed the existing political process."[119] The Michigan Populist whom I quoted in the opening pages of this chapter sought to underscore the magnitude of the proposed change when he mocked the antifusion proposition as a " 'law providing for the extinction and effacement of all parties but the Democratic and Republican.' "[120] Today, it is all but impossible to hear the sarcasm that this statement must have carried in the past. For the nineteenth-century third party is so long extinct, and today's voter so accustomed to choice between "the Democratic and Republican," that the effects of antifusion law have come to seem self-evident.

With fusion so far behind us, it is easy to mistake third-party failure for an immutable feature of United States elections and thereby to efface the politics of our two-party system. This chapter has sought to bring out that politics by narrating the two-party system as a turn-of-the-century power play. I have argued that antifusion legislation helped to create the two-party system as we know it in this one respect: the prohibition of fusion helped to reconfigure a winner-take-all system that counted the third party vote under certain conditions into one that redefined that vote as a ballot wasted.

Claims about the politics of this period have proven controversial because many reforms, the Australian ballot in particular, had the support of the very third-party activists who would discover only later that it worked to their disadvantage. Even the dominant-party political actors probably did not appreciate the full implications of what they were doing. Whereas Republican legislatures initiated the movement to ban fusion in order to secure their edge over the Democrats, antifusion legislation proved to benefit *both* establishment parties in the end. When fusion was legal there had been multiple-party competition in the United States—plurality rule and single-member districting notwithstanding. Its prohibition helped to transform a system of volatile competition between two closely matched dominant parties into an arrangement that guaranteed such wide margins of victory that third parties would never again pose an electoral threat. Antifusion statutes, then, helped entrench the "two-party system" as we know it: an electoral duopoly that locks out competition from alternative parties, mobilizes less than half of the electorate, and emphasizes national parties and elections over state and local organizations.

This argument stands in stark contrast to that of many party scholars. Whereas they date the United States two-party system to the 1840s, I maintain that this arrangement did not exist until it achieved its defining characteristic: locking out third party competition. If this contention holds, then there is a further irony. No sooner had this defining capacity emerged at the turn of the century than the very term *two-party system* became an anachronism. For the administrative expansion that fixed two-party duopoly in place also displaced party competition as the central mechanism of conflict organization.

To be precise, then, the two-party system as we *think* we know it has never existed. Throughout the nineteenth century, when competition between the national parties largely determined control of the government, this was not a *two-party* system, as we are accustomed to use that term, because a vote for a third party could—under certain circumstances—be significantly more than a protest. By the time the wasted vote maxim actually held true, this was no longer a *party* system because electoral competition was no longer its definitive feature. It had become a *pluralist* system, where party organizing was just one of many competing pathways to power. Why do we take the two-party system so for granted as a simple fact? The next chapter explores that question.

CHAPTER 3

The Two-Party System
Genealogy of a Catchphrase

Contemporary United States voters accept constraints on the "value of the vote" that would have appalled their nineteenth-century predecessors. We take it as a matter of course that a third-party vote is wasted, accepting it as axiomatic that third-party failure is a side effect of winner-take-all elections. To the voting citizens of the late nineteenth century, this was a *political* fact—a contingent effect of the turn-of-the-century political struggles that redefined the parameters of voter participation.

In chapter 2 I used the practice of fusion and the story of its prohibition to challenge the two-party doctrine, that complex of belief that sustains electoral duopoly as original, immutable, and necessary to democracy. Drawing on the work of historian Peter H. Argersinger and institutionalists such as Steven Skowronek and Frances Fox Piven and Richard A. Cloward, I detailed how ballot and voting reform helped to redefine the electoral system of the late nineteenth century into the two-party duopoly of today. Whereas that chapter aimed to disclose the politics of the *formation* of two-party duopoly, this chapter takes a different tack. I trace the lineage of the two-party system through twentieth-century American government and political party textbooks in order to disclose the politics of the *terms* by which this institutional formation is known and spoken about.

The *two-party system* is more than a name for a thing. A concept that we invoke casually, as if it did no more than name a feature of our reality, it forms the very fields to which it seems only to refer. The linchpin for a complex of observed facts regarding the inevitability of third-party failure, and deep-seated beliefs about the superior accountability and stability of two-party democracies, it serves both to orient action and to organize a field of knowledge. In short, the two-party system is a catchphrase.

I borrow this term *catchphrase* from party historian Ronald P. Formisano, who noted more than twenty years ago how scholars inevitably rely on "catchphrases and catchwords" to set the terms for what can be known, explained, and acted upon within their disciplines.[1] This makes any field of knowledge, in some respects, a "shared illusion." It is constituted not by common objects of inquiry but by "unresearched hypotheses" that orient action and speculation because they become "almost imperceptibly . . . imbedded in the conventional wisdom."[2] Formisano found this to be especially true in the field of party scholarship, which had converged on terms such as *party*, " 'party system,' 'democratization,' or the 'decline of deference' " that were generating error and ideology where scholarship claimed to be.[3] This chapter adds the *two-party system* to Formisano's list and undertakes a genealogical analysis to discern when—in the field of American government and politics textbooks—it came to be an object of knowledge.

This analysis is integral to the argument of this book because the operation of the two-party system as catchphrase plays a role in third-party failure. That journalists, citizens, and college textbooks use this term as a synonym for the United States electoral system reaffirms the two-party doctrine as an everyday certainty, a belief system that we trust not because we could make a case for it if it were challenged but merely because it comes so readily to hand. This chapter aims not to debunk this concept, for it is no simple falsehood, but to hold the political science discipline accountable for its part in producing it.

I do not imagine that party scholars invented the two-party system, nor do I charge them with having crafted their work to inculcate its doctrine. On the contrary, few self-respecting party scholars would embrace the two-party doctrine if you put it to them tenet by tenet. As for originality, they would tell you that the framers despised parties. Regarding immutability, they would assure you that single-member districting and plurality-win elections do not produce two-partyism as a matter of course (for, as I will argue, no one takes Duverger's Law *to be* a law except perhaps Duverger himself). And if you asked them whether the two-party system made the difference between democracy and totalitarianism, they would tell you—as Frank J. Sorauf already has—that party scholars' unconsidered "preference" for "a two-party system" is a cold war artifact.[4] If scholars had fixated on "two-party systems," Sorauf contended (with evident sarcasm), it was not because they were or should be normative but because their "infrequent occurrence . . . made them seem, like precious stones, the more valuable for their rarity."[5] Twenty years later Sorauf continued in this skeptical vein, noting that with the "new channels of political information and activity" that education and affluence have made possible, "the democracy of the mass political parties . . . is not necessarily democracy's pure or final realization."[6]

Party scholars are no less skeptical about the very "concept" of "*the* American two-party system" than they are about its doctrine.[7] Austin Ranney and Wilmoore Kendall have protested that it has no place in a proper science of politics. To begin with, anyone who undertook to gather data on *the* two-party system would find that there is not one "single over-all party system in this country" but *fifty* separate ones, as the Constitution leaves it to each state to determine—within limits—ballot design, ballot access, and campaign finance regulations.[8] And even if it were possible to generalize about the party system, two-party competition is hardly the feature these separate systems have in common. Up until the 1970s there were regions of the United States—such as the Solid South—where the second major party was so weak as to make it more like a one-party than a two-party system. That we imagine our democracy to be exceptional for its two-party competition is an ideological effect, the product of what Sorauf called Americans' tendency to forgive "their own one-party systems" and to overlook the fact that "single-party systems within democracies, such as the Congress Party in India or the Mexican party of Revolutionary Institutions (P.R.I.), bear much in common with the Democratic Party of the American Solid South."[9]

One might object that such claims may be *technically* true, but the simple fact remains: at the national level—unquestionably the most important one in our increasingly centralized system—two parties monopolize control of the presidency and the Congress. From any voter's perspective, and, more important, from any candidate's perspective, this is a two-party system. Such an objection reproduces the very commonsense understandings I am attempting to call into question and exemplifies the predisposition to forgive ourselves our one-party regions that so exercised Sorauf. It is simply the case, as Giovanni Sartori has observed, that "two-party system" and "electoral duopoly" are "by no means the same."[10] To qualify as a two-party system it is not enough that the dominant parties lock third-party competitors out of public office; they must be genuinely competitive with each other. Certainly, the United States has enjoyed a "two-party *format*" from its parties' inception because its third parties do not prevent its major parties from governing alone.[11] Nevertheless, it is not a two-party *system* because in a majority of the states, and a majority of elections, victory for just one of the two dominant parties is decided in advance. Thus two-party systems have been a rarity in this country, and "predominant-party systems" the norm.[12]

This is the puzzle. At least as far as the leading party scholars are concerned, the two-party system is not real in any straightforward empirical sense. And yet it has palpable effects on the way we speak about our electoral system and on the way we vote within it. It remains meaningful to refer to the two-party system, to define "rational" votes in its terms, to speculate about its "causes," to bemoan its shortcomings, to subject it to reform, and to debate the ethical and practical consequences of our interventions. Moreover, open to the "political parties" chapter of virtually any introductory text written in the past half-century. Not only will you find the two-party system defined (as if it were a proper object of political knowledge), you will also see it characterized in ways that elide the important distinction between two-party system and electoral duopoly. The two-party system is an electoral arrangement in which

1. the dominant parties "monopolize power, while the minor parties use . . . elections as an occasion for subsidiary political agitation that does not lead to power";[13]
2. "two parties dominate";[14]
3. "only two parties [have] any chance of winning nationally."[15]

It is worth noting that these definitions identify the characteristic feature of two-partyism in *negative* terms. It is defined not by what it achieves (i.e., competitiveness) but rather in terms of the one thing that it manages to exclude: alternate party challengers.

In the face of such criticisms we might well wonder why scholars have not followed Ranney and Kendall's injunction to "abandon" this concept altogether.[16] On this point a passage from Frank J. Sorauf's influential textbook proves revealing. Sorauf asks "how is it . . . that we refer so glibly to the American two-party system" when it is neither conceptually precise nor empirically valid.[17] Dissecting the catchphrase word by word, he rejects *party* system on the grounds that interest-group competition is at least as important to the democratic process as party activity, *two*-party system for "gloss[ing] over the issue of how unevenly [political] competitiveness is spread over the states and localities of the nation," and two-party *system* because interparty competition is but one of the many "relationships and interactions" that comprise the political *system*, as that word is properly understood.[18] It is significant that, although he distrusts it, Sorauf resigns himself to using this vocabulary anyway. He writes that "so ingrained in both everyday use and in the scholarly literature is this concept of the party system that *one has little choice but to work within its terms.*"[19]

This concession testifies to the discursive power of the two-party system. It demonstrates the power of habitually used words to form the facts to which they seem to refer—and to make such formations seem not just real but necessary and incontestable. As such, it also lays bare what I call the *empirical paradox* of the two-party system: we may *speak* of the two-party system but we cannot *know* it. Or, as one colleague put it to me, "Everybody *talks* about the two-party system but nobody really *studies* it."[20]

These remarks are the jumping-off point for this chapter. I contend that the two-party system is more than a term of reference. It is a *synonym* for the United States political system and an *organizing principle* for textbook knowledge of electoral democracy. This is what makes it a *catchphrase*, in Ronald P. Formisano's sense of the term. No proper object of inquiry, it is one of several "unresearched hypotheses" that orient action and speculation not because they are established in fact but because they have become "almost imperceptibly . . . imbedded in the conventional wisdom."[21] The purpose of this chapter is to trace how *two-party system* took hold as a catchphrase. How did it come to be an obligatory term of reference for the United States electoral system? How did it come to frame the delivery of information about that system? How did it come to be understood as necessary to democratic development? And how did it come to be the norm against which other democratic regimes would be compared?

This analysis complements the previous chapter's historical reexamination of the origins of two-party competition by historicizing the very concept of the two-party system. Such an analysis is crucial to the project of this book because it enables me to press beyond the commonsense understanding that a third-party vote is wasted in a two-party system to ask *when* that commonsense came to be. I will demonstrate that academic representations of the United States electoral system have changed over time, that the advent of its representation as a *two-party* system fed the two-party doctrine, and that such formulations as Duverger's Law and Downs's proposition regarding "rational voting" have helped the two-party system be taken for granted as an object of study. I do not propose that the two-party system is a consequence of misplaced beliefs, nor do I contend that if we want to overcome it we need only choose another set. Rather, I take its career in the field of party scholarship to help illustrate that what we say has empirical effects on what we believe to be real and normative effects on what we imagine to be possible.

Party Discipline

In 1922 noted progressive reformer and party scholar Charles E. Merriam observed:

> Although the party system is one of the characteristic features of American public life, it is a singular fact that no systematic description or discussion of the party developed until one hundred years after the sys-

tem had been established. The critical study of the party and its philosophy is practically the creation of the twentieth century.[22]

Why had parties so long "eluded careful and systematic analysis"?[23] One reason was that it was not until the twentieth century that there occurred "the general development of the systematic study of politics."[24] Universities began to detach the study of government and political economy from that of history, sociology, and anthropology in the 1890s, about the same time state legislatures enacted the ballot and civil service reforms that brought political parties within the compass of the emergent state administration.[25] By 1903 the new field had sufficient momentum to found the American Political Science Association. Within the first two decades of the twentieth century political science departments formed in all the major state universities.

Even with the advent of political science as field of study, academics were initially reluctant to turn their attention to the study of parties. Parties lay beyond the purview of the new science of politics because its earliest "practitioners tended to have constitutional, legal, and philosophical interests that excluded the study of political behavior and of less formal political institutions than those of the governmental structure itself." Not yet regarded "as institutional elements in a democratic system," because they had enjoyed no constitutional mandate and still had no legal place in the governmental process, parties were neither "entirely legitimate" as political institutions nor as objects of knowledge.[26] Once the states began to regulate party activity, however, it would not take long for them to be perceived as legitimate in both domains.

The 1920s saw a surge of academic interest in political parties and marked the publication of the first round of party textbooks.[27] Merriam argued that academics were moved to study parties "by the same general influences which brought about the insurgent and progressive movements in the first decade of the century."[28] Whereas Merriam did no more than call attention to the coincidence between party regulation and party scholarship, I suggest that the two were mutually legitimating. The *institutionalization* of political parties that made them respectable objects of academic inquiry relied in turn upon objective scholarly opinion to render that institutionalization legitimate.

What is interesting about the first party and politics textbooks is that the two-party system did not take pride of place in them. Writing in the wake of the institutionalization of political parties at the turn of the century, these scholars were much more concerned to account for what E. M. Sait called the "peculiar importance" of political parties as publicly regulated private associations. Their task was to justify the turn-of-the-century extension of state regulatory power to parties and to legitimate the parties' appropriation of state functions in turn.

Party scholars in the 1920s, then, were principally concerned with legitimacy—that of party activity, on the one hand, and its regulation by the state, on the other. The party institution, although unsanctioned by the Constitution, had become an "unofficial" or "double" government that conscripted citizens into the electoral process and worked the machinery of the state.[29] It was also, having been previously "unknown to law," now "overlaid by statutory prescriptions and mechanically articulated with the government."[30] This regulatory overlay was what most distinguished the American party system and most troubled these scholars who were writing barely two decades after the reforms that had brought political parties within the compass of the state. As Sait put it:

> Here, in the last generation, *a development has taken place which finds an analogy nowhere else.* American parties have ceased to be voluntary associations like the trade unions or the good government clubs or the churches. They have lost the right freely to determine how candidates shall be nominated and platforms framed, even who shall belong to the party and who shall lead it. The state legislatures have regulated their structure and functions in great detail.[31]

Merriam summed it up: "Nowhere has the power of party organization been greater than in the United States and nowhere has there been a more vigorous attempt to restrict and control the party organization than here."[32]

If the two-party system in these works was not yet a regulatory fiction, neither had it taken hold as a catchphrase. Two early scholars, James Bryce (1891) and Henry Jones Ford (1898), did not even use the term. Although the phrase does appear in Charles E. Merriam's *The American Party System* (1922), a leading text of the 1920s, it is only one of several ways that Merriam had of speaking about what he also called the "dual form," the "bi-party plan," and the "bi-party system."[33] He did not use the phrase "party system" as a synonym for "the two-party system" (as mid-century scholars would do). Nor did he make two-party competition a definitive characteristic of the American polity by representing the American party system *as* a two-party system in the way that later scholars would do. On the contrary, Merriam gave this characteristic little more than passing mention—and then only late in the book.

Thus although the phrase had some currency during this period, it was not yet an obligatory referent for United States electoral system. Neither was it the norm against which other democratic regimes would be compared.[34]

Scholars like Merriam, Ford, and Bryce certainly remarked upon the preeminence of the "two great parties."[35] And their work even prepared the way for the more celebratory aspects of the two-party doctrine, because they did tend to accord party dualism an originary footing in American society and temperament. They did not yet *applaud* party dualism, as later scholars would do, but merely remarked upon it.[36]

Charles E. Merriam is a good example of a scholar who took note of the binary tendencies of the United States electoral system without being caught up in the habit of using the term. Merriam presented it as a simple matter of fact that "on the Continent parties are organized upon a multi-party basis instead of the bi-party basis which has been common in England and the United States."[37] Merriam felt no compunction to warn that European parties were prone to instability and fragmentation, nor did he pass judgment on the relative merits of the two models. He mentioned only that the parties in the "bi-party system" are not class parties, and consequently that they were "less homogeneous than in the multi-party system where the party represents fairly definite class or economic interests."[38] In contrast to the pattern that would emerge in the mid-century textbooks, Merriam did not propose a theory of bi-partyism. He did not think it was a phenomenon that called for explanatory exertion. Nor did he set up bi-party and multiparty systems as binary opposites. On the contrary, he suggested that the two might complement each other, proposing that proportional representation "might find a place even in a two-party system," particularly in city elections, "as a means of obtaining fairer representation as between a majority and minority."[39] Although he linked multipartyism to proportional voting, he could not decide whether adopting proportional representation would "have the effect of developing multi-party system in place of the bi-party plan," or whether "proportional representation is . . . the consequence [rather] than the cause of multi-party groupings."[40]

These scholars drew comparisons between the political parties of the United States and those of Europe. It is striking, however, that the opposition between multiparty and two-party systems did not set its terms. Instead it turned on the matter of the proper relationship between party organization and power of the state. These scholars called attention to the precarious legitimacy of the turn-of-the-century party reforms and of party activity; this peculiar combination made the United States parties at once more regulated than their European counterparts and at the same time more central to the lives of its citizens.

This is not to say that the two-party doctrine was absent from this first wave of party scholarship, only that it was not yet hegemonic. E. M. Sait was an early cheerleader for two-party competition and stands out as an exception in this regard. By contrast to Merriam, who accorded two-party competition only passing mention and presented the distinction between the party systems of the United States and Europe as a matter of fact, Sait both devoted a discrete subsection to the two-party system and lent these differences a normative charge. Sait endorsed each tenet of the two-party doctrine. He promoted originality with the claim that "it is not altogether fanciful to trace the lineage of the existing major parties back to the time of the fathers,"[41] immutability by emphasizing "the very persistence of the major parties" and the "failure of successive efforts to displace them," and reserved his greatest enthusiasm for the tenet of democratic progress. According to Sait, the two-party system fostered democracy by distilling competing interests and policies into a single choice between clear alternatives and by facilitating compromise so that these alternatives were "likely to reflect the average point of view."[42] Then, as now, scholars embraced a version of the "wasted vote" maxim. As Sait put it, "Though the minor parties are many, their supporters are few; and the chief reason why they command so few votes is that, from practical considerations, perhaps from a mere sense of the futility of wasting votes on hopeless causes, Americans concentrate on the two major parties."[43] As to the voters in Britain and in the United States who agreed to concentrate their votes on one of the two major parties, Sait contended that they should be praised for their political "aptitude" and "practical bent," which he attributed to "a prolonged experience with popular government."[44]

In the earliest writings on political parties, and even in the first decades of party scholarship, the "two-party system" had not yet taken hold as a catchphrase. Although the term had some currency during this period, it was not yet an obligatory reference for the United States political system. More important, even though the tenets of the two-party doctrine had begun to emerge, two-partyism was not yet the standard against which all democratic electoral systems would be measured. Most important, these scholars could not imagine a two-party system functioning without third parties. To nineteenth-century scholars and voters alike, third parties were to be taken seriously as oppositional forces that raised urgent issues and promoted policies that were too controversial for the established parties to handle.

Party Patriotism

Between the first party textbooks of the 1920s and the mid-century textbooks in the "celebratory tradition" of political parties, there occurred a significant shift in scholarly representations of the two-party system. For an illustration of this change, we need look no farther than the dramatic opening pages of the third edition of Merriam's *The American Party System*. The new introductory chapter, authored by Harold Foote Gosnell (who joined as Merriam's coauthor in 1929), opens with a flourish, quoting a 1939 article from *Living Age* magazine called "As Nazi Tourists See Us":

> "Make the World Safe for Democracy." This is what the American doughboys were told they were fighting for in 1917 and 1918. . . . Fourteen years after the Versailles Treaty, Germany abandoned the democratic form of government. Has something gone wrong with the world we "made safe for Democracy"? Democracy, screams Hitler, is a "monstrosity of filth." Nazi German tourists who come to the United States find the American democracy "cumbersome, despicable" . . .
>
> "It can't happen here," say self-satisfied Americans. But a political scientist comments, "it is later than you think."[45]

Did Gosnell think that the complacency of the "self-satisfied Americans" was warranted? Yes and no. He crafted the chapter to impress on them what it was that separated American democracy from the failed democracies of Europe. This was, simply, "political parties of the American type"; one of the "outstanding characteristics" of that type was, of course, "that it is a two-party system, in contrast to the multiple-party systems which are found in the democratic countries of Continental Europe."[46]

Gosnell answered the implied question of his dramatic opening—*Could* it happen here?—in the concluding pages of his chapter. He offered fulsome praise for the "American two-party system," which he claimed had fostered a trust in "parliamentary methods," and "constitutional consensus" that Germany lacked.[47] Once a minor feature meriting only passing mention, the two-party system had been promoted to the front of the textbook *and* come to be celebrated as the bulwark of democracy in America.

No doubt, this transformation reflects the vagaries of coauthorship. There is no more persuasive testimony to the oft-proclaimed death of the author than the transformations that occur over multiple editions of a college textbook. As an established textbook ages, it is common to enlist a partner (often a junior scholar) to bring it up to date. The revisions tend to be done piecemeal. Rather than working new arguments and literatures through the volume, they are tacked on in ways that proliferate internal contradictions.[48] In the case of *The American Party System*, there is no way to know whether C. E. Merriam had changed *his* mind about the significance of what he had once called the "biparty plan." And this question is irrelevant in any case; textbook revisions register changing historical contexts and changing scholarly problematics.

The early party writings and first party textbooks were produced in the context of progressive reform, when patronage abuses loomed large in scholars' and citizens' perceptions of parties. Party scholars were frequently involved in the progressive movement, either as intellectual advisers or, in the case of Charles E. Merriam, active practitioners. Epstein has argued that whereas early political scientists' hostility toward parties has been exaggerated the "entanglement of political science with reform" in these early years did produce a degree of caution and suspicion toward political parties. This suspicion scholars would abandon—briefly—at mid-century.[49]

The 1950s and 1960s were the heyday of party scholarship in the United States. Parties were "the subject almost of a subdiscipline within the profession," with more political scientists declaring a specialization in parties and elections than in any other field except international relations and the *American Political Science Review* publishing more articles on parties (specifically between 1958 and 1969) than on any other single process or institution.[50] During that time, United States party scholars wrote as if the study of political parties began and ended with America.[51] The confidence in Anglo-American party forms derived, on the one hand, from the fact that by the mid-1930s multipartyism was firmly associated with fascism in Italy and Germany.[52] Whereas two-partyism could be celebrated negatively, *in contrast* to those regimes, it could also be positively vindicated by association with the New Deal, which was a triumph of policy engineering that made it "easier to be enthusiastic about the performance of parties and the rest of the American political system . . . than in either earlier or later years."[53] New Deal confidence together with cold war certainties elevated the two-party system to a catchphrase.

Simply put, the two-party system had become an obligatory term of reference. Scholars referred interchangeably to the two-party system, the American system, or simply the party system. And they began to represent it as the distinguishing feature of American politics. E. E. Schattschneider held "American politics [to be] *dominated and distinguished* by the two-party system," which he called its "most conspicuous and perhaps . . . most important fact."[54] The Committee on Political Parties of the American Political Science Association declared it a "fact" that "the two-party system is part of the American political tradition."[55] And *Government by the People*, the leading American government textbook of this time, declared that "the vital feature of our party system is that it is a two-party system."[56]

Schattschneider and other scholars of this period no longer troubled themselves with the question of legitimacy that had produced the 1920s preoccupation with the "peculiar importance" of parties. By the 1950s few textbooks saw fit to mention that political parties had once produced their own ballots. If state regulation of party activities was presumed legitimate, so were parties and two-party competition. That parties lacked constitutional sanction no longer troubled scholars. Parties and the two-party pattern were established by their longevity. E. E. Schattschneider (undoubtedly their most ardent promoter) represented the "American major parties" as venerable elders who "deserve to be treated with great respect . . . for their age if for no other reason."[57]

The transformation of party scholarship during the postwar period occurred in response to contradictory imperatives. On the one hand was the academic imperative of behavioralism, which signaled the emergence of a new commitment to a "scientific outlook" on the study of politics.[58] A "protest movement within political science," it was led by "revolutionary sectarians . . . who shared a strong sense of dissatisfaction with the achievements of conventional political science," especially its scholasticist preoccupation with textual analysis.[59] Not a research method, although the term was sometimes used that way, behavioralism was something more like a term of art employed to proclaim political scientists' aspiration to bring to the study of political behavior the rigor and predictive capacity of the modern empirical sciences.[60] This ideal presupposed that human behavior exhibits "discoverable uniformities" that can be tested empirically by survey research methods and explained—perhaps predicted—by rational choice and systems theories.[61] By these methods the behavioralists aimed, in David Easton's words, to lead "political analysis away from 'common sense' to 'scientific' sense."[62]

The ethos of behavioralism animated party scholarship in many ways. Up until the 1940s it was typical for parties to be studied descriptively and "as actors in American history rather than as institutional elements in a democratic system."[63] During the postwar period, scholars made a new commitment to precision in defining the fundamental terms of inquiry. Maurice Duverger conveyed a pervasive view of this time when he underscored the importance of "methodical classification," insisting that the discipline "will make no true progress so long as its investigations are scattered and individual, empirical rather than scientific."[64] Party scholars were also "among the first to expand and refine the empirical methods and newer statistical analysis that American political science now takes for granted."[65] Finally, scholars who had previously merely presumed there to be a necessary relationship between democracy and two-partyism began to render this presupposition explicit and couch it in scientific form. They undertook to specify the version of democracy that they understood parties to serve and to search for systematic regularities to justify the association.[66] Ironically, it was during this period that scholars formulated the tenets of the two-party doctrine and sought to formalize them.

How could the attachment to two-partyism intensify at a time when political scientists had initiated a revolution against common sense? It was motivated, in part, by the political imperative that emerged alongside behavioralism and in competition with it: to vindicate mass democracy in the wake of totalitarianism. Two-partyism presented itself as an answer to this imperative. Both a fundamental difference that insulated the United States against the instability and extremism of the mass regimes of Europe and a simple political fact, the two-party system stood at the intersection of a changing conception of political science as a discipline and a postwar confidence in the achievements of American democracy. It was taken up at once as an occasion for optimism and a site for the practice of political science *as science*.

To be sure, behavioral analysis should have worked to discredit belief in the two-party system. And for scholars like Frank Sorauf, it did exactly that. Remember, however, that behavioralism was more than an approach or method. It was also a movement that popularized new ways of speaking about political phenomena. As these ways of speaking crept into the vocabularies of scholars and journalists who did not share its methodological aspirations, the effect was paradoxical. Behavioral method aimed to test our nationalist attachments to such institutions as two-partyism; behavioral discourse proved to legitimate them wherever it enabled the expression of party patriotism in dispassionate terms. As Sorauf observed, in a masterstroke of Socratic irony,

> American scholars of government and political parties have not hesitated to show their preference for a two-party system. It has seemed, *almost as a matter of logic*, more compatible with democracy's need for majorities, responsible opposition and alternatives, and stability and structure in the political dialogue. Just *as a simple matter of association*, two-partyism has accompanied two of the most enduring of the democracies, Great Britain and the United States. Multi-partyism, on the other hand, has plagued some of democracy's most awesome failures, those of Weimar Germany and interwar France. . . . This relationship between democracy and the viable two-party system has been *clear enough* to send political scientists *scurrying in search of the causes and conditions of the two-party system.*[67]

The very term *system* played a critical role in this transmutation of value into fact.

A term of art in cybernetics, system connotes a social world that is orderly, integrated, and self-regulating. The "idea of a political system," according to David Easton, who appropriated the term for political science, assumes "that the study of political life . . . constitutes a distinctive theoretical field."[68] He called the *political system* an "analytical tool designed to identify those integrally related aspects of concrete social activity that can be called political."[69] Is the political system a theoretical construct or an empirical field? Frederick Dolan has remarked that Easton used the term both ways, as a "metaphor" to enable behavioral analysis and as "an actually existing thing, an 'adaptive, self-regulating, and self-transforming system of behavior' " to establish behavioralism as the master form of political analysis.[70] In the context of behavioralism, the ambiguity in the term *system* had the powerful ideological effect of constituting value-laden political phenomena as value-neutral objects of inquiry.

When scholars took up the *two-party system* as a catchphrase (however mistakenly, in the view of Sorauf or Ranney and Kendall) they inherited this ambiguity between word and thing, together with its ideological effect. It helped them represent work that entrenched the two-party doctrine as if it made a break from the vague speculations and national chauvinism that biased the scholarship of the past. In their 1952 textbook Burns and Peltason invoked Gilbert and Sullivan (a "high" cultural reference that would never be allowed into a 1990s textbook) to mock earlier explanations for two-partyism:

> Why do we have a two-party system? Nobody knows for sure. Jefferson thought that men naturally divided into whigs and tories. Lord Bryce said they inevitably split into nationalists and states-righters. Some have said that "advanced Anglo-Saxon peoples" sensibly adopted tidy political systems; perhaps the sentry in *Iolanthe* was mocking them when he sang:
>
> Now let's rejoice
> that Nature wisely does contrive
> That every boy and every gal
> That's born into the world alive
> Is either a little Liberal
> Or else a little Conservative.[71]

Their point, of course, was as ironic as the lyric itself: whatever else it may be, the two-party system is surely no natural (nor naturally superior) political formation.

Schattschneider also went out of his way to discredit those who had explained the two-party system as "a mark of the 'political maturity' of Anglo-American peoples." He countered, "We are reasonably certain that *definite circumstances*, easily identified, make this system inevitable in the United States regardless of the personal preferences of individual critics."[72] What was this definite circumstance? The "American election system."[73] Schattschneider argued that the invincibility of the major parties was "the direct consequence" of the constitutional prescription for single-member districts and plurality voting.[74] Anticipating Duverger's Law (although he self-consciously refrained from expressing it "with the precision of a mathematical formula"), E. E. Schattschneider explained the tendency of a single-member district electoral system to "exaggerate the victory of the strongest party and to discriminate radically against lesser parties," *especially* against "the third, fourth, and fifth parties," whose chances of victory it extinguishes "altogether."[75] As a consequence of this structural framework, Schattschneider contended that "the gap between the second major party and the greatest minor party is enormous and insurmountable; no minor party in American history has ever become a major party, and no major party has ever become a minor party."[76]

Schattschneider obviously departs from the chauvinism of some earlier writers. But there is a second departure here, one that makes possible a far more insidious form of chauvinism. In contrast to earlier writers, for whom it was clear that the bi-party pattern was a relatively recent legislative effect, Schattschneider took the politics out of the two-party system. He represented the "monopoly of power by the major parties" as a *structural* inevitability that had nothing whatsoever to do with politics and culture.[77] What's more, he represented the two-party system as self-creating, as an arrangement that could remain legitimate altogether without third-party activity.

Mid-century party scholars did not discover the two-party system, nor were they suddenly converted to the two-party doctrine. As I have shown, these were present in the study of political parties from the beginning. What did happen at mid-century, however, was that the two-party system was *repositioned* in the field. No longer can scholars give this arrangement only passing mention, postpone it to the end of a chapter or monograph on parties, or contrast it against the multiparty systems of Europe in a casual or matter-of-fact way. They are compelled to represent it as a synonym for American democracy. It had taken hold as a catchphrase. Surprisingly, given the ideological power of this association, the two-party system also proves to lend itself to the disciplinary transformation that occurred at this time: it fostered a science of politics that wanted to look and sound like a positive science.

Political Parties and the Science of Politics

In 1954 something momentous occurred in the career of the two-party system as a catchphrase: the birth of Duverger's Law.[78] This proposition, that "*the simple-majority single-ballot system favours the two-party system,*" was formulated by French sociologist Maurice Duverger in *Political Parties*, the study that he wrote in order to shift the field of party scholarship from studying the "social composition of parties," and their "doctrines" to structural analysis of the "nature of [party] organization," and "their place in the state."[79] In the opening pages of the second volume Duverger turned his attention to the subject matter that would make his name a household word (at least in the households of American political scientists): the relationship between electoral systems and "the number of parties."[80] Duverger proposed to study a contrast that was considered to be "of much less importance" than that between "the multi-party and the single-party systems," and that had understandably been "neglected" by the field. This was the contrast between "the two-party and multi-party systems."[81] In the United States today, where we have grown accustomed to chart significant differences in terms of the multiparty/two-party distinction, it is surprising to learn that the multiparty/single-party distinction was once the "commonplace" and that scholars once understood it to divide West from East, democracy from totalitarianism. Moreover, it is ironic to read this claim in the work of the theorist who is renowned for having focused so much attention on the multiparty/two-party contrast.

Duverger's Law was a momentous event in the career of the two-party system as a catchphrase because it brought two-party systems into the forefront and it constituted the two-party system as a problem for political scientists *as scientists* to explain. As V. O. Key skeptically observed in 1952, "the 'causes' of the dualism of the American party structure . . . ranks as a favorite question for political speculation."[82] Duverger's Law elevated this favorite question in two ways. He focused attention on the role of electoral rules in producing two-partyism as opposed to the more easily discredited (because obviously chauvinist) political culture and national character. In so doing, Duverger provided United States political scientists with an empirically testable proposition on which to practice "normal science," just as the discipline—in the throes of the behavioral "revolution"—sought to establish itself as a proper (read positive) science.[83]

Duverger's Law proved to be ideally suited to this enterprise not because it was, as Duverger claimed, "a true sociological law."[84] The significance of this proposition was, as William Riker would later put it, that it enabled knowledge to be "accumulated" in the field of political science.[85] It did not matter whether it was accurate, or even whether it qualified as a law (as opposed to a mere empirical observation). Duverger's Law caught on in the 1950s because it was a scientific-sounding proposition; true or not, it was a testable hypothesis that appealed to political scientists who aspired to practice their craft as positive scientists.

Even in its very name *Duverger's Law* mimics positive science; it appears, like an axiom of physics, to be called after the scientist who discovered it. In fact, as William H. Riker has observed, Duverger did not originate the proposition that bears his name. Since the 1880s politicians and scholars had maintained that single-member districting tended to produce two-party competition. Whereas the proposition that would be called Duverger's Law was part of the working knowledge of nineteenth-century English political practitioners, they did not speak of it as an axiom.[86] Riker emphasizes that it was not Duverger's contribution to discover this proposition but to take up a "commonplace" and "assert it as a law."[87] We remember him because he "was the first to dare to claim it was a law. The memorial honors, therefore, a trait of character as much as a scientific breakthrough."[88] What Riker terms "character," I would call a turn of phrase, and add that the memorial testifies that it is not just *what* we say but *how* we say it that has consequences for what we take to be real. In short, Duverger's achievement was discursive: he contributed a scientific-sounding proposition to party scholars at a time when they aspired to practice their craft as positive scientists, and thereby formed an object for that practice.

Duverger's Law was as much an emblem of the movement to render the study of politics a positive science as it was a substantive contribution to knowledge about the dynamics of the two-party system. This is the central thesis of the remarkable 1982 essay by William H. Riker from which I have been quoting, "The Two-Party System and Duverger's Law: An Essay on the History of Political Science." Riker wrote the essay in order to demonstrate that political science could indeed be practiced as Kuhn's "normal science."[89] He chronicles "a particular series of reformulations called Duverger's law" with the

> intention . . . to demonstrate that a history [of political science] does exist. . . . I am not undertaking this demonstration out of chauvinism, merely to claim for students of politics the name and privilege of scientists, but rather to show that the accumulation of knowledge is possible even when dealing with such fragile and transitory phenomena as political institutions. This is also why I deal with Duverger's law, *a not very well accepted proposition* dealing with institutions of only the last two hundred years. If it is demonstrated that knowledge has accumulated, even in this not yet satisfactorily formulated "law" about an

> ephemeral institution, then I will have demonstrated at least the possibility of the accumulation of knowledge about politics.[90]

I quote Riker at length here because his work so beautifully illustrates the notion of "party discipline" that frames this chapter. It is not that parties are the sole focus of political science but rather that the two-party system has been a highly charged object of inquiry, one that has assisted the project of discipline formation in moments of crisis.

This is clear from the principal objective of Riker's essay, which was not to *prove* Duverger's Law but to use it as a call to arms. In Riker's hands the history of Duverger's Law becomes a parable for giving succor to those researchers who, in "despair" of producing "scientific generalizations" about politics, were in danger of succumbing to "the movement toward phenomenology and hermeneutics and other efforts to turn political science into a belles-lettristic study."[91] A classic manifesto, it calls upon political *scientists* to recognize themselves as participating in the "accumulation of knowledge in the form of more or less verifiable propositions about the natural world" and narrates the development of Duverger's Law in such a way as to give them reason to take up the call.[92] With all due respect to Riker, it is no small irony that a formal theorist (whose usual stock-in-trade is game theory and regression analyses) would write a manifesto—an explicitly normative declaration—on behalf of positive science; Riker took up the practice of what he called "belles lettres, criticism, and philosophic speculation" in order to close ranks against it.[93] But there is more here than irony.

Duverger's Law advanced the career of the two-party system as a catchphrase by taking what had been an object of speculation and making it an object of scientific inquiry. Duverger could not make the two-party system exist in fact, of course (despite his own belief that two-party systems were grounded on "natural political dualism").[94] He did succeed, however, in lending it credibility as a catchphrase—that is, something for everyone to talk about and no one to really study—by causing it to exist in theory.

His work also reaffirmed the two-party doctrine. When Duverger's Law is stated, as it typically is, as an unqualified fact, it makes two-party competition a historically constant feature of the United States electoral system. This puts two-party competition beyond politics, so that it seems to be both impervious to political challenge and innocent of partisan content. It also represents third-party failure as inevitable by virtue of the "mechanical" tendency for winner-take-all systems to overrepresent the majority party and the corresponding "psychological" tendency of voters to "realize that their votes are wasted if they continue to give them to the third party."[95]

The publication in 1957 of Anthony Downs's *Economic Theory of Democracy* had a similar effect that further bolstered the two-party system as a catchphrase.[96] Downs's book, which he described "as a study of political rationality from an economic point of view," took a very different approach to the study of parties than Duverger's. Nonetheless, it put forward a similar picture of two-partyism as an extrapolitical tendency due not to the electoral structure of winner-take-all but rather to "the logical structure of the voting act."[97] Downs's economic model proceeded from two assumptions. First, he posited an instrumentally rational voter who casts a ballot "for the party he believes will provide him with a higher utility income than any other party during the coming election period."[98] Second, he stipulated that elections are to be regarded "solely as means of selecting governments" and that rational behavior with respect to voting is defined exclusively in terms of that end:

> A rational voter first decides what party he believes will benefit him most; then he tries to estimate whether this party has any chance of winning. He does this because his vote should be expended as part of a selection process, not as an expression of preference. Hence even if he prefers party A, he is "wasting" his vote on A if it has no chance of winning because very few other voters prefer it to B or C. *The relevant choice in this case is between B and C. Since a vote for A is not useful in the actual process of selection, casting it is irrational.*[99]

Downs further entrenched the two-party system by stripping it of historical and cultural specificity. Not only did he claim to have identified "*the* logical structure of *the* voting act" as if it were constant over time and place, he extrapolated this logic from the conditions that governed voting in the mid-twentieth century without acknowledging their specificity. Downs's "economic logic" recast the tenet of immutability from a historical fact to a game theoretic proposition. In turn, he could make the tenet of democratic progress seem value-neutral; by establishing the "rationality" of major party voting, Downs reaffirmed two-party voting as the index of progress toward an apparently objective measure of superiority. Any citizen who accepted the premises of "rational voting," that voters are instrumentally rational and that elections are means for selecting governments, would not bother voting for a third party; likewise, any candidate who accepts those premises would never run on a third-party ballot line.[100] One could now single out the two-party system as evidence of "political maturity" without risking the charge of chauvinism.

A centerpiece of Downs's economic theory was an argument that had the potential to undermine the very premise that voting is an instrumentally rational act. This began from his observation that elections are costly for voters and parties alike. Downs argued that whereas citizens aim to spend their ballot on the party that will best represent their interests, parties aim to win control of government by expending as little capital (from campaign promises to money spent on publicity and turn out) as possible. In a perfect world of cost-free information, these aims would not conflict. But the real world of electoral politics is one "beclouded by uncertainty."[101] And a winner-take-all system gives parties an incentive to turn uncertainty into electoral advantage. By contrast to a proportional representation system, where parties stand to gain by distinguishing themselves from each other because they do not need to capture a majority, winner-take-all "forces both parties to be much less than perfectly clear about what they stand for," which raises the cost of information-gathering for the average voter.[102] In short, there is a conflict between party rationality and voter rationality in a two-party system. In such systems "rational behavior by political parties tends to discourage rational behavior by voters."[103] Put differently, if the citizen's objective is to maximize influence and minimize wasted expense, in a two-party system it is irrational to vote *at all.*

Had Downs stopped there, he would have dropped a bombshell on the "celebratory tradition" that held democracy to be "unthinkable" without political parties and lauded the two-party system for making "elections meaningful and even exciting to millions of voters who know how to choose between a few alternatives but not among a bewildering variety of men and platforms."[104] Even his own project would be untenable. For if citizens vote in spite of the fact that it is demonstrably inefficient and ineffective, then perhaps they cast their ballots with something more than "utility income" in mind; perhaps elections are something more than "means of selecting governments" and political rationality does not lend itself to study from an "economic point of view" after all. Downs recuperated the fundamental premise of his project by displacing the irrationality of voting onto multiple-party systems, and onto third-party voting within a two-party system.

Downs argued that rational voting is much more complicated in a multiparty system, where the governing coalition forms *after* the election, because it depends on calculating how other voters are most likely to cast their ballots, and on being able to predict how the governing coalition will take shape, knowing which parties will most likely enter it and what they will be willing to compromise to hold it together.[105] Under such conditions, a vote for a party is not a vote for a government. According to Downs's model then, which stipulated that elections should be understood as means of selecting governments, rational voting is precluded by definition. Multiparty systems cannot guarantee accountability, responsiveness, and representation because voters have no way to anticipate the coalition-building phase. We are left with the two-party system as a fallback.

But within the two-party system, of course, the proportion of "wasted" votes is much higher. How to recuperate its rationality? Downs's solution was to displace the charge of vote wasting onto third parties by emphasizing that a vote for a third party candidate is an act of support for someone who "has no chance of winning." By this turn of argument, Downs both presupposes that the value of the vote derives exclusively from the competitiveness of the candidate and forestalls the conclusion that it may be equally a waste to cast a vote for a dominant-party candidate whenever that candidate is assured of winning (which is often the case in today's two-party system, with its pronounced incumbency advantage) or represents "the lesser of two evils," as voters so often put it.

Downs leaves us with a theory of rational voting that is purely negative. That is, rationality is assured not by what two-party voting accomplishes—e.g., provide for popular sovereignty—but by what it does not do, which is waste a vote. The bottom line is that voters in a two-party system can always vote for a winning candidate, even if they cannot always cast a ballot for a candidate who most nearly represents their views.

Downs's "rational voting" principle was taken up and tested by behavioralist political scientists just as Duverger's Law had been. Like Duverger's Law, it proved to be more influential for the fact that it could be put into play as a falsifiable hypothesis than for any substantive insight it could yield. And, as was also the case with Duverger's Law, the fact that rational voting existed only in theory did nothing to diminish its powerful discursive effects. Thus, Downs achieved for the wasted vote maxim what Duverger achieved for politicians' intuitive appreciation of the strategic effects of electoral rules; his "rational voting" reformulated a commonplace notion as a legitimate hypothesis.

Together, Downs and Duverger offer new insights into the workings of party discipline. Both represent the two-party system *as a system*—extrapolitical, ahistorical, and strategically constant. The effect of their work is to lend credibility to that aspect of the behavioralist turn that called for a shift from historical analysis and normative theory to abstract modeling. By answering the call to produce testable generalizations about political behavior, they promoted systematic thinking about politics at the expense of theoretically informed historical inquiry. Both fund the empirical paradox of the two-party system by constructing elaborate formulas that perpetuate the life of this construct *in theory*—regardless whether it can be operationalized in empirical investigation. Over the course of the twentieth century the catchphrase *two-party system* has emerged in United States political practice and scholarship as the predominant way of ordering and speaking about mass political consent—the elusive, ephemeral, and risky form of human agency that is taken to distinguish this political system as a democratic system. Although we take it for granted today, it was not a catchphrase prior to the turn of the century. It became common currency only after the turn-of-the-century reforms that brought parties, campaigns, voting, and elections within the compass of the state, discouraged third parties, and stabilized two-party competition. At mid-century the two-party system enjoyed a brief tenure in party scholarship as a virtually sacred object. It allowed citizens to reassure themselves that mass democracy would work, and political scientists to practice the methods they hoped would unify the field. Few party scholars today would maintain that the health of democracy depends either on the parties or on two-party competition; interest groups have displaced political parties as the focal point of both the discipline and the democratic process.

The two-party system retains its popular currency, nonetheless. This may testify to the fact that behavioralist ways of speaking about politics have proven to be more tenacious than behavioralist methods of studying it. As Dolan has put it, the "jargon" of behavioralism—"a rhetoric in which particular political associations are treated as 'systems' with varying degrees of 'stability'—has become firmly entrenched in the metaphysical language of journalists," not to mention that of politicians and Supreme Court Justices.[106]

One purpose of this chapter has been to demonstrate the interplay between political institutions and disciplinary knowledge formation. I have shown how the academic study of politics helped at its outset to affirm the legitimacy of political parties and confirm the two-party system as a touchstone for common sense. In turn, I have also demonstrated how the academic discipline of politics was contingent, in part, upon the institutionalization of parties at the turn of the century, which helped to provide the social stability that such a modern academic discipline would require in order to practice a particular kind of science. To be sure, political scientists did not invent the two-party system. But, in taking it up as a catchphrase, they have helped to naturalize it as an organizing frame for the way that United States citizens think about their own democracy, and for the prescriptions they make to others.

As the institution that the Supreme Court could praise for—to borrow from the *Timmons* ruling—bringing "stability" to elections and "integrity" to ballots, the two-party system is both a catchphrase and a commonsense parameter of United States electoral politics. As such, it has had material effects on the practice of political science and on the practice of democratic citizenship. It has participated in defining what political scientists have at once contested and accepted as an object of knowledge and what journalists, politicians, and voters in the United States take to be real constraints on elections. As such, the two-party system can be said to have *disciplined* voting. It has "given epistemic shape" to mass democratic agency by positing major party voting as legitimate, rational, and calculable behavior and as a criticizable phenomenon.[107] At the same time, it has marginalized other forms of institutionalized opposition (such as community organizing and protest) and other forms of voting (such as fusion or stand-alone third party candidacies) by rendering them inefficient, incomprehensible, or patently illegitimate.

The interconnection between state regulation of political parties and the formation of political science as an autonomous field exemplifies the distinctively modern linkage between the organization of knowledge production and the organization of social institutions. This is "discipline" as Michel Foucault uses the term, a "positive" power that does not rely on a monopoly over the legitimate uses of force.[108] In contrast to corporal punishment or statutory fines, prohibitionary forms of power that must emanate from a sovereign in order to be legitimate, discipline is a process rather than an act or injunction. It forms objects of knowledge, designates canons of relevance, institutionalizes techniques and methods of investigation, and recognizes those who may speak, know, and act with authority.[109] This is to say that disciplinary power is productive. The division of academic fields of study is one site for its production. Discipline in Foucault's sense calls our attention to the "continuity between the *internal organization of knowledge production* at the level of academic disciplines and the *institutional structure of society*."[110]

The two-party system has been an exceptionally potent transfer point between the organization of the academic study of politics and the social organization of mass political participation. The turn-of-the century ballot and civil service reforms, which helped to precipitate two-party duopoly into being, helped to stabilize electoral contests by frustrating third-party competition and suppressing the participation of those who chose third parties as their vehicle. Reform at once stabilized the electoral system and rendered political behavior amenable to systematic analysis. For whereas the two-party system was an effect of the regulation of parties by the state, that regulation in turn provided some of the requisite conditions for the formation of political science understood as a field in its own right. At its outset, then, political science was a party discipline; the two-party system, though no inheritance of the American founding, was intimately bound up with the founding of a new scholarly regime.[111]

It should be clear that in calling political science a "party discipline" I do not mean to suggest that the field has devoted itself exclusively to the study of parties, nor that it originated in order to do so. Party discipline, as I understand it, is on the one hand a complex of regulatory acts that tamed the corrupt and competitive electoral system of the late nineteenth century and, on the other hand, the field of knowledge whose formation was made possible by those acts of regulation. The institutionalization of parties at the turn of the century supplied the routinization and control of political behavior that the modern academic disciplines (especially the human sciences) require in order to produce "objective knowledge about agents."[112] It is to this linkage between knowledge production and the productivity of power that I mean to call attention when I call political science a "party discipline."

To point to this interplay between knowledge and power is not to *conflate* the two, as some have charged. Rather, it is to propose that if the modern academic disciplines (especially the human sciences) are to fulfill their promise to produce generalizable propositions, they "require a level of social stability that derives from institutions capable of providing the requisite controls." Cultural theorist John Mowitt puts it this way, "*That* we know has a great deal to do with *what* we know, and this has everything to do with the general social function of power."[113] The two-party system, like the military, the hospital, the education system, and the law, forms bridges between social power and academic knowledge. Like each of these, it orders human behavior so as to render it amenable to such characteristically modern forms of analysis as statistics and quantitative analysis. As such, it is what Mowitt calls a "regulative fiction."[114] This is neither to say that it is a chimera nor that it somehow defrauds citizens of their capacity to act. Rather, it is an academic construct with material effects. Conjoining the organization of academic knowledge production to the ordering of mass society, it "*really* works to orient research within a particular field [that] may actually lead to [practical political] interventions."[115]

Many third-party scholars, proponents of proportional representation, and third-party advocates emphasize the institutional obstacles to third-party organizing. I emphasize how this catchphrase is an obstacle, too, not to deny the importance of other institutional factors but rather to underscore how the very terms in which we have come to speak about this system render us less likely to question it. As a catchphrase the two-party system is both an organizing frame for the practice of political analysis and a commonsense parameter of United States electoral politics. It has powerful normative effects on what the citizens of this polity imagine to be possible. Specifically, it leaves neither room nor need for third-party activity. As I will explore in the next chapter, it not only writes fusion out of the narrative of United States party history but also renders its strategic advantages inconceivable.

Chapter 4

The Two-Party System and the Ideology of Process

The history of democratic government is virtually synonymous with the history of parties. When the countries of eastern Europe gained their freedom a few years ago, one of their first steps toward democracy was the legalization of parties. When the US was founded two centuries ago, the formation of parties was also a first step toward the erection of its democracy. In case after case, *democracies have found that they cannot do without parties and for the simplest of reasons: it is the competition between parties that gives popular majorities a chance to determine how they will be governed.*

—Thomas E. Patterson, *The American Democracy (emphasis added)*

The alternating of power and influence between the two major parties is one of the most important elements in American politics. *Party competition is the battle between Democrats and Republicans* for the control of public offices. Without this competition there would be no choice, and without choice there would be no democracy.

—George C. Edwards II, Martin P. Wattenberg, and Robert L. Lineberry, *Government in America* (emphasis added)

We often refer to the United States as a nation with a "two-party system." By this we mean that *in the United States the Democratic and Republican parties compete for office and power.* Most Americans believe that party competition contributes to the health of the democratic process. Certainly, we are more than just a bit suspicious of those nations that claim to be ruled by their people but do not tolerate the existence of opposing parties.

—Theodore J. Lowi and Benjamin Ginsberg, *American Government: Freedom and Power* (emphasis added)

Although we have been focusing on major parties, we must not lose sight of all the exotic third parties in American history: abolitionists, populists, antiliquor, Bull Moose, Communist, the Citizens' Party of 1980, and John Anderson's Independent party. Third parties are described by some scholars as "a response to major party failure," *but the crucial aspect about third parties is how often they charge into the national political arena and how they never win.*

—James MacGregor Burns, J. W. Peltason, and Thomas E. Cronin, *Government by the People* (emphasis added)

Imagine a politico from the 1890s—let's call him Ignatius—enrolling in a 1990s "Introduction to American Government" class. Ignatius would be the kind of student that every teacher hopes for, one who reads the newspaper, works on election campaigns, and likes to talk about politics. When the class reached its week on political parties, it would have surprised Ignatius to see such praise for the two-party system. To begin with, the very currency of this phrase would have sounded odd because, as we have seen, in Ignatius's time the two-party system was not yet the obligatory term of reference that it is today. It would be stranger still to see two-partyism affirmed as a "traditionally" American pattern[1] and have it dated to the "rivalry . . . between Thomas Jefferson and Alexander Hamilton."[2] Strangest of all would be the confident assumption that democracy is the purpose and direction of the American experiment, and that competition "between the two major parties" is what keeps this experiment on course.[3] No respectable party analyst of the late nineteenth century would have so happily labeled the United States of America a democracy, nor accepted party competition as contributing to its "health."[4] To praise the "formation of parties [as] a first step toward the erection of democracy"—that would have been unheard of.[5]

Albert Stickney, a turn-of-the-century journalist and party critic, exemplifies the distance between party scholarship then and now. Stickney maintained that parties had no part in any of the founding moments of the American republic: "We went through the war of the Revolution without parties. Some men were royalists, others were rebels; but there were no organizations that could be called parties."[6] As Stickney saw it, parties played no role in forming the Constitution, contributed nothing to the "great work" of organizing a government, and took no part in building up a treasury; it "was, in fact, almost entirely due to the absence of parties and party contests that men, in the thirty years from 1770 to 1800, were able to carry out any one of the points of policy . . . [that were] necessary to accomplish the freedom of the colonies and the formation of the new national government.[7] Stickney even went so far as to doubt whether the nation "would ever have had an existence" had parties come into being "within the first twelve years of our national history."[8]

Stickney's claims are debatable. The groups he cites might with good reason be called precursors to parties, if not parties proper. And this is precisely my point: Albert Stickney (and others) represented party politics *differently* than contemporary textbooks do. Whereas textbook authors today go out of their way to mention an inherent national propensity for a two-party system, the leading voices of Ignatius's time were equally adamant that the institution had no constitutional warrant. Coming from a time when the dominant parties had yet to establish their monopoly on electoral power, and when textbooks had yet to applaud them, an Ignatius would see something in today's party textbooks that a contemporary reader would be primed to overlook: textbook histories lend two-party politics an original status and timeless permanence by glossing over the partisan struggles that brought this arrangement into being.

This chapter continues my analysis of the two-party system as a catchphrase, this time shifting from its empirical effects on what we take to be real to its normative effects on what we imagine to be possible. I contend that when introductory and even advanced-level political science texts depict two-party competition as a motor of democracy, they write third political parties out of its history. They also script the two-party system into a narrative of advancement over time that imputes to United States party history what sociologist William H. Sewell has called a "teleological temporality," a sense of time as linear, moving ineluctably forward toward an outcome that was "foreordained by the necessity built into [an arrangement] from the moment of its creation."[9] To be sure, such linear, progressive views of the United States party system have their critics among leading party scholars. William Nisbet Chambers identifies the "notion of continuity" as a "simplistic account," one characteristic of "an older historiography" to which "no reputable student" subscribes today.[10] Theodore Lowi has emphasized the break that occurred in party history around 1840, once the party system was institutionalized. He contends that institutionalization "was accompanied by *a change in the direction of party function from liberal to conservative, from innovation to consolidation, or from* [promoting] *change to a resistance to change.*"[11]

Lowi's argument refutes the belief that the parties are democratic entrepreneurs, together with the sense of time as continuous forward movement. Party scholars have even accepted it as a "general hypothesis."[12] Nonetheless, as the passages I cited at the outset of this chapter attest, there remains in circulation what Chambers would call a "simplistic" and outdated view that connects political parties to democratic progress. Chambers has remarked that "older conceptualizations die hard, particularly in the popular mind."[13] I would add that they die hard in the judicial mind—as evidenced by the *Timmons* decision—and even in the minds of political scientists as well.

How better to debunk the myth of parties as agents of progress than to tell the story of the maneuvers by which third political parties were forced out of the United States electoral system? That story, because it features a break in the history of the party system, helps to make the case against continuity. Even such critics as Chambers and Lowi fail to do so. In fact, Lowi effectively scripts this episode out of his account of the parties' conservative turn by dating that shift to 1840. There are many scholars who would consider the turn of the century to be an equally significant breaking-point for the United States party system and who would count the forced extinction of third political parties as a contributing factor to its growing conservatism. For example, political historian Alex Keyssar, who makes a point of emphasizing that neither of the two major parties has "an unblemished record of embracing democratic principles," singles out the late nineteenth century as a time when the two collaborated to reduce turn out by passing "laws designed to keep citizens from the polls and to prevent popular dissident parties from effectively contesting elections."[14] Scholars who gloss over these antidemocratic initiatives miss an opportunity to dismantle an outmoded historiography; they even help to perpetuate a "simplistic" faith in the permanence of the two-party system as we know it, together with the corroborating fiction of inevitable third-party failure.

Such beliefs, and the teleological temporalities that underlie them, are not just outmoded; they also have normative effects. Lawrence Goodwyn has argued that they are critical to forming the culture of resignation on which industrial democracies depend to persuade their populations "to define all conceivable political activity within the limits of existing custom."[15] By fostering an inchoate sense of advancement, teleology produces a "condescension toward the past" that discredits the expansive democratic vision of movements like the Populists.[16] It also casts suspicion on protest movements in the present.

I contend that textbook accounts that write third political parties out of party history have participated centrally in producing this culture of resignation. Textbook histories that represent democracy as the truth of this electoral system and celebrate two-party competition as its motor force have limited what United States citizens expect from electoral democracy. They make third-party failure seem inevitable, and such oppositional strategies as fusion inconceivable. Whereas chapter 3 focused principally on what scholars have said about the two-party system, this one takes on the more difficult task of analyzing what they have failed to say about third political parties. My assumption is that textbooks generate resignation as much by the episodes they leave out as by those they choose to celebrate.

Textbook Time

How should we interpret the fact that today's textbooks omit most of what an Ignatius would count as the most controversial battles of his time—ballot reform, voter registration, and even fusion? Any textbook publisher would explain that there is no great scandal in this, especially where fusion is concerned. A short-lived, regionally specific practice that has been out of use for more than one hundred years, it is hardly textbook worthy. Moreover, as fusion ended with the party ticket system, it could only seem obscure to a voter who knew no other instrument than the Australian ballot. There is very little to be gained by making it accessible. Except in New York, there is no practical context for a twentieth-century citizen to put it to use. Fusion was not written out of party history; on the contrary, it was appropriately forgotten.

Such arguments are irrefutable on one level. Esoteric historical episodes have no place in the American government textbook of today, which has developed elaborate strategies for efficient information delivery. Fifty years ago even introductory textbooks were dense with copy; shaped like books, they relied on little more than an occasional political cartoon to break up the page. Now they are like magazines. Designed to appeal to students who are not readers in their spare time but internet surfers and television watchers, the contemporary textbook does more with pictures than it does with words. Publishers rely on full-color photos, charts, graphs, and trivia quizzes—all gimmicks to keep a student moving from one page to the next (when it is assumed that the force of prose alone will not do). Historical narration loses the most by this format. Relegated to sidebars as supplementary to the facts at hand, it is at most optional reading.

If introductory-level textbooks can be forgiven for forgetting fusion, why is it that even advanced-level party textbooks and specialized studies of third parties fail to feature it in much detail? As for the story of the struggle by which it was outlawed, Peter H. Argersinger has remarked that party scholars have not regarded it as a struggle at all but as one among many "structural modifications [that are] essentially apolitical or nonpartisan."[17] A leading work on third parties mentions fusion only in passing as a Populist strategy that created strife within that party.[18] Another specialized third-party study relegates fusion to a footnote, calling it—accurately but parsimoniously—a nominating strategy that gives third parties "a role, but a peculiarly auxiliary one" in influencing a major party's choice of candidate.[19] An analyst of voter turn out mentions fusion as a local strategy, limited to "certain states and certain elections," whose prohibition had little effect on the definitive trends of the twentieth-century electoral system.[20] An influential advanced-level party textbook dismisses fusion as a "classic instance" of "quirks in local election laws" that give third parties an electoral foothold unwarranted by their own numbers.[21]

Of the various political scientists who analyze third-party politics today, only Daniel Mazmanian takes care to explain how fusion enables third parties to beat the "wasted vote" maxim and to detail its mechanics and contemporary use. But even he does not mention its history. And in choosing to refer to fusion as the "modified two-party system," Mazmanian represents the strategy within the terms of the very system that it once challenged.[22]

My concern is with the normative effects of such omissions. Would scholars be so certain about the insignificance of fusion, and the irrelevance of third parties generally, if it were not for the *two-party system*? As a catchphrase this construct helps party scholars determine what counts as relevant and important, just as it helps journalists determine what is newsworthy. It is not that the fusion story was suppressed (that would make it a hidden or covert event and suggest the presence of a conspiracy or cover-up); authors simply judged it inconsequential. This was no conspiracy, only a lapse of historical imagination. But it was a telling lapse, for it would have taken a narrative exertion to make fusion interesting. Fusion's import is simply inconceivable to any scholar who takes the two-party system for granted as a fact of United States politics, a sign of progress toward democracy. The fusion story both contravenes textbook narratives of party history and debunks what Thomas Kuhn has called their "unhistorical stereotype" of time.[23]

Although he is better known for the concepts paradigm, scientific revolution, and incommensurability, concepts establishing that facts follow from theories and cannot be used to test them, Thomas Kuhn deserves renown as an astute critic of the conventions of textbook writing. Specifically, Kuhn upbraided physics textbooks for representing the history of science teleologically, as a process of "development-by-accumulation."[24] Kuhn argued that this misrepresents how knowledge advances, which is not by accumulation but discontinuously. He argued that the history of science is punctuated by the scientific revolutions (or paradigm shifts) that interrupt the course of research in a field to redefine its "legitimate problems and methods."[25] Kuhn emphasized that these revolutions make so complete a break with what preceded them that it is as if "the proponents of competing paradigms practice their trades in different worlds."[26] Textbooks gloss over these disjunctures. They represent "the scientists of earlier ages . . . as having worked upon the same set of fixed problems and in accordance with the same set of fixed canons that the most recent revolution in scientific theory and method has made seem scientific," thereby inscribing the norms of the present into the very "technical structure of the text."[27] For this mode of representation, which effectively writes the history of a discipline "backward" to fix and validate the present, Kuhn called them "pedagogic vehicles for the perpetuation of normal science."[28]

Kuhn's observations hold just as true for textbooks in political science as they do for those in physics. The introductory American government textbook writes party history backward whenever it calls "the two-party system" original, accepts it as inevitable, or celebrates it as state-of-the-art technology for mass democracy. Such representations are pedagogical vehicles for perpetuating what we might call *normal citizenship*. This is not to say that textbooks aim to brainwash the public, to produce "docile" voters who carry on the party identifications of their parents. On the contrary, today's introductory textbook presents a wide range of political activity as legitimate, from peaceful protest, to letter writing, to lobbying, to campaign contributions. At the same time, however, texts present the history of the ballot and party system as if it had been uneventful. By failing to hand down the story of fusion (and other alternative practices such as proportional representation and cumulative voting), they help to socialize students into the practice of citizenship according to the reigning paradigm, which holds the two-party system to be unbeatable (if not altogether desirable) and guarantees that a third-party ballot is a ballot wasted.

To accept this paradigm is, in Kuhn's terms, to perpetuate an "unhistorical stereotype" that writes the breaks, or events, out of party history. I use the term *event* here in the sense that some historians, sociologists, and anthropologists have defined it, as a *rare* occurrence, an act or incident that alters the "going order of things."[29] To speak of an event is never simply to claim that "something happened." It is also to assert a counterfactual judgment about a phenomenon; it is to affirm that had this "x" not occurred, a now established pattern of relationships could or would have been otherwise. Although an event can be regarded empirically as an occurrence, it is not reducible to an empirical register because eventfulness turns not only on what happens but also on the significance that attaches (or fails to attach) to it in a particular historical context.

For this reason Marshall Sahlins has argued that a judgment regarding eventfulness is both empirical and "anthropological."[30] Recognizing an event involves, besides discerning the facts of the matter, "a work of cultural signification" to interpret an incident as meaningful and consequential in a historically and culturally specific context.[31] The capacity to interpret "a 'something-happened' as an event, as well as [to identify] its specific historic consequences, *must depend on the structure in place*"[32] That is, judgments about eventfulness are inevitably guided by notions of salience that take their measure from the present. Consequently, it is possible that what one generation considered an event may be altogether overlooked by another. Uneventfulness, then, is not an intrinsic property of the past but an interpretive effect that carries normative consequences. Those incidents we write off as uneventful, even more than those we memorialize as events, foster resignation toward the present.

I find the concept uneventfulness useful because it helps me explain what I mean by asserting that fusion has been written out of party histories. Consider: when the contemporary textbook narrates the history of political parties in the United States in terms of the development of the two-party system, it is telling a story that renders fusion a nonevent. Granted, it is difficult to see fusion bans as altering an electoral paradigm if we imagine the state-sponsored ballot and single-party nominations to have been with us from the start. It is more difficult still if we accept third-party failure as a foregone conclusion. In short, if we treat today's two-party system as "simply or necessarily the continuation of a given historical trajectory," then it will be difficult to conceive antifusion law as anything worth noting: it made a trivial contribution to something that would have occurred anyway.[33]

It should be evident from the arguments of previous chapters that judgments that fusion was insignificant, quaint, and bizarre are effects of what the electoral "structure in place" today counts as eventful. Fusion did make a difference within the highly decentralized state structure of the nineteenth century; consequently, from the vantage point of players within that regime, its prohibition was eventful. There were regions of this country where electoral fusions figured centrally in party strategy. Dominant parties maneuvered their ballots to capitalize on third-party constituencies. Third parties, in turn, timed their nominating conventions to gain maximal independence from, and leverage over, the dominant parties. Certainly, the fusion bans themselves did not cause two-party duopoly, nor were they solely responsible for the precipitous decline in the numbers of significant third parties that have featured in twentieth-century electoral politics. Nonetheless, banning the practice extended state regulation into a previously lawless domain of competition and strategy. Its prohibition was consequential for the turn-of-the-century augmentation of state capacity and hence eventful in a way that is difficult to discern if we take state regulation of parties for granted, narrate party history as the history of the two-party system, and assume that third-party efforts are bound to fail.

My point is that uneventful historical narration has helped to reproduce the two-party system as a catchphrase and has thereby promoted resignation to the present limits of electoral democracy. This begs a further question: what explains scholars' practice of uneventful narration? Are we to assume that they are inherently predisposed toward the status quo? Not exactly. I contend that uneventful narration is a practice of American exceptionalism.

I turn now to explicate that ideology and to explore its history and relationship to American political science.

American exceptionalism connotes a patriotism that no proper scientist would own up to. Herbert Croly once described it as the national myth that figures America "in the imagination of its citizens as the Land of Promise"—a place where time brings material and moral advancement.[34] At once self-congratulatory and normative, exceptionalism assigns United States institutions a "vanguard role in world history."[35] It is, as Dorothy Ross has aptly described it, a "world of mirrors in which the generic and the American, the ideal and the real, come together."[36] Notwithstanding protests to the contrary, Ross maintains that it is also the "national ideology" to which "American social science owes its distinctive character."[37] Ross argues that, from their beginnings as academic disciplines in the 1850s, politics, economics, and law have "consistently constructed models of the world that embody the values and follow the logic of . . . exceptionalism."[38]

Does Ross charge that social science, since its inception, has rallied to promote the ideals and institutions of American liberal democracy? This would be the case if exceptionalism were a simple formula from which to derive political certainties. Ross corrects this stereotype of exceptionalism, together with the stereotype of social science that follows from it. She emphasizes that exceptionalism has been contested over time, and that, far from promoting complacency toward all things American, it hosted a "continuing quarrel with history," one in which "liberal market values" contended against "Protestant and republican ambivalence toward capitalist development and historical change."[39] As Ross tells the story, America's "promise" was not the founding premise of exceptionalism but its central problem.

I contend that eventfulness figured centrally in resolving this problem. The very notion of an event, of an occurrence that would alter the order of things, conflicted profoundly with the early exceptionalists' belief in American perfection. In its first iteration, in the early nineteenth century, exceptionalism was teleological and profoundly unhistorical. The early exceptionalists prided themselves on inhabiting a nation without the class conflict, violence, and the social strife that was the motor force of change in the Old World. Believing that America stood "at the westernmost culmination of European history," they envisioned America's progress in static terms as "a *quantitative* multiplication and elaboration of its founding institutions, not a process of *qualitative* change."[40]

The nineteenth century brought democratization, civil war, emancipation, industrialization, and urbanization, undeniably qualitative changes that marked the irruption of eventfulness into exceptionalist time. This presented twentieth-century social scientists with a challenge: how to reconcile these events with the nation's faith in "the promise of American life"? They had not only to contend with the violent departure from America's agrarian republican beginnings but also with the rupture of that unhistorical sense of time that had imagined progress happening without change. Scholars needed to come to terms at once with these particular events and with eventfulness *itself* as the possibility of qualitative change. Social scientists met this challenge with two revisions of exceptionalist doctrine, producing an exceptionalism of *progress* at the turn of the century and an exceptionalism of *process* in the wake of World War I. Both of these, in different ways, evaded the challenge of the event.

Progress exceptionalism simply hitched itself "to the great engines of modern progress: the capitalist market, social diversification, democracy, and scientific knowledge."[41] The idea, according to Herbert Croly, who was one of its architects, was to recognize that the American "national Promise" was not "an inexorable national destiny" but a political responsibility to be undertaken as "a conscious national purpose."[42] Realizing this purpose called for active participation from citizens as well as from political scientists, who were to shift from normative prescriptions about the proper foundations of politics to empirical analysis of institutions as history made them. This was "historical realism"; it brought "the study of political parties, administration, and city government, the black sheep of American politics," within the compass of the discipline.[43] Historical realism was evidence of a break from the early exceptionalists, who had feared change, to a liberal historicism that saw time as a "progressive historical force."[44] By contrast to their predecessors, these Progressive-era revisionists welcomed eventfulness insofar as they welcomed change. Nonetheless, they domesticated the event by scripting change as progress. Theirs was a first formula for writing history according to the "unhistorical stereotype" that appropriates the past to justify the present.

Progress exceptionalism did not last long. The First World War demonstrated how easily the "great engines" of modernity could be put to use in mechanized warfare and how popular democracy could betray the promise of reasoned self-government. This prompted a second revision of exceptionalism whereby the liberal humanist orientation toward progress ceded to a scientistic orientation toward "natural process."[45] This was a radical revision. Whereas progress exceptionalism had conceived of history as a succession of events to which human intentions and meanings are significant (if not determinative), process exceptionalism rendered history as flow, "a process of continuous, qualitative change, moved and ordered by forces that lay *within itself*."[46] The idea was that history could now be studied like nature, "as a series of ordered changes working toward some result."[47] That result was no longer, as progress exceptionalists like Croly had defined it, a "conscious national purpose"; it was merely the outcome of anonymous, contingent processes. The beauty of process exceptionalism (at least for social scientists who were increasingly committed to value neutrality) was that it affirmed humans' capacity to study order in history but let them off the hook for originating it. Events and eventfulness have no place in the conception of process; it imagines time as a continuum and scripts change as a moment in a sequence.[48]

Progress and process exceptionalism help to illuminate the cultural context within which American government textbooks are written and to explain how third political parties are written out of them. If, as Ross argues, social scientists have constructed models of the world that embody the values and historical logic of American exceptionalism, then I contend that, for political scientists, "the two-party system" has been one such model. Russell Hanson has made a similar claim. Invoking progress exceptionalism, he observes that party scholars plot the story of political parties as a "history of the *advance* of democracy in America."[49] Hanson's observation holds true for mid-century party scholarship, and for many introductory-level textbooks. As I have noted, however, more recent party scholarship eschews progress, denouncing "our party system today [as] a laggard in political development on both the national and state levels."[50] Even though party scholars have long ceased to regard the major parties as agents of progress, I contend that contemporary party scholarship persists in an exceptionalist frame by virtue of their attachment to *process*—an ideologically charged notion that is all the more powerful by virtue of seeming not to be one.

Taking instruction from Ross's nuanced treatment of exceptionalism as a site of contest over the meaning of progress, I demonstrate how party scholarship became a terrain on which the contending republican and liberal versions of American national identity did battle. Contests over the legitimacy and proper place of political parties were caught up in struggles to reconcile the faith in America's unique destiny with the fact of its departure from the political, economic, and social conditions that were to have guaranteed it. They were also caught up in the battles between historical and scientistic conceptions of social science. Third political parties took a beating in these disputes. Once held up as a corrective to the dominant parties' tendencies toward corruption, by mid-century they would be repositioned on the one hand as simply ineffectual and on the other hand as potentially threatening.

For the remainder of this chapter I set changing twentieth-century representations of political parties in the context of the disputes about the limits and possibilities of popular government that were so central to defining both American national identity and the scope and methods of American political science. My main concern is to show that representations of third parties have changed over time with changes in beliefs about what made American popular government unique, what it should achieve, and how political scientists—as *scientists*—could best study it. Scholars have not always regarded third parties as they do today, as "exotic" failures[51] that have "an uncanny ability to divert our attention from the routines of America electoral politics."[52] This view is an effect of the exceptionalist turn to process, which not only shunted third parties to the margins of political science as a discipline but linked "the two-party system" to a truncated conception of democracy.

Progress Exceptionalism and Responsible Popular Government

Third political parties figured centrally in the early Progressives' vision of American democracy. Breaking with what Herbert Croly pointedly termed the "formulas consecrated in the sacred American writings," these scholars proposed a new vision that joined a republican concern for public interests with a democratic ideal of popular self-determination.[53] This was "responsible popular government," which Frank J. Goodnow described as "a system of government in which decisions as to political conduct are the result of the conscious deliberations of the people."[54] In place of a system of checks and balances that was "calculated to thwart the popular will," responsible popular government called for citizen action to be paired with political centralization.[55] Citizens would "stand and vote together for what they think is paramount."[56] That vote would empower the state to take "any action, which, in the opinion of a decisive majority of the people, is demanded by the public welfare."[57]

Political parties complemented this new, popular vision of republican government in ways that they could not complement the elite republicanism of the founders. Following the work of Henry Jones Ford, the early Progressives recognized "party organization" as an "extra-constitutional means" that filled a void in a republican architecture of the founding.[58] The founders had made no provision for linking the people to its representatives and had even sought to thwart the formation and expression of public purposes. Following Ford, Frank J. Goodnow sought emphatically to legitimate the party system, which he described as an "extra-legal" institution that has "come to supplement—we must say indeed to amend—the Constitution."[59] Whereas Ford and Goodnow were correct in emphasizing the need for party organization, the party machines and party bosses could hardly be praised for their responsiveness to popular demand. This was where third political parties would come in. Their role in "responsible popular government" was to act as watchdogs over the party machines. When bosses used the dominant parties to put their own interests ahead of the public good, third parties could right their course by "enabling a considerable body of political opinion to find rational expression at the ballot-box."[60]

James Albert Woodburn, whose prominent party textbook was first published in 1903, made a forceful distinction between the dominant party machines and "third party agitations" which he praised as "positive and aggressive forces" that could reassure citizens "that party history, after all, is not entirely machine made."[61] Woodburn not only praises third parties for "doing a great service in enabling voters to stand up for their opinions," he actually denounces as "absurd" and "illogical" the "idea that men must vote with one of the two parties":

> It leads citizens to vote for men whom they do not trust, and to subscribe to principles in which they do not believe. It is often an obstacle to healthy political education and development. It tends to induce men to subordinate their real convictions for the mere idle purpose of rallying under a traditional party name to carry an election. . . . to go with a party which the voter thinks is fundamentally wrong or is headed entirely in the wrong direction, merely because the other party is worse, is not calculated to make for wholesome politics or for the ultimate benefit of the country.[62]

Although Woodburn expressed it with uncommon eloquence, the belief that responsible popular government rested not on "the two parties" but on third parties was not an uncommon position at the time.

In this, and in many other respects, the Progressives' perspective on third political parties stands in stark contrast to that of the present. For example, if political analysts today caution citizens that third parties promise more than the two-party system will permit them to deliver, Progressive-era analysts warned that "the significance and effectiveness of the third party movements is *underestimated* by the casual observer."[63] Leading party scholar and reformer Charles E. Merriam credited such parties with having scored "notable" electoral victories: "From 1896 to 1916 there were chosen by the minor parties some six Governors, 116 Senators and Representatives; and 1,761 members of the various state legislatures. In addition to this many members of city and county and town officials were elected by the independent or minor groups."[64] He also praised them as "advance guards of new issues," singling out the Free Soilers for playing "a very important, some would say the major role in the slavery struggle," the Greenbackers and Populists for advancing currency reform, and the Progressive party for fostering gains toward women's suffrage and "various issues of social and industrial justice, notably that of child labor."[65] Even E. M. Sait, though an early enthusiast for the two-party doctrine, could agree that the "potential usefulness" of third political parties was not open to dispute.[66]

Actually, Sait went farther than endorsing the instrumental value of third parties. He suggested that the dominant parties depended for their very legitimacy on a symbiotic relationship to minor party insurgencies because, without them, the established parties tend to fall behind the times. For example, Sait observed that the dominant parties had "aroused much critical comment" by their silence "on the highly controversial subjects of prohibition and woman suffrage" and that "such momentous changes as were embodied in the Eighteenth and Nineteenth Amendments . . . [took] place without [their] intervention."[67] He argued that minor parties, acting as strategic adjuncts to the dominant parties, could quiet those criticisms. Whereas the major parties would choose their issues "as a merchant replenishes his stock," sticking with the policies that are a proven sell with the voters, they would rely on third-party movements would test market new ideas, moving the major parties forward when they found a good one.[68]

Renowned party critic Moisei Ostrogorski put the failure of the major parties even more forcefully. In a sarcastic aside to those who thought it a virtue to model the American system after the "two great parties" of Britain, he remarked, "There seems to be no inkling that the great parties are like the proverbial Roland's mare, which possessed every good quality, but had the misfortune to be dead."[69] What had killed the major parties was what Ostrogorski called "political formalism."[70] A tendency of the dominant parties in a two-party system, formalism occurs when parties become "stereotyped" organizations, digging their heels into outworn "political principles and ideas" for fear of losing their base.[71] Ostrogorski argued that it was thanks only to the interventions of those third parties—at least those that managed to tap into a suppressed issue cleavage of *genuine* import—that the dominant parties were ever forced to bring their "endless prevarications" to a halt.[72]

It is interesting that Ostrogorski is infamous today for advocating the abolition of parties, because that was not the thrust of his argument.[73] He did call for reforms such as proportional representation that would make it easier for third parties to do their work. In the broader context of his argument, this was opposition not to parties generally but to electoral duopoly in particular. David R. Mayhew has observed that Ostrogorski's reputation as a party critic is undeserved, testifying to the "American political science community's firmly held belief that American parties somehow or other must be functional."[74] It also highlights the tendency of that community to conflate parties, the two-party system, and democracy.

What stands out in the work of scholars such as Merriam, Sait, and Ostrogorski is their insistence that two-party competition is structurally flawed. None could imagine the major parties achieving popular government as "rational" government *without* the periodic intervention of third parties.[75] They understood third-party insurgencies to be integral not only to the smooth functioning of the two-party structure but also to its legitimacy. And they acknowledged fusion as a third-party strategy. Charles Merriam noted that many third-party victories were secured by means "of various types of fusions between independents and regulars."[76] James Bryce explained that the strategy gave third parties a means to influence the major parties' choice of nominees, observing that it "helps to keep a minor party going, and gives to its vote a practical result otherwise unattainable."[77] It is noteworthy that Merriam and Bryce treat fusion as a simple matter of fact. Although its existence neither excited nor worried them, its absence might well have. Whereas Bryce wrote in advance of the assault on fusion, Merriam wrote directly in its wake, too soon to see the consequences antifusion legislation would have for the kinds of third parties he admired. They might well have counted antifusion legislation as an event, had they anticipated its impact.

These scholars offer an alternative vantage point on our own time. They did not take it for granted that third parties waste votes and they emphatically did not consider the two-party system to be sufficient guarantee of competitive elections, nor of responsible popular government. Consequently, they might well regard the absence of third parties in our time as a setback to democracy rather than an advance.

Process Exceptionalism and Process Democracy

In the post–New Deal, post-WWII period scholars' expectations for democracy changed, as did their expectations about the role of political parties in producing it. E. E. Schattschneider, in 1942, published *Party Government*, a classic work "devoted to the thesis that the political parties created democracy and that modern democracy is unthinkable save in terms of the parties."[78] As Schattschneider tells it, political parties single-handedly piloted the nation into modernity. They were "political entrepreneurs" that "got the law of the franchise liberalized," "presid[ed] over the transformation of the government of the United States from a small experiment in republicanism to the most powerful regime on earth," and made it "vastly more liberal and democratic than it was in 1789."[79] Robert MacIver echoed that "where parties flourish we have in effect passed from a pre-democratic mode of representative government to a genuinely democratic one."[80] Even Ranney and Kendall emphasize that party development promoted the development of democracy in the nation and in the party organization at once. They describe each step in party development as a step "toward democracy and away from absolutism," "each subsequent step toward democracy . . . result[ing] in . . . a corresponding change in party organization."[81]

These passages construct a blatantly teleological model of party history that imagines time moving forward toward emancipation and casts parties as its agents. This was the height of exceptionalism as an ideology that celebrated the idiosyncratically American two-party system as a generically democratic form. As such, it makes a remarkable change from the disposition of Progressive-era scholars, who had so much to say about the structural failings of two-party competition.

But it is important to recognize that this approval for the *form* of two-party democracy was not accompanied by complacency toward its practice. There was real disagreement regarding what democracy could be, what parties could or should contribute to it, and how political scientists as *scientists* could position themselves both to study parties and foster democratic political forms. The postwar period is distinct, then, both for an exceptionalist consensus regarding the exemplary status of American political parties and for impassioned argumentation that linked together the future of parties, the future of American democracy, and the future of American political science. Although third political parties were not seen as crucial to any of these debates, they were crucially repositioned by them.

At the confluence of these concerns about parties, democracy, and the discipline stood the 1950 report of the Committee on Political Parties of the American Political Science Association, *Toward a More Responsible Two-Party System*. This document, which was meant as an expert blueprint for party reform, turned out to do much more to focus academic debates about the future of the discipline than it did to guide political debates about the future of the parties.[82] The dispute between the authors of the report and their critics has frequently been cast as a contest between normative and empirical approaches to party scholarship. I maintain that it staged a confrontation between contending versions of American exceptionalism and that this confrontation is interesting for two reasons. First, it illustrates how the discourse of "process" works to disavow ideology at the same time as it perpetuates exceptionalist ideas. Second, it reveals a sea change in the evaluation of third parties. Whereas party scholars of the early Progressive era considered them integral to two-party democracy, most mid-century party scholars (with one important exception) counted their absence as a sign of American political health and maturity.

Can democracy survive without strong parties at its core? This was the central question of the "responsible parties" debate, to which the APSA Committee on Political Parties answered an emphatic "No!" The committee argued that America's "big tent" parties jeopardized the integrity of popular government because they were unprincipled, opportunistic, and decentralized. Absent reform, its members predicted that citizens would lose faith in voting and that the power to speak for "the people" would concentrate in an increasingly demagogic (and potentially authoritarian) presidency. They proposed to remake the parties after a British parliamentary model of responsible party government. This called for parties to be deliberative, organized around "well-considered programs," capable of marshaling "widespread public support" behind a clearly articulated conception of the public good, and sufficiently disciplined to enact a coherent program once in office.[83] This was, as David Ricci has noted, "a throwback to the days when liberals had routinely believed in the postulates of rationality and responsible government."[84]

Critics objected that those postulates were discredited by the history of parties in the twentieth-century United States and, moreover, that even the British parties did not live up to the committee's romanticized vision of responsible government. They countered with a vision of democracy and conception of political parties they claimed to derive from observing the United States parties in practice. Contrary to the committee's wish that the parties would articulate a unifying national purpose, these self-proclaimed empirical theorists put competition—not doctrine—at the core of popular government. Theirs was a "process theory of democracy"[85] that called upon the party organization only to "achieve a working alliance of interests and bring support to leaders who desire both to control the government and to tolerate a loyal opposition."[86] If the committee worried that United States political parties functioned as "*mere* brokers between different groups and interests," its critics found this to be perfectly appropriate.[87] Parties that aimed to discipline their members and to define themselves by a cohesive doctrine would not be an asset but an impediment to this alliance-building process. In fact, to E. Pendleton Herring, whose work inspired the critics' response, the absence of "responsible" parties would not have been a flaw but a virtue, for it is only in "totalitarian" states where "the more natural social and economic ties of community have been broken" that solidarity needed to be imposed by a strong party from above.[88]

Running alongside the contest between these rival visions of party organization, and intensifying it, was a dispute between apparently radically different conceptions of the practice of political science. Whereas the committee has been almost unanimously denounced for answering a call for practical advice with a normative vision (and a romantic and anachronistic one at that), its critics have been allowed to claim the mantle of science for themselves.[89] They were credited with producing an "empirical" theory that premised its expectations for democracy on its actual practice despite the fact that this theory was shot through with ideological commitments. It embraced liberalism, with its trust in party competition, and pluralism, with its confidence in the fluidity of group membership. If these ideologies have ever seemed neutral, it would not have been in 1942 when, as Jeffrey C. Isaac has observed, popular government raised the specter of totalitarianism. At that time liberal pluralism was by no means the real-world description that it claimed to be but rather a "*prescription* about the only kind of halfway decent politics that might, it was believed, avoid the evils of totalitarianism."[90] In passing off their own normative vision as simple fact, the committee's critics achieved what Isaac terms an empirical "subterfuge."[91] I suggest that an exceptionalist conception of process assisted this maneuver.

Mid-century critics of responsible parties disavowed the Progressive-era faith that the American people could function as a public, conscious and deliberative. If popular government were to produce democracy in America (as opposed to fascism) it would be thanks to process alone. Competition, between political parties and among interest groups, would assure the stability and continuity of party government and safeguard the people against ideological extremism. This was the genius of process, which, unlike progress, lacks *overt* enthusiasm for things American: it could enable mid-century social scientists to perpetuate exceptionalism while appearing to have left ideology behind.

Thus far, I have argued for seeing the committee and its critics as partners in exceptionalism rather than as opponents on either side of the normative/empirical divide. Nowhere is their kinship more clearly borne out than in their treatment of third political parties. Both the committee and its critics rely on third political parties to mark the difference between American democracy and the unstable popular governments of Europe. They represent the *absence* of third political parties as testimony to the superiority of United States democracy.

Given their concern to reform every other aspect of the party system, it is noteworthy that the committee enthusiastically accepted the two-party system as a parameter of debate. Members were unabashed in declaring that in speaking generally of "the parties . . . we mean throughout our report the two major parties."[92] From its title to its concluding sentences, the report invoked the "two-party system" and the "American two-party system" as its object.[93] No document from this period is more adamant about the "fact" that "the two-party system is part of the American political tradition," a "fundamental" prerequisite of political accountability, and so "strongly rooted" in both tradition and "public preference . . . that consideration of other possibilities"—such as adopting proportional representation instead of or alongside party reform—"seems entirely academic."[94] It was not that they "consider[ed] third or minor parties undesirable or ineffectual within their limited orbit"; they judged them relatively inconsequential for having left no "lasting imprint upon [either] the two-party system [or] the basic processes of American government."[95] What is striking about these statements is the conviction that the two-party system is self-sufficient. It puts the mid-century proponents of responsible government significantly at odds with their Progressive-era predecessors, who could not imagine the major parties performing responsibly *without* the intervention of third political parties.

By contrast, their pluralist critics did not celebrate the two-party system; they did, however, cheer the *absence* of third political parties as proof of a healthy group process. As they saw it, third parties would come and go; their going should be read as proof of major party success at "harmonizing and adjusting the economic and social forces of their communities."[96] Conversely, "the rise of a third party to any position of influence would be a portent of serious rigidities in our political system. It would not indicate a movement to be frowned upon but would suggest rather that our party leaders had failed in their [conciliatory] task."[97] Ranney and Kendall put it even more plainly, writing that the absence of "strongly supported *and* long-lasting minor parties" should be read as proof "that our party system, and the pluralistic politico-governmental system it animates, are succeeding more than ever in the past in making people feel [that it is worthwhile not to leave the political mainstream]."[98] Historian Richard Hofstadter summed up the celebratory view when he famously wrote that "third parties are like bees: once they have stung, they die."[99] Hofstadter, Herring, and others took it as a sign of a healthy liberal democracy that though it would permit its bees a periodic sting, they were never more than gadflies on the rump of the polity.

I have shown how American exeptionalism survives on both sides of the responsible parties debate. To be sure, neither the committee members nor their critics endorse an overtly ideological temporality of progress; they manage to fuel a condescension toward the past that nonetheless encourages resignation toward two-party politics. Whereas the committee lost sight of the role that third political parties were once expected to play in responsible government, its critics celebrated their failures as testimony to the success of the consensus-building group process. It would not do to close this discussion without mentioning the work of V. O. Key, a mid-century party scholar who stands out both for valuing third political parties and for breaking with the textbook stereotypes that write them out of United States party history. What accounts for Key's unorthodox perspective? He was a critic of both "progress" and "process" whose pathbreaking theory of "critical elections" amounts to a profound challenge to exceptionalism (although he would not use the term).[100]

A "critical election" is an electoral event. It is a hotly contested election that effects so "sharp and durable" a *realignment* of partisan alliance as to change the balance of power between the dominant parties.[101] Critical elections have been accompanied by institutional reform that redefines the very practice of electoral democracy, such as the shift from the caucus to the convention, from restricted to universal white male suffrage, from the party ticket to the secret ballot, and from multiple-party to single-party nominations. These events do more than shift voters from one party to the other; they alter the terms of electoral competition. So different are the political alliances, electoral rules, and voting behavior in the wake of a critical election that scholars conceive the intervening periods as distinct party systems.[102]

Critical elections theory mounts a thoroughgoing challenge to textbook histories of the United States party system. First, it reveals that what we think of as a "system" is not one but rather many.[103] Second, it reveals that the continuity of this country's major political parties is deceptive. Each one has been periodically remade by the electoral upheavals that have redefined their issues and reorganized their constituencies. As Walter Dean Burnham has put it, the major party organizations "*on one level* have undergone no basic transformations since they achieved characteristic form in the 1840s"; this continuity, however, "is only part of a larger dynamic or dialectical process."[104] Third, it suggests that scholars may put too much stock in continuity as the secret to the stability of democracy in the United States; it has depended as much or more on this dynamic or dialectical process as it has on incremental, cumulative change.[105]

There are obvious affinities between this "critical elections" reconceptualization of party history and Kuhn's argument about scientific revolutions. Just as a paradigm shift sets a new agenda for electoral research, electoral realignments redefine the "broad boundaries of the politically possible."[106] These electoral events have made possible large-scale policy initiatives such as the New Deal, which could not have been enacted even a few years earlier, and have redefined the trademark commitments of the dominant parties and the voters who affiliate with them. Most important, critical elections depend on third-party activity as a catalyst.

Key maintained that it was difficult to appreciate the significance of third political parties if scholars insisted on reducing them to "miniatures of a major party."[107] Like Merriam, he argued that they are not to be judged by their longevity, nor by such quantitative measures as "whether this or that 3 per cent of the vote polled by a minor party constituted a balance of power and swung the election in this or that state)."[108] To dismiss third parties for their slim showings at the polls was to assimilate them to a measure of success appropriate to the dominant parties alone. Key urged scholars to appreciate the difference between doctrinal third parties that were, paradoxically, long-lived but insignificant and "transient third-party movements" (such as Populism) that may "deeply affect the party system" not by taking office but "by demonstrating the existence of a block of voters for whose support a major party may bid."[109] For V. O. Key, third political parties are more than "bees" who give the major parties a periodic sting. Instead, they are "integral elements of the so-called two-party system [that] . . . spring from the center of the political melee, and . . . affect the nature of the major parties and the relationships between them as they cumbersomely make their way from election to election.[110] Like Sait and Merriam before him, then, Key emphasized the symbiosis between the major and minor parties, even suggesting that this interdependency ought to call our very terminology—"the *so-called* two-party system"—into question.[111]

Key also stands alone among his colleagues in devoting space to fusion as a legitimate third-party strategy. An early edition of his textbook explained how Fiorello LaGuardia was elected mayor on four distinct ballot lines, due to the "New York system of nominations [that] makes it possible for a minority party to fuse with a major party without losing its identity and also to prove the dependence of the major candidate upon its support."[112] By 1952 he added a much more comprehensive explanation of the mechanics of the strategy, emphasizing the importance of separate listings and separate tallies so that "minor-party leaders can . . . point to their party's contribution to the total vote of the victorious candidate, [and] . . . also demonstrate that if their party had named its own candidate or endorsed the opposing candidate, the outcome would probably have been different."[113] If this is fusion's advantage to third political parties, its benefit to voters is that it "circumvents the ancient dilemma of third parties—that if they nominate a candidate of their own, they might thereby contribute to the defeat of the major-party candidate most nearly agreeing with their principles."[114] Key further elaborated that New York politics was unique not only for permitting multiple nominations but for sustaining third parties as *fusion* parties. In contrast to La Guardia's time, when alternative candidates used multiple nominations to secure public office, by the 1950s and 1960s New York's third political parties were content merely to influence elections. These parties existed as electoral arms of organized labor. With their power base assured independently of the party system, their leaders sought neither to challenge the dominant parties nor to "win office themselves."[115]

Key stands out for giving prominence to third political parties, for featuring fusion, and, most important, for putting forward an account of party history that challenges notable features of American exceptionalism. Although Key did not set out to refute this ideology, his theory of critical elections rebuts the "unhistorical stereotype" of cumulative time that underlies it. By contrast to both progress and process exceptionalism, which premise stability on continuity and incremental change, Key emphasized discontinuity, conflict, and abruption. His work also defies classification in terms of the responsible parties debate and its attendant methodological contests. He was a rigorous empirical scholar who relied on statistical and historical analysis, an impassioned critic of one-party politics, and a student of democracy who regarded both political parties and pressure groups as necessary to popular government.

By 1964 scholars agreed on the need to make a more scientific approach to the study of political parties. This would entail quantitative analysis, treating the party itself as "an organizational system," and breaking with the "semi-empirical strategy" of approaches that focused on the "statutory and legal status" of parties at the expense of analyzing their political functions and substituted "the narration of historical background, together with impressionistic, uncontrolled observation and much anecdotal reference" for the formulation and testing of generalizable propositions.[116] It would also entail putting the political parties in perspective as elements in the political system, and not the most critical ones at that. In 1964 Samuel Eldersveld noted with disdain the leading party scholars of the postwar period who "accepted as incontrovertible truth that the historical development of democracy would have been impossible without the concomitant appearance of political parties."[117] In 1980 Frank J. Sorauf dedicated his advanced-level party text to defending the "proposition that the political parties have lost their preeminent position as political organizations and that competing political organizations now perform many of the activities traditionally regarded as the parties' exclusive prerogatives."[118] If the dominant parties lost their position of preeminence during this period, third parties fared even worse.

Frank J. Sorauf stated the case against third political parties most powerfully in *Political Parties in the American System*, the 1964 precursor to his widely read textbook. Writing as an advocate for what Sheldon Wolin, who wrote the foreword to that volume, called the "new methods of the political scientist,"[119] Sorauf urged his colleagues toward greater precision in defining their terms and toward the study of phenomena that could yield generalizable propositions about *mass* political behavior. Sorauf objected to his colleagues' disproportionate attention to third-party efforts, which he claimed preoccupied them "to the almost total neglect of the major parties." He pointedly observed that the fascination with these movements was at odds with the scientific aspirations of the discipline: it "seems to indicate that the canons of relevance and importance have given way to a fascination with the *quaint and bizarre* in American politics."[120] For Sorauf, it followed that proper scientists should regard the study of third parties to be almost as quixotic as the movements themselves.

This is American exceptionalism, even though Sorauf neither celebrates the two-party system as proof of America's progress nor holds it up as the world's most perfect democratic form. In praising party scholarship for having outgrown its "preference for 'hard-headed' practical description and activism and . . . suspicion of theoretical propositions," Sorauf represents political *science* (not politics) as progressing incrementally toward more comprehensive understanding.[121] He insists that political scientists study party process, focusing on "party structure," and on "the ways in which parties contest elections and organize political power," at the expense of historical narration and analysis.[122] The effect is to fix the "canons" of structure and functionalism, thereby endorsing that which the most recent scientific revolution had rendered credible.

Scholars' orientation toward process promoted an ahistorical approach to the study of political parties that reaffirms the two-party system as a timeless truth of United States electoral politics—even among scholars who would never celebrate it as a bulwark of democracy. The determination to study process, and to conceive process as, above all, conciliation and incremental change, did more than any explicit affirmation of two-partyism to establish third political parties as inconsequential to electoral democracy. It also carried with it a preference for uneventfulness that produces resignation toward the "process conception" of democracy, that vision which holds self-government to work perfectly well without citizens. This is the normative effect of *the two-party system:* in producing what we take to be real it also limits what we imagine to be possible through the electoral process.

In chapters 3 and 4 I have emphasized how this term is contested in the discipline. I have shown how it figures into competing conceptions of democracy and emphasized the importance of events such as fusion for their potential to call attention to the politics of its formation. If the two-party process and the process conception of democracy discourage electoral participation, what norms and institutions would promote it? Would fusion and third parties have a role in fostering a more participatory electoral regime? I turn to these questions in the next chapter.

CHAPTER 5

Oppositional Democracy and the Promise of Electoral Fusion

Decades ago, E. E. Schattschneider observed that political parties "occupy a blind spot in the theory of democracy."[1] *Blind spot* was a good choice of words, for it names at once an impossibility and a fantasy. The blind spot marks an impossibility because it refers not to those things we just happen to overlook but to that which we are precluded from seeing by the architecture of the eye or by the design of the vehicles that we trust to move us forward. Whereas a driver *learns* to correct for the blind spot and so is quite conscious that there is a failure of vision built into the mechanics of driving, it is otherwise with the eye itself. We never know where the eye fails, or even *that* it fails, because the brain compensates by filling in what it imagines must be there. That compensatory imagining, necessary as it is to seeing sensibly, is a hazard when it comes to institution building.

In theories of democracy today, as in those of forty years ago, visions of participatory democracy propel themselves forward through a dynamic of blindness by design and compensatory fantasy. Citizen participation has become the watchword for small-d democrats on both the right and left who lament Americans' declining civic commitment. It has become commonplace to argue that the United States is in the throes of a crisis of public life that is, at base, a crisis of political participation. Academics have advanced numerous proposals for bringing citizens back into politics. These include James Fishkin's "deliberative opinion poll,"[2] Robert Dahl's citizen-policy expert "minipopulus,"[3] Benjamin Barber's neighborhood assemblies and public service programs,[4] and Amitai Etzioni's interactive televised electronic town hall.[5] These proposals have at least one feature in common. Nowhere do their architects attend to the first question of political organizing: how will you turn out the people? It is as if citizens who are uninspired by the charade of representative government would flock to the new age agora on the strength of the infinitely more rewarding (albeit more time-consuming) practice of citizenship it demands.

It is also noteworthy that political parties typically have no place in these participatory visions. In stark contrast to enthusiasts like Schattschneider who celebrated parties as democratic "entrepreneurs," today's proponents of deliberative and participatory democracy, schooled in the movement politics of the 1960s, hold party politics to be opportunistic, bureaucratic, and antithetical to citizenship.[6] To Hannah Arendt, political parties quash "action and participation in public affairs" by making politics the business of "career" politicians and choosing leaders "according to standards and criteria which are themselves profoundly unpolitical."[7] Continuing along this vein, Benjamin Barber holds party politics to exemplify everything about liberalism that is "deeply inimical to real democracy." In his view they have "consistently diminished rather than enhanced self-government."[8] As for voting, Barber memorably (if scatalogically) compares it to "using a public toilet: we wait in line with a crowd in order to close ourselves up in a small compartment where we can relieve ourselves in solitude and in privacy of our burden, pull a lever, and then, yielding to the next in line, go silently home."[9]

If there is one thing to be learned from the presidential election of 2000, it is that casting a measurable vote involves a good deal more than pulling a lever. For a well-educated, efficacious middle-class citizen, voting may be so straightforward a task as to be discharged like a biological function. For the poor, for the elderly, and for those who cast ballots on antiquated machinery, getting to the polls and registering a choice is not quite the reflex that Barber makes it out to be. On the contrary, Barber's analogy (which, admittedly, is a caricature) represents as a norm what is, in fact, a privilege. Political parties, whatever their shortcomings, are foremost among the associations that offset that privilege. They subsidize the cost of voting by registering votes, dropping campaign literature, door knocking and phone banking to increase turn out, and driving voters to the polls. As Walter Dean Burnham once put it, "Political parties, with all their well-known human and structural shortcomings, are the only devices thus far invented by the wit of Western man which with some effectiveness can generate countervailing collective power on behalf of the many individually powerless against the relatively few who are individually—or organizationally—powerful."[10]

I contend that critics of liberalism who celebrate participation but shun parties have a blind spot for the costs of political action, together with the political labors by which they are offset. This blind spot legitimates their antipathy toward political parties and gives rise to a compensatory fantasy of spontaneous citizen action that, ironically, reproduces a core assumption of the liberal individualism they set out to criticize. The assumption is that participation is self-generated: whereas the liberal counts interest as the fount of the will to act, the democrat seeks to cultivate civic mindedness in its place.

By contrast to their Progressive-era predecessors, today's architects of responsible public citizenship define political parties out of their field of vision by discounting the labors they perform. This chapter aims to alter the sight lines of contemporary democratic theory by taking the cost of action and the labor of organizing seriously. Drawing upon the work of E. E. Schattschneider, I propose an alternate diagnosis of the crisis of public life, which I argue is not simply a crisis of participation but, more specifically, a crisis of *de*mobilization driven by the bias of the forms of political organizing that the present conflict system prefers.

Scope of Conflict/Scope of Democracy

E. E. Schattschneider once wrote that "the role of the people in the political system is determined largely by the *conflict system*, for it is conflict that involves the people in politics and the nature of the conflict determines the nature of the public involvement."[11] I have been critical of Schattschneider throughout this book as an enthusiast for the two-party system. At the same time, I am drawn to his writing because it lends itself to thinking about the politics of institutions and procedures, about the ways that the putative frameworks of politics order conflicts, and the ways that conflicts, in turn, organize people into and out of politics. This is especially true of the phrase *conflict system.* Although he never defined it precisely, Schattschneider used this concept by turns to denote the principles (such as universal rights), governing mechanisms (such as markets and states), and modes of organizing (political parties, social movements, interest groups) that set the context within which some issues are more easily politicized than others. I hold this term to make a significant intervention into debates about political participation and abstention, one whose implications for today's crisis of public life have been largely ignored. I propose to draw out those implications and thereby reframe the crisis of public life to better comprehend the forms of organizing that might ameliorate it.

Schattschneider called attention to the "conflict system" to criticize the midcentury pluralists, whose marketplace model of politics insisted on the neutrality of such institutions as parties and interest groups, and even pluralist ideology itself.[12] Schattschneider emphasized that institutions are not indifferent to the groups that form and last or to those that are repeatedly frustrated. This was his central insight: the capacity to mobilize certain forms of opposition and participation is *already* institutionalized in any form of political organization by its "bias in favor of the exploitation of some kinds of conflict and the suppression of others."[13] Moreover, institutional "frameworks" are never politically neutral. They organize issues and people into and out of politics by virtue of what Schattschneider called the "mobilization of bias," without which there can be no organization at all.[14]

These terms, *conflict system* and *mobilization of bias,* forcefully refuted the pluralist fantasy that state power is open to any organized group that succeeds in winning either mass support or agency sponsorship. But they were equally an indictment of what Schattschneider called "classical" theorists of democracy, whom he accused of doing the "worst possible disservice . . . to the democratic cause" when they posited a "self-generated impulse of people to participate in the life of the political community."[15] Schattscheider countered that citizens do not participate in politics unless they are organized. They form groups in answer to the call of conflict, and institutions shape that call. Thus the classical democrat's "disservice," according to Schattschneider, was to imagine that political participation is spontaneously generated at "the grass roots."[16]

Schattschneider rejects the naturalistic fiction of participation that animates both participatory and pluralist conceptions of democracy by emphasizing that citizen engagement is an effect of what a conflict system exploits. As Schattschneider understands it, conflict never simply happens; it is, rather, an effect of the bias toward certain forms of opposition and participation that is *already* institutionalized in the conflict system by the modes of organizing it prefers. This bias may be as patently obvious as an explicit ideology; it may be quietly written into the most innocuous procedural detail—such as the configuration of a ballot. The point is that however participatory it aspires to be, no institution treats "conflict impartially, [any more than] football rules . . . treat all forms of violence with indiscriminate equality."[17] Just as football is a game of managed violence, politics is a game of managed conflict in which political leadership aims to mobilize battles that reproduce long-established cleavages and to tax those that might generate unconventional alliances.

Thinking about the mobilization of bias calls forth a very different image of the public than circulates in the work of many participatory and deliberative democrats. In such work it is common to figure the public as a "space" or a "realm," as if it were a container that fills with citizens whenever a particularly compelling problem emerges. Schattschneider displaces this open sphere with one crosscut by competing ideologies and policy preferences. Mobilization is a strategy for identifying the issues or clusters of issues that cleave it into unequal parts. Its object is not to unify the public, nor is it even to carry a majority and win the battle. More important is to win the battle to *stage* the battle and thereby secure the capacity to define its "scope" in your favor.[18]

E. E. Schattschneider compels us to look into the blind spot of contemporary democratic theory. He establishes that action costs. He shows that it costs more for some groups than it does for others. And he argues that it is a most "important strategy of politics" to manipulate the costs of political action by affecting its scope.[19] This is a distinctively political way of thinking about institutions and procedures that opens up a novel perspective on the crisis of public life, one that looks not to citizens but to conflict to explain the pathologies of this democracy. If we are concerned to understand why citizens do not vote, Schattschneider counsels us to analyze the conflict system, to look at "the way in which the alternatives in American politics are defined, the way in which issues get referred to the public, the scale of competition and organization, and above all [at] *what* issues are developed."[20] For what keeps nonvoters away from the polls is not that they are ignorant, nor that they are content, nor even that they are unfulfilled by the kind of participation that voting affords. It is, rather, that they are demobilized by the forms of political organizing that the present conflict system prefers.

Schattschneider helps us conceive of nonparticipation as an *effect* of mobilization rather than as its antithesis; it is a pathology of the conflict system that "reflects the suppression of the options and alternatives that reflect the needs of the nonparticipants."[21] In 1998 a National Public Radio listener echoed this view, explaining on a call-in to *Talk of the Nation* that nonvoters abstain not just because they are "apathetic [or] throwing their vote away because . . . they have something else to do." Some make a considered decision to stay away from the polls "because [we] understand nobody's really representing us anymore."[22] If this listener and his political science advocate are correct, the problem of public life is not that liberal, privatized, individualistic institutions have imposed obstacles to public participation; it is, rather, that such institutions *produce nonparticipation* as an effect of the forms of organization they prefer.

Schattschneider's reframing of our crisis of public life calls for a new way of thinking about power that he himself touted as a "revolution in our thinking about politics."[23] Contrary to what he called "the familiar simplistic calculus based on the model of a tug of war," Schattschneider proposed to conceive of power not as a measurable property but as an "*unstable relation*" that extends beyond the parties to a conflict to its spectators.[24] The instabiliy of power follows from what Schattschneider deemed the "central political fact in a free society": the "contagiousness of conflict."[25] The principle is that, in a free society, conflict is catching. In politics as in street fighting, sport, and theater, Schattschneider maintained that the "excitement of the conflict *communicates* itself to a crowd"; the crowd figures centrally into the calculus of power, in turn, because its participation changes the "balance of the forces involved."[26]

To accept this "central political fact" is to effect a shift from treating power as leverage—defined as such by Robert Dahl who famously held power to consist in "A's capacity for acting in such a manner as to control B's responses"—to conceiving it as a process.[27] This process works not exclusively or even primarily by proscription but, rather, by *communication*. It is crucial to note that communication, as Schattschneider defines it in the context of the contagion principle of conflict, is not to be confused with speech, dialogue, argumentation, or any other means by which humans come to mutual understanding. Schattschneider's conflict "communicates" not like reason but more like a virus. To follow the contagion metaphor, it is communicable (rather than communicative). Power consists as much in exploiting the contagious properties of conflict as it does in containing them.

For Schattschneider, as for many contemporary political theorists, power is *productive*. It is at work not only in the struggle to *win* a conflict but also in the struggle to determine the "*scope* of its contagion."[28] Contests over scope sometimes happen concurrently with a fight over a substantive issue, as a struggle to define it, which is *framing*, in scholarly terms, or *spin control*, in common parlance. But it may also take the form of struggle over the "*organization of politics*."[29] This is struggle over the conflict system itself, over such procedural provisions as same-day voter registration, public campaign financing, and ballot access law that indirectly affect the matters that can be fought publicly insofar as they either foster or constrain modes of organizing that open the electoral arena to new participants. Although procedure rarely seems political, procedural change inevitably effects "change in the scope of conflict." Even procedure "has a bias; it is *partisan* in nature."[30]

Manipulating the scope of conflict has profound implications for that most basic democratic principle of majority rule. For the narrower the scope of a conflict, the less it takes to win. To understand this is also to understand how it is possible for a conflict system to *produce* nonparticipation as one of its principal effects. We should expect nonparticipation to increase wherever the bias of a conflict system selects mobilizations that *narrow* the scope of conflict, wherever its preferred procedures, forms of organizing, and substantive issues tend to stage conflicts among a minority of the public.

I have argued throughout this book for understanding the two-party system as a *conflict* system that narrows the scope of conflict.[31] I have contended that today's two-party system, in contrast to its nineteenth-century configuration, demobilizes third-party opposition. I have also argued that this demobilization is a legacy of electoral reforms that began at the turn of the century and continued through the Progressive era. I turn now to examine that legacy in greater detail.

Political Rationalization

Ours is a conflict system in which labor-intensive organizing has ceded to technology-driven electioneering. Broad-based organizing strategies such as door-to-door canvassing, neighborhood potlucks, and stump speeches to low- and middle-income groups have given way to "a highly sophisticated mix of detailed polling, focus groups, targeted direct mail, and television and radio commercials precisely tailored in response to the flood of information concerning public attitudes."[32] Political consultants use these techniques (borrowed from consumer research) to test-market issues, find the niches where they resonate, and then deploy ad campaigns in the markets where they will bring the greatest returns at the polls. Meanwhile, establishment candidates reserve their labor-intensive mobilization for the areas where it is most likely to pay off, saving personal contact for "people who are known to them, who are well placed in social networks, whose actions are effective, and who are likely to act."[33] Small donors are drawn into the fray by fund-raising tactics (such as direct mail solicitations) that rely on fervent appeals that mobilize uncompromising, single-issue constituencies. Even for state legislative races, candidates and parties are pressured to raise funds expediently and to make them pay off at the polls.

In a system that sets a premium on the "capacity to mobilize money, not people," is it any wonder that a majority of the citizenry declines to vote?[34] Any citizen can see that donations are more powerful than ballots, and that politicians are more concerned to speak to the ideologically motivated sectors that they can "hecto[r] into the voting booths" than to their more moderate constituencies.[35] In this respect it is revealing that the contemporary crisis in participation, although widespread, is not universal. It is a selective malady that is concentrated, like unemployment, illiteracy, malnutrition, infant mortality, and other such conditions, among the poor and less well-educated.[36] These are the citizens who are least likely to *be* counted, as their voting rates are the lowest, and are least likely to *count*, in the sense of warranting a personal contact by an office seeker.[37]

Where did this conflict system come from? It is, in part, a legacy of the institutional transformation that took place at the turn of the twentieth century. Few would dispute that the reforms of that period remade this nation's conflict system, and that the electoral system was a foremost vehicle in transforming the principles, governing mechanisms, and modes of political organizing that prevailed during the nineteenth century. As I have already detailed, the reformers aimed to modernize the highly personalized regime of courts and parties by putting a centralized bureaucratic administration in its place. Whereas they did succeed in curtailing the power of the political parties, they did not anticipate how much the new administration would mimic the regime it succeeded. Grafted onto the decentralized regime of "courts and parties," the new state was no streamlined machine but, in Stephen Skowronek's words, "a hapless administrative giant . . . that could spawn bureaucratic goods and services but that defied administrative control and direction."[38]

This transformation had significant effects on political organizing. First, as I have discussed in chapter 2, party organization weakened as party bosses lost control over the rewards (patronage, municipal services, and bribes) they had used to mobilize their constituencies. Second, the explosion of new government agencies proliferated access points to power, so that the new state apparatus elicited new forms of organizing "where individuals follow[ed] scripts of self-interested utility maximization" in place of the tribalist group formations of the nineteenth century.[39] These two changes diminished the significance of elections, as "the arena of political decision making had shifted to one in which organized interests and their financial resources counted, rather than ballots."[40] The irony is that these purported good government reforms had a devastating effect on electoral participation. Reformers curtailed the power of the parties, extended the suffrage, and expanded other formal political rights in the name of putting more power in the hands of the people. Without strong parties to mobilize it, public participation declined. Thus "democratic" reform proved to diminish the practice of citizenship, especially by lower-income, less educated voters.

About fifty years later the emergence of new communications, survey research, and transportation technologies accelerated the shift from a labor-intensive party politics to a capital-intensive politics of interests.[41] Although it is tempting to blame television, the internet, and the notorious "soft money" exemption of post-Watergate campaign finance reform for the turn to consumer advertising strategies in electoral campaigns, the fact is that Madison Avenue technologies took hold as they did by virtue of the context in which they developed. This was a context defined by a new round of reforms that aimed to further curtail party organization by weakening the influence of local party leaders over the presidential nominating process, adopting rules to increase the proportion of minority delegates to conventions, and setting strict limits on party-controlled campaign finance.[42]

Like those of the Progressive era, these reforms were intended to democratize the parties and make the electoral process more responsive to the people. Also like those of the Progressive era, the new reforms had unexpected effects on political participation. By diminishing the power of local party officials, reforms to delegate selection further decimated ward- and district-level party organization. This, in turn, detached candidates from the mediating institutions (community organizations, labor unions, black and progressive churches) that had connected them to their popular constituencies.[43] Even the political parties lost their grip on candidates, as changes to the committee structure in Congress coupled with campaign finance reform to encourage entrepreneurial relationships between office seekers and organized interests.[44] In response to the tighter controls on party-sponsored resources, there was an "explosion" of political action committees (PACs), especially those sponsored by corporate, as opposed to union, interests.[45]

For a time, it looked as if capital-intensive organizing would displace the political parties altogether. Rather than wither, however, the parties abandoned their traditional labor-intensive modes of organizing to look more like PACs. The party of the late twentieth century is no longer a presence in the "daily life of citizens" but a fund-raising machine "in service" to its candidates.[46] It serves principally as a conduit for soft money, donations that the parties are supposed to use for voter education, which come largely from a "donor class" of extremely wealthy individuals.[47]

This transformation from labor-intensive to capital-intensive organizing helps to account for how the conflict system produces nonparticipation as one of its principal effects. Parties no longer need to put their principal energies into the mass mobilization efforts that were crucial to winning the highly competitive contests of the late nineteenth century. In present-day elections efficiency dominates what has fast become the *business* of vote getting to an unprecedented degree. This means hunting funds among wealthy individuals and corporate PACS and hunting voters at the extremes. This amounts to a rationalization of the conflict system such that reforms that might have enhanced the *value* of the vote proved to *commodify* it instead.

Rationalization is a loaded word. A synonym for efficiency, it is typically identified with technological development, the differentiation of tasks, specialization of knowledge, and the preeminence of an instrumentality that promotes economic profit at the expense of more humane ends. Walter Dean Burnham has defined rationalization in just this way, and has cast it as a turn-of-the-century legacy. Burnham charged that Progressive era reforms "rationaliz[ed] politics" by bringing elections "into harmony with procedural electoral democracy and with the imperatives of the 'corporate' ideal," which aimed to replace "politics by administration." The result was a deformation of democracy, as "lateral conflicts and bargaining among equals" were displaced onto "technocratic (and implicitly hierarchical) modes of conflict adjustment."[48]

Burnham's vision of the Progressives is not without grounds. The reformers did seek a "bureaucratic remedy" for the antagonisms generated by the pairing of industrial capitalism with liberal democracy.[49] This remedy may well have foreclosed movement toward a more socially egalitarian, politically populist democracy. As Stephen Skowronek has observed, the new administrative order "proved more serviceable for politically salient groups in society, and it *preempted all radical alternatives in political and economic organization*."[50] However, to blame the damage to democracy on bureaucratization alone is to promote a caricature of rationalization that makes the turn-of-the-century transformation difficult to understand; it also renders the pathologies of contemporary democracy difficult to diagnose.

It is often assumed that rationalization went wrong by virtue of the authoritarian strains inherent in bureaucracy and technology. I contend that its pathologies have as much to do with a flawed conception of *democracy* as they do with efficiency carried to an extreme.[51] Turn-of-the century reformers aimed not only to create a value-neutral bureaucracy; they sought to couple it to a popular will that was unsullied by partisan interest. Whereas the nominating primary and direct election of senators were to give citizens more control over party decision making, initiative, referendum and recall gave them the power to act in place of the legislature, and even to dissolve an elected body. As I argued in chapter 4, they wanted "responsible popular government," which, to them, meant self-government *without* partisan motive.[52]

Consequently, at the same time as they pursued administrative expansion, Progressive reformers also promoted political revitalization by explicitly direct democratic means: popular election of senators, candidate selection by nominating primary, initiative, referendum and recall, extension of the franchise to women. Not since the 1820s had reformers stripped away so many of the obstacles that our republican political framework maintained against popular participation. And yet the result was not an *increase* in political participation but a sharp, dramatic decline.

Both sides of reform—bureaucratization and promoting direct democracy—were moves toward rationalization; it was not the rationalization of efficiency and instrumental thinking as the caricature holds, however. The reformers conceived of rationalization in such terms as Max Weber would later conceptualize it: a process involving efficiency *and* legitimacy.[53] It involved promoting industrial development in tandem with the development of democratic institutions that would pair value-neutral bureaucratic administration with direct popular decision making.

This aspiration succumbs to a different kind of rationalization, one bound to an ideology that James Morone has called the "democratic wish": the ideal of self-government by "a single, united people, bound together by a consensus over the public good which is discerned through direct citizen participation in community settings."[54] Like the desire to settle political conflict by bureaucratic means, the democratic wish yearns for "choices untainted by politics."[55] It aims not only to transpose "ideological conflicts into matters of expertise and efficiency" but to purify them as well, by taking parties out of the picture.[56]

The democratic wish does sabotage citizen participation but not quite as the caricature of bureaucratic rationalization would have it. Even as it aimed to open up the electoral process to popular control, reform began to shut down forms of organizing that had mobilized disadvantaged populations and to close off pathways for organized insurgency (such as fusion). In place of these, reformers promoted an ideology of spontaneous participation. Wishful thinking about direct democracy guided electoral reform that weakened the dominant political parties and extinguished the institutionalized third-party altogether. This left broad-based political opposition to be sprouted from the grass roots—as if citizens could simply *act* in concert without the laborious organizing that brings them together and motivates them to do so.

In this kind of reform the Democratic Wish finds its counterpart in the Organizer's Dream, a fantasy of spontaneous association that imagines, "If we hold it, they will come." The result is an idealization of popular self-government that actually undermines broad political participation because it lends legitimacy to efforts to dismantle the institutions—such as parties, unions, or social movements—that mobilize and sustain citizen action. Progressive-era reforms did indeed set the rationalization of the conflict system in motion; this occurred not simply because they put too much trust in bureaucratic efficiency but also because they were animated by a fantasy of democracy that is oblivious to the preconditions for mass political mobilization.

The contemporary conflict system is a twofold legacy from the past. It has inherited from turn-of-the-century reforms a bias toward capital-intensive electioneering, together with disincentives for labor-intensive organizing. It has also inherited the organizer's dream, which explains what I have called its blind spot for the costs of political action. Whereas the consequences of this first inheritance are much debated under the guise of campaign finance reform, controls on media advertisements, and more, those of the second are typically overlooked. I turn next to their exploration.

The Party and the Public

The legacy of the organizer's dream is especially pronounced in the work of citizenship theorists who are influenced by the republican ideal of a public realm or sphere. Idealizing the public as a locus of either free action or disinterested deliberation, these theorists tend to denigrate political parties for engaging in bargaining and compromise and to forget any importance they may have for the hard work of political mobilization. I propose to reconsider the opposition between parties and publics. I contend that, if their relation to power is properly understood, the idea of citizens acting in cooperation as a *public* should not undermine but rather underscore the need for particular kinds of *party* organization. To see why this is so, it is necessary to look briefly at the two postwar normative political theorists, Hannah Arendt and Jürgen Habermas, whose work has done the most to carry the ideal of the public space or public realm into contemporary theories of citizenship.

For Arendt and Habermas, both critics of interest-group pluralism, publics are alternatives to stalemated forms of political organization such as mass parties and corporate lobbies.[57] For Habermas (as for Dahl), the public stands for the ideal of *deliberative* democratic self-government. This ideal calls for principled collective decision making by procedures that enable private persons to join together to discuss public issues or norms under the stipulation that they set all strategy aside and agree to concede to no force other than the better argument.[58] In contrast, Arendt defines the public not as a realm of debate but (like Barber and others) as a place of action that exists "when people gather together and 'act in concert,' [and it] disappears the moment they depart."[59] For an event to be public in Arendt's terms does not require that it involve deliberation. It needs, rather, to be "seen and heard by everybody" who is or could be involved and to engage their plurality of contending viewpoints.[60] For Arendt, as for Schattschneider, public spectacle generates a grassroots power that is not a capacity to be "possessed like strength or applied like force" but rather a "potentiality in being together."[61]

Insurgent speech and action that challenge state power—such as the Charter 77 movement that helped to prepare the way for democratization in Czechoslovakia, the Green movements in Europe and the United States, and even block clubs or PTAs—exemplify the Arendtian public.[62] So do cultural productions that test the limits of what is traditionally considered to be political, the "die-ins" and "kiss-ins" staged by ACT-UP, performance art, films, and such everyday resistances as straights refusing to marry or gays staging elaborate weddings.[63] For examples of the Habermasian ideal, we need look no farther than the debates, town hall meetings, and internet voter information services that have infiltrated the contemporary political campaign.

This is the strength and the paradox of publics: they are unauthorized in the fullest sense of that term. Voluntary and self-selected, they cannot speak for, allocate, sign on, or otherwise bind. They do not represent and they cannot legislate. This does not make them impotent; on the contrary, it allows them to be insurgent and surprising. It does mean, however, that they do not—in themselves—wield democratic power. In fact, they are *twice* removed from it.

When people gather together to deliberate or take action on a problem they want to politicize—pesticides on fruit, drunk drivers, sexually explicit lyrics—they have reformulated a private concern into a public opinion. Publicity, the effect of gathering in common, carries a *potential* for power that must gain influence in order to be realized. Influence can be bought, of course, as the 1990s eruption of "issue advertising" into United States policy making attests. But those who cannot buy influence must earn it, first by striking a chord with a broader public, and then by winning the struggle to define the terms in which this common problem is both posed to a national audience, and resolved.[64] Changing public opinion is difficult enough for an already public figure (just remember how President Clinton's universal health care initiative devolved into a battle over choice of doctors and access to technology). Even if a popular association should become an influential public, it has won only half the battle: it must then convert its influence into political power. This occurs only when popular opinion "passes through the sluices of democratic procedure" (i.e., the policy-making process in Congress) and from there "into legitimate lawmaking."[65] This passage from opinion to law is difficult to effect without the resources to sustain mass public organization and interest-group pressure.

Political parties once subsidized this passage in the United States. Today, in multiparty systems, they still do. Publics rely on the "activity of political parties and general elections" to convey insurgent views from the innovative "periphery" to the routinized center of a democratic regime.[66] Jürgen Habermas has argued that third political parties are particularly important in this regard, for it is their surprise showing at the polls that can enable an issue to "make its way . . . [onto the] expanded platforms of 'established' parties, [or] important court decisions" and thereby "into the core of the political system and there receive formal consideration."[67] The important thing to see here is that whereas publics are not themselves institutions, political parties (third or otherwise) are not themselves public spaces. Proponents of public participation who denigrate third parties, together with political parties more generally, for being opportunistic, strategic, and even hierarchal are asking them to *be* publics. In turn, when they celebrate publics for affording an ephemeral but potent vantage point on "the system" *because they operate outside it*, they misunderstand *democratic* authority.

I dwell on this point to prompt a reconsideration of the antagonism that proponents of participation have for political parties. This antagonism stems, in part, from a more general antipathy toward institutions, one rooted in the belief that they inevitably compromise public associations. The fear is that once such associations are drawn into the mechanisms of interest-group liberalism, they become either the "target constituencies of politicians" or the "supplicants of judges and bureaucrats."[68] Either way, they are transfigured from sites of insurgency into objects of propaganda, pity, and policing.[69] Jeffrey Isaac contends that this "tension between meaningful participation and strategic effectiveness is . . . *built into*" any participatory politics that aims to "irrigate the deserts of liberal democratic mass politics."[70]

There can be no doubt that the tension between action and institutionalization is real. However, to imagine that insurgent publics are *inevitably* corrupted by institutionalization is to forget E. E. Schattschneider's important lesson about power, that publics do not appear and disappear at random. That some gain influence while others dissipate depends on the interests, ideologies, and forms of organizing that a conflict system prefers. As Schattschneider emphasized, conflict systems solicit some participants and exclude others by the very nature of organization, which *is* the "mobilization of bias."[71] Following Schattschneider, I wonder whether the tension between participation and strategic effectiveness is really endemic to "liberal democratic mass politics," as Isaac claims. Perhaps it is heightened in this mass liberal democracy today, which has systematically dismantled the forms of organization that once served to conduct the problems raised by oppositional publics from the periphery to the authoritative core of the political system.

Political parties would ideally be one of the "sluices" that would shuttle movement opposition "from the periphery into the center of the political system."[72] Indeed, they once were. During the late nineteenth century, when there existed fewer obstacles to third-party competition, there was greater reciprocity between movement politics and party politics. Free Soilers, Greenbackers, and Populists all succeeded in communicating some of their demands from the periphery to the center of the system. Could it be the two-party system as we know it, more than electoral politics per se, that frustrates that passage today? Might electoral politics be a more fruitful option for political movements in a conflict system that neither discredited third-party efforts as both fringe and futile, nor drove the dominant parties toward what a few influential organized groups define as the political center?

In a cultural and institutional context defined by political rationalization—efficient, technology-intensive campaigns coupled with the fantasy of a self-organized, unified public—third political parties are easily dismissed as agents of fragmentation, petty grievance, and political extremism. It is not surprising to find them considered a liability to wishful democracy. They might be an asset to a conception of democracy that valued the kind of opposition the nineteenth-century third political party made possible.

The Centripetal Force of Two-Partyism

Opposition does not figure centrally in the work of contemporary citizenship theorists. Instead, their various proposals for deliberative and associational publics exhibit a preoccupation with self-government that, as Ian Shapiro has argued, overshadows an equally significant democratic "milestone": political opposition.[73] Looking to such movements as the "nineteenth-century English Chartists and socialists" (not to mention the Free Soilers, Farmers' Alliance, and Populists), Shapiro emphasizes that struggles "to abolish or limit . . . an unjust hierarchy" have been as crucial to the development of democracy as the attempt "to foster participatory politics."[74] Drawing from this legacy, he contends that democracy must afford "opportunities for those affected by the operation of a collective practice [not only] to participate in its governance [but also] to oppose its results when they are so inclined."[75] Opposition is a crucial aspect of citizenship because there are always forms of domination at work, even in advanced democratic polities. Actually, it is in democracies that domination may be most insidious because it is manifest not as overt force but in that which presents itself as a matter of fact or necessity. Shapiro sees domination wherever "avoidable hierarchies . . . masquerade as unavoidable ones; involuntary subordination is shrouded in the language of agreement; unnecessary hierarchies are held to be essential to the pursuit of common goals; and fixed hierarchies are cloaked in myths about their fluidity."[76] He recommends party competition, which ensures that the apparatus of government can change hands, as a means to resist it. Surprisingly, he praises "two-party-dominated-plurality systems" for producing "significant institutionalized opposition."[77]

Opposition can be difficult enough to spark and sustain under conditions where power shows its face. How to foster it when power is so fully institutionalized that it need not squelch dissent but rather stops at rendering it merely inconvenient or inconceivable? The challenge here is to resist what William E. Connolly calls the "pressures to normalization" that work to "depoliticize consensual conventions that injure many.[78] By "pressures to normalization," Connolly means the tendency over time for priorities, social relations, and institutional arrangements that are contingent preferences to become entrenched as natural, necessary, and incontestable conditions of democratic governance. Connolly complicates the challenge of opposition. Whereas Shapiro stops with the competitive party system, Connolly emphasizes the importance of cultivating an intellectual and popular culture to estrange us from beliefs that pass for natural, necessary, and normative.

In my view the two-party system would be a prime target for such intellectual and cultural work, for it is precisely the kind of thing that Connolly would deem "normalized" and that Shapiro should recognize as an "unjust hierarchy." A contingent political arrangement that masquerades as a necessary hierarchy between minor and major parties, it bears all the signs of having atrophied into a system of domination. Whereas the wasted-vote maxim naturalizes this hierarchy, the two-party doctrine justifies the maxim by perpetuating the belief that third-party failure is necessary, incontestable, and requisite to stable and healthy democratic government. And by cloaking the *fact* of one-party rule in the *myth* of electoral competitiveness, it holds out a false promise of opposition.

The uniquely institutionalized third political parties of the nineteenth century once afforded a means to challenge this unjust hierarchy and to conduct insurgent interests into authoritative democratic fora. I do not propose to idealize them as sites of authentic citizen participation. On the contrary, to recognize their contribution to electoral democracy it is imperative not to romanticize the work they once did. Noteworthy neither for reasoned deliberation nor for rigorous commitment to principle, the third parties of the nineteenth century did not change the modus operandi of the dominant parties so much as they affected their *strategies*. They identified voting blocs that could be moved from one party to the other. No doubt third-party movements have championed significant reforms before dominant parties were willing to touch them. But the Free Soilers certainly did not discover slavery, nor was the People's Party first to see agrarian unrest at the gold standard, land speculation, and price gauging by the railroads. Instead, these third parties demonstrated the power that contentious issues could have at the polls by mobilizing constituencies whose capture could change the balance of power between the dominant parties. By putting problems in words that moved people to act, they have "telegraphed" the "basic issue-clusters" for the next electoral era.[79]

The rationalization of the contemporary conflict system, together with social transformations beyond the bounds of the electoral system, rendered that unique third-party form extinct. This precipitated a loss to democracy many citizenship theorists cannot appreciate because they define all parties out of their field of vision as impossibly bureaucratic and hierarchal. Ironically, in doing so they confirm assumptions that are a mainstay of the liberal pluralism they set out to criticize. Just like the party enthusiasts and the basic American government textbook, they accept the major party as the standard of parties generally, dismiss third political parties as insignificant, and so reproduce the two-party norm.

I argue that the nineteenth-century third party has a place in a conception of democracy that regards opposition and self-government as co-equal modes of citizenship. The closest this democracy came to realizing both, at least electorally, was during the nineteenth century, when the conflict system institutionalized third-party opposition as part of responsible popular government. Third political parties provided an institutional home for organized opposition that widened the scope and contested the bias of the conflict system. Because I value the uniqueness of the nineteenth-century third-party form, together with its institutionalization of political opposition, I hold the futility of third-party efforts today to be more than a problem for would-be third-party voters. It is a problem for electoral democracy more generally: the extinction of the institutionalized third party at the turn of the twentieth century deprived voters of their only electoral corrective to the pathologies of two-partyism.

It will be objected, of course, that third parties do not correct the pathologies of mass democracy but contribute to them in at least three ways. First, they destabilize political systems by winning undue influence for extremist constituencies. Second, as it has no chance of winning, a third party candidacy is false promise: it does not *amplify* the voices of those who feel ignored by the dominant parties but marginalizes them still further by "wasting" their votes. The better the third party does in the general election, the worse this situation becomes. A third party that polls well is more than likely to be a "spoiler," one who fosters the election of the dominant-party candidate that is *least* preferred by a majority of the electorate. Spoiler candidates threaten the legitimacy of the electoral process by producing outcomes that do not represent majority preference. Even a third party that polls well but does not "spoil" harms the electorate by cutting into the winning margin of the victor and thereby denying the president's claim to a "mandate."[80] Third, a great virtue of our major parties is that they are "big tents," broad-based coalitions that have to mediate among conflicting interests; third parties are narrow, often single-issue organizations that serve only to disaggregate what their more responsible major party counterparts have put together.

These are familiar objections. Rather than rehearse the equally familiar responses, I propose to meet them with a question: What do we in the United States have most to fear from our two-party elections? Destablizing the government and exaggerating the influence of extremist minorities is not the threat to us that it is in parliamentary systems. It is excess *consensus*, not fragmentation, that threatens electoral democracy in the United States. In this rationalized system of conflict, the forces to be feared are centripetal rather than centrifugal.

It has been a defining trope of American political thought to fear that "turbulence and contention" would tear this experiment in self-government apart.[81] The *Federalist Papers* are filled with metaphors of tempests, fires, battles, and other images of turmoil. Contrary to that classic text, subsequent political scientists have found inertia to be at least as significant a threat by virtue of the dynamics of winner-take-all elections. In such elections, as Anthony Downs famously argued, the parties have an inexorable tendency "to converge ideologically upon the center."[82]

It misunderstands Downs to imagine that this convergence is a virtue that stabilizes popular democracy and moderates ideological extremes. The Downsian center is not the Aristotelian mean of the ideological spectrum. On the contrary, it is the electoral jackpot—a politically contested location that will be fixed by those interest-group leaders who can claim to deliver the largest voting blocs.[83] Parties in a winner-take-all system need to woo such voting blocs in order to maximize their polling power with minimal effort. In a socially stratified society, however, their pursuit of majority voting blocs compounds inequalities of voice and access; thus, Downs observes, the logic of vote seeking will be at odds with "the equality of influence which universal suffrage was designed to ensure."[84] The drive to the center, then, is not a moderating force but, as Downs acknowledged, a force that moves parties and public policy "a long way from political equality among citizens."[85]

Downs's analysis of the dynamics of two-party elections busts the myth that the United States major parties can be "big tents" as they claim. To borrow an argument that Iris Young has made in another context, in socially stratified societies the promise of inclusive consensus turns out in practice to mean that the "perspectives and interests of the privileged" predominate, effectively defining the Downsian center.[86] Meanwhile, the interests and perspectives of those groups that are less well organized and well funded are systematically shunted aside. In the big tent major parties, then, it never fails that some acts get more attention than others, and still others are best described as sideshows.

This is precisely where third parties come into the picture. They are barkers for the sideshows. Parties in a winner-take-all system do not innovate of their on accord. As E. M. Sait and others have argued, they rely on the periodic eruptions by third parties, protest movements and other insurgents to precipitate change.[87] Consequently, Walter Dean Burnham has observed that "the truly 'normal' structure of American electoral politics at the mass base" is characterized not by incrementalism but by a "dynamic, even dialectical polarization between long-term inertia and concentrated bursts of change."[88] If, as Burnham argued, third parties are catalysts of this process, they are integral to the "normal" workings of United States electoral democracy and even crucial to its stability.

It is customary to praise two-partyism for bringing stability to the electoral system. This it has done. But with stability has come a tendency to stall, to equivocate, and to amplify the interests of the privileged. If it is not fragmentation but this tendency toward inertia that is most to be feared in United States electoral politics, then it may well be that voters need third-party movements to protect the democratic milestone of opposition. Periodic third-party interventions are one important way that voters in a winner-take-all system secure their right to both participate in collective self-governance and to oppose the results of collective decision making. The concluding chapter looks at reforms to bring third-party opposition back into being.

Conclusion
Against the Tyranny of the Two-Party System

The tyranny of the two-party system is this: that a regulatory system born of politics comes to be taken as a defining feature of American political identity, that an ultimatum—vote for one party or the other—stands as the epitome of democratic choice. Would it "collapse in an instant if the tubes were pulled and the IV's were cut"?[1] Probably not. Although electoral duopoly *is* a regulatory system, it is not *merely* one. It is also a common sense that persuades most of the United States electorate to either vote within its terms or not vote at all. This is its most tyrannical aspect. It resigns us to the choice between the two dominant parties, and even threatens to punish us if we refuse that choice (our vote will either be "wasted" or "spoil" the election for the dominant-party candidate we would otherwise prefer).

That United States party scholars have held competition to be the gold standard of electoral democracy and yet also promoted two-partyism as competition's perfect form is odd. For many citizens, to be confronted with an option of voting for one of only two viable parties is to be forced to cast a ballot (if we vote at all) not *for* the candidate we want but *against* the candidate we least prefer. On these terms voting becomes a double bind that makes our consent almost impossible to withdraw. Vote for a third-party candidate and your ballot is "wasted." Refuse to "waste" your ballot and you sign on to the establishment. Refuse to vote at all and you will be assimilated into the nonvoting mass whose abstention is not read as a reflection on the conflict system but as a reflection on you—as proof of your apathy, alienation, laziness, or even tacit affirmation.

The contemporary United States electoral system allows no protest to be counted within its terms. It makes voting a ritual of consent performed by citizens who reproduce the system even as they are persuaded by the trappings of the campaign that they are making a choice. It might be different if there were a way to express dissatisfaction with the framing of that choice, as in Israeli parliamentary elections where citizens cast a white or blank ballot to signify "none of the above." There is no such option in the United States.[2] Instead, today's would-be protest voter must accept that her vote will either be insignificant or—in a close election—that it risks the very legitimacy of the electoral process by producing a winner who was *not* the preference of a majority.

Some would call this the "dilemma of the third-party voter," a catch-22 that has purportedly plagued alternative parties since the founding. I call it the "tyranny of the two-party system," a partisan formation that is no age-old problem. An effect of rules, habits, and beliefs that have been with us since the turn of the twentieth century, the two-party system is an entrenched hierarchy that affords established parties a political embargo against challenger candidacies. Whereas the dominant parties legislated this arrangement into being, it is the voters who shoulder the blame for its dysfunction.

We who worry about "wasted" votes and "spoiler" candidates take the "dilemma" of third-party voting upon ourselves. Given no responsible alternative to a two-party vote, we tend to vote responsibly—unless we are assured of doing no harm. This book has asked how "responsibility" has come to be defined in terms that so discourage citizen engagement. I have told the story of fusion in order to recast what passes for "responsibility" as domination, thereby to persuade readers to think twice about citing the two-party system as a simple political fact. I have labored to depict that arrangement as a system of meaning, complex of rules, and common sense that not only shuts down third-party opposition but casts third parties as aberrations to the United States electoral system. I have revisited nineteenth-century electoral politics to put the common sense of the present into perspective. I have argued that third political parties not only have a history in the United States but that they are structurally necessary to its normal functioning: they are catalysts for the dynamic of inertia and abrupt change that has characterized its electoral process. But I have also argued that third parties as we know them today fall far short of what we need them to be. For that reason, I have suggested, it may be time to revive aspects of the third-party tradition of the past.

There could be no better illustration of my argument than the 2000 presidential election. On its face this claim might seem absurd. Not one but two third political parties mounted nationwide candidacies in the 2000 election. Both confirmed the worst prejudices that United States voters hold against such efforts. In 2000 a third-party vote was *worse* than wasted: it was a folly that muddied the outcome and compromised the legitimacy of the electoral process.[3] And for what? Ralph Nader's candidacy drew precious votes from Gore without achieving the 5 percent that would have qualified the Greens for public financing; Patrick Buchanan split the Reform Party and burned over twelve million in taxpayer dollars.

If the third-party showing in 2000 confirmed every stereotype, the outcome of the major party vote was a surprise. It shook the faith in the two-party doctrine just as surely as Buchanan and Nader proved the truth of its corollary. If it is true, as Douglas Amy has remarked, that political scientists view the study of voting procedure like good detective fiction, where the hero "takes on what looks like a routine divorce case only to see it quickly develop into a more elaborate case of blackmail, murder and drug running," then the great thing about the 2000 presidential contest is that it got ordinary *citizens* reading beyond the first page.[4] Not since the turn of the century has the United States electorate seen so blatant a war of maneuver on the "contested terrain" of electoral procedure. Those who followed the contest, and many did, received an object lesson in the tyranny of the two-party system. Read in the most radical terms, everything we learned from the 2000 presidential election can be taken to contradict everything we think we know about two-party democracy.

First, we cannot trust the two-party system to present a clear-cut choice between candidates. Election 2000 was bizarre: a close election not because the electorate was sharply divided (as some proclaimed in its aftermath) but rather because the majority of voters *perceived* little difference between candidates who were, in fact, quite different. They held significantly different political philosophies regarding whether government or the market is the best provider of the social goods that we call social security, welfare, medicaid, and medicare. They held different views regarding which constitutional rights are fundamental to individuals. They also disagreed regarding the need for federally supported initiatives to protect the environment. Whereas the parties gave us distinctly different candidates, these differences blurred over the course of the campaign.

Both candidates wagered that the liberal and conservative wings of their parties would stay with them in the end; consequently, they played down the issues that would have set them apart (such as gun control, environmental protection, and reproductive rights). They ran on issues to which no one can object (such as education), and conducted themselves throughout much of the campaign as if it were a contest to determine who was most amiable. This race for the Downsian center was the trademark effect of two-party competition, amplified by today's high-technology, candidate-centered, personality-driven elections. Thus, election 2000 suggests that even when the parties offer up competing candidates the two-party system fails to bring out the differences between them.

Second, *the* two-party system is not *one*. What could possibly make it plainer that we have *many* party systems than the aftermath of election 2000, when the process stood with its several ballots, voting technologies, and ways of counting revealed? No standard, no matter how clearly specified, could possibly have made these ballots commensurable, as long as they had been designed in different formats, and marked in myriad ways. Much as scholars have praised *the* two-party system for producing decisive outcomes, it turns out that it cannot even orchestrate a vote. This one was not just too close to call (as it looked at first) but mathematically inconclusive.

Finally, two-party duopoly does not secure democracy; it frustrates it. This was evident in the most startling feature of election 2000: the disparity between the vote of the citizenry and that of the electoral college. There was no concealing the fact that George W. Bush won the presidency not because more voters chose him but because those who did choose him were distributed so that he captured a majority of districts by plurality rule. His was a "manufactured majority," an artifact of the electoral college that gave him the White House despite the fact that he lost the popular vote.[5]

Although there had not been so glaring a discrepancy between the popular vote and the vote of the electoral college for over a century, it is a mistake to think that such discrepancies are unusual. On the contrary, the process by which the United States elects its presidents is designed to produce two outcomes: a popular vote and an electoral college vote that comes after (and supercedes) that of the people. Whereas it is unusual for the two to conflict (as they did in 2000), it is quite *typical* for them to diverge, as when a president garners a slim popular majority but claims a landslide based on the electoral college. Here the system produces not a manufactured majority but an exaggerated one: it overstates a mandate.

In contrast to the manufactured majority, which strikes fear in the hearts of all electoral college fans and dogs all but the most imperturbable of presidents with the stain of illegitimacy, the exaggerated majority proves to be the politician's best friend. It turns out that everybody loves a mandate. Political scientists applaud the two-party system for "produc[ing] majorities automatically."[6] Even the media succumb to its bandwagon effect. How many voters know that when Ronald Reagan took office in 1980 "he received only 50.9 percent of the popular vote [while] the winner-take-all system gave him 89.9 percent of the electoral votes—and thus the impression of a huge landslide"?[7] The trouble with the exaggerated majority is that it is not *visible* unless the media (unlikely) or the officeholder (inconceivable) calls attention to it. Wherever a close victory masquerades as a decisive outcome, it discredits an opposition that has a right to expect concessions because it came so near to winning.

It is supposed to be a virtue of the two-party system that it produces governing majorities as a matter of course. But if these majorities are artifacts of a winner-take-all rule that systematically discounts votes, it should be difficult to call them democratic. This is what election 2000 discloses, when read in the most radical light: the tendency of the two-party system to discredit opposition by *forging* consensus in the fullest sense of the word. It forces unity by painting a false portrait of majority support. This centripetal tendency had its critics in the past. Progressive-era party scholars understood it to compromise democratic legitimacy by putting the dominant parties at odds with "controversial subjects" and out of touch with "momentous changes."[8] E. M. Sait saw that it tempted some party critics toward the "wrecking of the major parties" and worried that it could be "inimical to the public interest"—if not for the ways that "minor parties and other organized groups" stepped in to champion "neglected issues."[9]

Should election 2000 return us to this century-old perspective on electoral democracy, to its skepticism about two-party democracy, and to its appreciation for the symbiotic relationship between the established parties and their challengers? Much has occurred to justify such a comparison. Our voting process is, once again, suspect. This time the trouble is not overt partisan corruption. Rather, it is a more insidious trouble with aging voting machines and insufficiently staffed polling places that need not be intentionally partisan to have obvious partisan effects. The trouble is that our federalist system leaves the value of the vote to be determined by whatever tax dollars a given county can afford to invest in it.

We live, once again, in a time when the major parties cannot command a majority at the polls, and when they are almost unanimously denounced for being captive to monied interests. The smoke-filled rooms of the past are gone, only to be replaced by a torrential flow of money into politics that is no less distasteful for being more public. This is an era when corporations underwrite campaigns, conventions, and even inaugural ceremonies in almost the same spirit as they sponsor sporting events. It might not be too outlandish to imagine an "Exxon Republican Convention" or "Microsoft State of the Union Address" taking its place alongside the "Tostitos Fiesta Bowl."

If our troubles echo those of a century ago, should our solutions as well?

There is no doubt that Progressive-era remedies have come back into vogue. Initiative and referenda come to mind as the most notorious examples. Since 1978, with Proposition 13, California's infamous property tax limitation measure, ballot initiatives, and referenda have served as vehicles for more tax protests, anti-immigration legislation, attacks on and defenses of gay and lesbian civil rights, campaign finance reform, and more.[10] These campaigns cloak themselves in the democratic wish, appealing, as Daniel A. Smith has noted, to the American citizen's "faith that the direct participation by the people is somehow a purer form of democracy than representative democracy."[11] And they are sabotaged by the organizer's dream, which, with its blind spot for the work and the costs of mass political mobilization, permits "the organizational and financial resources of interested economic groups" to run these purportedly grassroots movements as if they come together spontaneously. Media-intensive, poll-driven, and orchestrated by political consultants from the top down, these movements have not provided a "procedurally purer" alternative to our high-tech, high-rolling representative democracy.[12] Instead, they have opened an alternate passageway for the flow of money into politics, one that represents itself as above suspicion by claiming to be powered by the "people."[13]

These putatively "direct" democratic electoral remedies feed political rationalization, exactly as I have argued we should expect them to. They were conceived by reformers who distrusted the parties of their time and designed without taking the costs of political action into account. Thus it is not surprising that they have ushered more money than people into the electoral process.

Precisely because it is not a direct democratic but a *party-centered* strategy, fusion stands in stark contrast to these reforms. It neither falls prey to the democratic wish nor plays into the organizer's dream, but mobilizes organized opposition via the pathway of a third-party ballot line. By institutionalizing electoral protest, fusion helps to subsidize its costs. It thereby ensures that dissent is not an elite prerogative and that *legitimate* opposition is not an exclusive title for those who define themselves within the mainstream.

To begin with the most straightforward argument in its favor, fusion resolves the usual dilemmas of third-party voting. A vote cast on the ballot line of a third party that has joined forces either with an established party or with several alternative parties can reasonably expect to elect a candidate. Thus it is not fated to be a "wasted" vote and need not risk throwing the election to the established candidate that is everyone's third choice. Simply put, fusion gives dissenters a protest vote that counts.

Fusion also poses a counterforce to the centripetal tendencies of the two-party system that is unique for working within the principle of the American major party, which aims to create a broad-based coalition in a two-sided political universe *before the election.* By the device of the autonomous ballot line, fusion enriches this coalitional practice. It forges an alliance that is more adequate to the idea of coalition than the big tent because it marks the differences between the partners to a candidacy. Moreover, votes cast on the fusion line quantify the threat of exit that E. E. Schattschneider took to be so central to electoral democracy. They tell winning candidates exactly how much they stand to lose if they do not make good on their promises and alert rival parties to what they stand to gain by presenting a real alternative. If two-party competition sacrifices choice for stability, and proportional systems multiply choice at the cost of instability (because coalition building takes place after the election), then fusion may be the best of both worlds. It manages to be more specifically representative than the two-party system, while avoiding the uncertainty and volatility of multiparty governments because parties decide their partnerships before the vote.

It is possible to make this argument too well. For, compared to an autonomous third-party candidacy, the fusion strategy seems all too compatible with two-partyism. How much does it really multiply choices at the polls to lend alternative-party ballot lines to establishment-party candidates? Might fusion not have the opposite effect of fortifying two-partyism by assimilating every vote—even a would-be protest vote—to the terms of the establishment? Such objections, which circulated during the fusion era, cast this practice in its most unflattering light as a strategy of capitulation that does more to secure the two-party establishment than to perturb it. It may be even more conventional than two-party voting in this respect: whereas a two-party contest simply *wastes* third-party opposition, fusion candidacies actually *enlist* it by stamping established party candidates with a radical imprimatur.

The force of such objections is undeniable. They serve to remind that there are no simple ways of turning back the clock. A return to fusion today would have to contend with a media- and money-intensive electoral arena that would tilt this strategy, as it does every other, toward groups that mobilize more dollars than people. In this age of increasingly candidate-centered elections, fusion is undeniably quaint as well. It is a strategy of alliances between parties that assumes parties to be principled decision makers and voters to identify with them on principle. In the contemporary electoral arena the party is an umbrella for political entrepreneurs who may have little else in common than the desire to win. Fusion would do much more than mark the differences within these vast coalitions; it would serve to underscore their incongruities. In a state like Minnesota, for example, one might well find Green/Democrat fusions in the urban districts offset by Right-to-Life/Democrat alliances in the northern part of the state (a hold-out for Democratic voters with strong working-class *and* religious convictions). How long could a party of such extremes maintain itself as a party if it had the fusion strategy to call attention to them?

Seen from this perspective, fusion seems bound to erode party organization from within. Looked at from another angle, however, fusion might actually fortify the major party organizations. In today's elections, where contestants find it more profitable to run as an "outsider" than as the standard-bearer for either party, it might be an advantage to court an alternative party ballot line. In doing so, establishment candidates could market themselves as breaking with politics as usual, thus earning new credibility with disaffected voters.

What would it take to resurrect fusion? First, it is important to recognize that relegalizing fusion alone would do little to alter the dynamics of party politics in the United States or to open up new possibilities for political opposition. To accomplish those broader goals, fusion would need to be partnered with a comprehensive program of electoral reform that would address the inequities of balloting and campaign finance alike. But, to practice fusion, United States citizens would have to expect more out of voting than they do today. And they would have to trust third political parties in ways they currently do not. Changing citizens' disposition toward third parties first requires changing their predispositions about two-partyism.

Often as we hear it said that a ballot cast for a third party candidate is a ballot wasted, the fact is, in many United States elections voting for *any* party is a waste of time. Low turn-out rates attest that many citizens see it so. How will the 2000 presidential election affect this perception? Because it was a startlingly close election (a rarity for the twentieth century), it should communicate the potential for every vote to be the deciding one. And yet the events of Florida showed voters in tax-poor counties everywhere just how likely their votes are to *be* wasted even if they take the trouble to cast them. Contrary to one of our most prominent copybook maxims, then, it seems that third-party voting has not cornered the market on "wasted votes" and political irrationality.

Election 2000 succeeded in achieving what no third political party has managed to accomplish: it laid bare the futility of a major party vote. In so doing, the election opened a window onto the precarious legitimacy of this winner-take-all system. It remains to be seen how far the federal government will go toward prescribing uniform balloting standards and how much state legislatures will invest in new voting technologies. There is a danger in allowing this debate to remain at the level of hardware, for it leaves unchallenged the presumption that the proper technology can put the vote right. This assumption, with its characteristically American faith in machinery, threatens to close the window on meaningful reform.

Even if we outlaw confusing ballot designs, prescribe a uniform ballot format, and upgrade every voting machine, we will still have not remedied an unfairness that has nothing to do with counting ballots but everything to do with *wasting* them. For if we imagine that all we need is a quick fix to the standards for reading disputed ballots, or even if we go so far as to call for uniform ballot design and touch screen voting in every county, we would still have succumbed to an illusion. The trouble with our electoral system lies only superficially in how we tally our votes; it resides more deeply in how we value them.

I have already cited E. E. Schattschneider's claim that the fight for democracy today continues in struggles over the "kinds of things that make the vote valuable."[14] In the aftermath of the 2000 presidential election this quote bears repeating, if only because that contest so plainly revealed how the value of the vote has declined. What Schattschneider had in mind when he wrote these words was not the mundane details of voting machinery and ballot design but rather the (in his time) more pressing question whether two-party competition could be made to prevail in the one-party states of the Solid South. Schattschneider pegged the value of the vote to the presence or absence of competition in the party system. The worth of the vote is discounted wherever elections afford voters little choice at the polls.

Choice is the appeal of third-party candidacies, and it is part of the rationale behind the fusion strategy. My goal in writing this book, however, has not been to argue for the proliferation of third parties generally, as if more parties meant more choices. In the electoral arena, as in the supermarket, it is possible to clutter the aisles with so many variations on what is, deep down, all the same. Whether you take your orange juice with pulp or without, your toothpaste with teeth-whitening baking soda or tartar control gel, your high-finance, media-intensive political party on an established line or a new one—you've changed very little about the way you organize your morning or your electoral system. My purpose has been to advocate resurrecting the distinctive form of electoral opposition that third political parties once made possible. In my view, today's third parties extend to voters a false promise.

Take the candidacies of Ross Perot. Perot ran candidate-centered, money-intensive, media-savvy campaigns that were no alternative to major-party politicking; he merely gave the major parties a run at their own game. Even the Green Party candidacy of Ralph Nader in 2000 proved to be conventional in many respects. Although some hoped that his would be the kind of third-party campaign that would enlarge the scope and shift the bias of the conflict system, Nader did little to organize the unorganized or challenge the terms of the debate. Instead, he ran for the votes of disaffected white progressives, appealing to them with the trademark third-party message that there's not a dime's worth of difference between the corporate-funded establishment candidates. On this point many Green Party activists parted with their standard-bearer, protesting that Gore and Bush differed a great deal about signature issues of the left. Nader betrayed his base as major party candidates betray theirs. Moreover, he seemed to take on "spoiling" as a strategy, as if to stand behind his claim that the established candidates were interchangeable. This was Nader's tactical blunder. He competed hardest in erstwhile Democratic strongholds where his numbers were highest but where they would be least likely to hold on election day, when voters would reconsider casting a vote for Nader if it would throw the state to Bush. Had he campaigned for Democratic votes in states that Bush had already captured, the Greens might have cleared the 5 percent threshold.

Indeed, if this were their primary goal in backing Nader, fusion would have been a less costly way to achieve it. Were fusion legal, votes cast for Gore-Lieberman on a Green Party line would not have sent Bush to the White House. Relieved of that risk, more Green-leaning Democrats would have felt free to support the insurgent effort. Fusion is clearly an expedient remedy for the very palpable dilemmas of third-party voting in a winner-take-all system. It is a tactic that transforms the way voters align with the established parties. The question is whether it can be more than that. Can it mobilize new constituencies to alter the bias and change the scope of two-party politics?

Possibly. But to do so, fusion parties would have to mature into autonomous actors, capable not simply of influencing the major political parties but of beating their candidates. Such a goal would be difficult to achieve within the confines of the single-member plurality system, where no fusion party has ever grown into an independent challenger. Fusion would pack a more potent punch if it were to be partnered with a modified form of proportional representation. For such a partnership cumulative voting presents an especially promising option.

Like fusion, cumulative voting has a history of practice in the United States. It even made a brief splash in the mainstream media by virtue of its prominence in the work of Lani Guinier, who makes an especially interesting case for this tactic as part of a broader argument about voting equality, race-based districting, and gerrymandering. Against the hallowed standard of "one-person, one-vote," Guinier contends that formal equality means little in practice to those voters who find themselves perpetually in a numerical minority. Guinier counters with a more rigorous standard, one that requires "as many votes as possible [to] count . . . in the election of representatives."[15] She defends this standard as Schattschneider might, presenting it as a means to enrich the value of the vote and even calling it "one vote, one value."

Guinier argues that single-member plurality systems compromise "one vote, one value" by the very process of districting, which incumbents use to produce as many *safe* seats as possible. She demonstrates how districting—whether race-conscious or not—is tantamount to gerrymandering; it is the manipulation of geographic boundaries to bias the outcome of the election and to minimize the number of votes that really matter. Thus, in single-member plurality systems, the interests of citizens and those of incumbent parties are profoundly at odds. Although the vote has its greatest value to a citizen in a contested election, contested elections are precisely what legislators have the motivation and the prerogative to forestall.

If the 2000 election revealed the scandal of the many ways that the United States electoral system fails to count votes, Guinier's argument brings to light something even more disturbing. Even when the balloting works *properly* and most votes cast are counted, they cannot count for much. In a majority of districts they are either cast for someone who had no chance of winning or for someone who could win without them.

Guinier proposes cumulative voting to remedy this situation. A modified form of proportional representation, cumulative voting creates multimember districts and accords citizens one vote for each seat that is up for election. Citizens have the option either to disperse their votes, distributing one to each preferred candidate, or to cumulate (or "plump") them, assigning two or more to a single candidate whom the voter wants to elect but believes will receive only minority support. Vote plumping gives numerical minorities a chance to make up with strategy what they lack in numbers by concentrating their support on a single candidate. But it does more than this. Cumulative voting also takes districting out of the hands of those who have the most to gain by limiting electoral competition. It makes the act of voting itself a kind of "self-defined apportionment based on shifting political or cultural affiliation and interests."[16]

By contrast to the current United States system, where voters are grouped from the top down, and their interests defined by (geographic or partisan) proxy, cumulative voting lets voters group themselves according to priorities they define and change. Cumulative voting has the potential to alter the bias and enlarge the scope of the electoral system because it gives "politically cohesive groups" the power to constitute themselves across district lines and in defiance of prevailing categories of identity and partisanship.[17] Susan Bickford captures what makes this tactic so radical when she observes that it would transform voting into a genuinely active form of participation and provoke a corresponding "change in the character of public discourse . . . [which] would no longer take the form of 'Vote for me' or 'Who are you going to vote for?' but rather 'How will your votes be distributed?' (Or, in more everyday language, 'What are you going *to do* with your votes?')."[18]

The fact is that our single-member plurality system gives us very little to do with our votes. It produces so many landslide victories (elections where the victor prevails by more than a 20 percent margin of the vote) and so many *uncontested* races that electoral outcomes are practically determined by the districting process rather than the vote.[19] Whereas winner take all virtually *guarantees* that oppositional organizing by minorities (numerical and otherwise) is not worth the effort, the plumping option almost ensures it will bring results at the polls. The tactic makes it possible to mobilize groups against the prevailing bias of conflict, thereby realizing opposition in the different ways that I have argued William E. Connolly and Ian Shapiro understand it: it enables even a numerical minority to displace the party in power and holds out the possibility of disturbing naturalized categories of identity.

To use the "plumping" option well, however, citizens must vote strategically. They must cast their ballots in accordance with the intensity of their preferences and with their calculated estimate of the relative strength of their constituency. To make such calculations, numerical minorities must have some idea about where like-minded voters will likely be concentrating their votes. If they do not coordinate their voting, they risk negating the advantage of the plumping strategy by dispersing their votes across multiple candidates, or multiple parties. Whereas elite minorities will have the resources to offset this risk (through television advertising, phone banking, and door-to-door canvassing), minorities without such resources will need to rely on oppositional organizations, such as social movements or third political parties, to guarantee the value of their votes.[20]

The strategy gap is significant because it has the potential to subvert cumulative voting from challenging the two-party system to reinforcing it. It turns out that, in the absence of alternative organizations, the most efficient way for less well-financed groups to coordinate their vote is to concentrate or plump it on the ballot line of the second major party. Ironically, then, as Douglas Amy has observed, cumulative voting proves not to bring new oppositions into being but to ensure "representation only for the largest minority political party—not the full range of minority political groups."[21] It also serves to intensify that party's *monopoly* on political opposition.

This is where the partnership with fusion comes in; together, the two tactics combine to offset each other's weaknesses. Fusion complements cumulative voting in an intriguing way: it depicts vote plumping on the ballot itself. Just as plumping involves casting multiple votes for a single candidate, fusion involves listing the same candidate on multiple party lines. Those party lines could serve as a cue for the plumping strategy. In effect, they declare, We're all concentrating our votes *here*! If the ballot itself could teach voters this new form of organizing, vote plumping could pay off even for those groups that cannot afford to buy expensive television advertising. And it would not need to reinforce the default opposition of the second major party. Cumulative voting offsets a principal weakness of fusion, in turn. It can give third political parties a foothold in an electoral system *without* requiring them to lend their ballot lines to established party candidates. Because plumping enables numerical minorities to vote like majorities, it would make it viable for coalitions of third parties to mount opposition against *both* established parties. Whereas fusion would enable such parties to join forces behind a single candidate, the plumping option would give them real power at the polls.

This is a democracy that systematically devalues voting. It is a conflict system defined by electoral rationalization, one where the money-intensive campaign locks out challenger candidates who are not independently wealthy, where advertising has replaced organizing at the ward and district level, and where "grassroots" politicking has become the province of organized interests. It is also a conflict system that intensifies the financial obstacles to successful third-party movements, despite increased third-party voting and a trend (until *Timmons*) for the Supreme Court to strike down some of the most egregiously protectionist ballot access laws. This system is sustained, in part, by a political culture in which market mechanisms are identified with freedom and government regulation (of campaign contributions, of hiring, of health care, etc.) is regarded as partisan interference with the free play of competition. Such conditions make it especially difficult to call the terms of the conflict system itself into question by pointing to its "bias in favor of the exploitation of some kinds of conflict and the suppression of others."[22] It is more difficult still to change those terms by agitating for procedural reform.

My concern throughout this book has been to politicize a feature of our contemporary conflict system that we all too readily take for granted. As I see it, what we think of as the two-party system is deeply, invisibly, and, therefore, insidiously antidemocratic. It is a political and historical formation that regulates organized opposition out of the electoral process, while at the same time presenting itself as a *system*—a self-reproducing framework that is insulated from politics and immune to challenge. Since its consolidation at the turn of the century as a duopoly, two-party competition has suppressed the electoral participation of dissenting groups and thereby exaggerated the consensual basis of American public policy. Third political parties have been one means of resisting the biases of two-party conflict. They have traditionally mounted opposition to its substantive policy commitments and challenged its pretense to be above politics.

The trouble is that third political parties can no longer mediate between peripheral publics and mass institutions as they once could do. Whereas

Alexander Bickel praised them as "an outlet for frustration . . . a creative force and a sort of conscience, [and] as an ideological governor to keep major parties from speeding off into an abyss of mindlessness," today they are campaign vehicles that tend mindlessly to concentrate their efforts on the presidency—the one office where third-party challenges have been least effective and most likely to confirm their reputation as spoilers.[23] Moreover, today's third parties do not so much complement and correct the dominant parties as *mimic* them. As Ross Perot's 1992 candidacy demonstrates, they are most successful when they eschew grassroots mobilization for the money-intensive, media-intensive, one-shot presidential campaign.[24] And, if Jesse Ventura's success is any indication, the twenty-first century third party is more likely to intensify the libertarian leanings of liberalism than to challenge such fundamental separations as those between public and private, state and market, national order and global order.[25]

If Bickel is correct that the "minor party would have to be invented if it did not come into existence regularly enough," then perhaps it *does* need to be invented again.[26] Fusion is just one strategy for initiating that reinvention.[27] It captivated me, but not because I think it is the only or even the most effective way to promote a third-party revival. Fusion captured my imagination as a story, the kind of lost history that reverses the polarity between the preposterous and the ordinary.

One hundred years ago, a third-party vote was a viable vote. And the basic premise of fusion, though controversial, was understood to be well within the competencies of the average voter: one candidate, two (or more) ballot lines. Today that premise strikes us as esoteric, cumbersome, or even suspect; imagine, however, what a nineteenth-century Populist would say about elections today. Remember the horror of the editorialist in Michigan who anticipated that in a winner-take-all system *without* fusion "there could *only be two parties* at one time."[28] If we fear fusion as disorderly and destabilizing, they feared duopoly as tantamount to tyranny.

We may look to fusion as a model ballot reform, one that orients us toward a future where this winner-take-all system is more open to third political parties and to the dissenters who organize them. To my mind, it is even more significant for the way it orients us toward the present. As a once familiar electoral practice that only now seems out of place, the story of fusion dislodges our two-party common sense. It prompts us to consider that democracy as we practice it today may not be an improvement over its practice in the past. It teaches us that a third-party vote is not necessarily wasted, even in a winner-take-all system. And it may even inspire us to work to change what we have regarded as the simple facts of our political world.

Notes

Preface

1. Raymond Seidelman, "Political Scientists, Disenchanted Realists, and Disappearing Democrats," *Discipline and History: Political Science in the United States*, ed. James Farr and Raymond Seidelman (Ann Arbor: U of Michigan P, 1996), 313.

Introduction: The Tyranny of the Two-Party System

1. William Grimes, "After You, No, After You. Ouch!" *New York Times*, 19 July 1998: WK2.

2. "Our Perspective: The Ventura Vote," Editorial, *Minneapolis Star Tribune*, 8 November 1998: A26.

3. Stephen Dornfeld, "Jesse's Election Not a Victory for Reform, But a Triumph for Trivialization of Politics," *St. Paul Pioneer Press*, 9 November 1998: 10A.

4. Ventura ran against two popular, respected establishment candidates. Running for the Democrat-Farmer-Labor Party was Hubert H. Humphrey III, who had just come off a significant victory against the tobacco industry as attorney general. Running for the Republicans was Norm Coleman, the popular mayor of St. Paul, who had recently been reelected by a strong margin.

5. E. E. Schattschneider, *The Semisovereign People: A Realist's View of Democracy in America* (New York: Holt, Rinehart and Winston, 1975 [1960]), 128.

6. Pam Belluck, "A 'Bad Boy' Wrestler's Unscripted Upset," *New York Times*, 5 November 1998: B10.

7. Twelve percent of people surveyed in exit polls reported that they would not have voted at all had Ventura not run. This sentiment was even more pronounced among voters eighteen to twenty-four years old, fully one-quarter of whom stated that they turned out only for Ventura. See Sarah Hallonquist,"Exit Polling Indicates That Many People Would Not Have Bothered If Ventura Had Not Been Among Their Choices for Governor," *Minneapolis Star Tribune*, 5 November 1998: A24.

8. Theodore J. Lowi, "The Party Crasher," *New York Times Magazine*, 23 August 1992: 28.

9. Garry Wills debunked these and other misconceptions about the Ventura election and also criticized the exclusively cultural explanations of his success.

Garry Wills, "The People's Choice," *New York Review of Books*, 12 August 1999, http//: www.nybooks.com/nyrev.

10. E. E. Schattschneider, *Party Government* (New York: Holt, Rinehart and Winston, 1967 [1942]), 69.

11. V. O. Key, *Politics, Parties, and Pressure Groups*, rev. ed. (New York: Crowell, 1952), 299.

12. Cass R. Sunstein, *Democracy and the Problem of Free Speech* (New York: Free, 1995), 98. I borrow the term *regulatory system* from Sunstein, who introduced it to challenge the free-market ideology in campaign finance jurisprudence that imagines the contemporary domain of free speech to be spontaneous and rebuffs efforts to limit and otherwise regulate campaign contributions as state interference.

13. John D. Hicks, "The Third Party Tradition in American Politics," *Mississippi Valley Historical Review* 20.1 (June 1933): 3.

14. Ibid.

15. Ibid., 4.

16. Ibid., 3–4.

17. Ibid., 27.

18. Indeed, fifty years later the authors of the leading political science study of third parties made a similar observation. Only the terms of the analogy had changed: United States voters hold "the two-party system [to be] a sacred arrangement—as American an institution as the Congress, the Super Bowl, or M*A*S*H." Steven Rosenstone, Roy L. Behr, and Edward H. Lazarus, *Third Parties in America* (Princeton: Princeton UP, 1996), 40.

19. Robert Dahl, *Pluralist Democracy in the United States* (Chicago: Rand, McNally, 1967), 214.

20. Schattschneider, *Party Government*, 66.

21. Theodore J. Lowi and Benjamin Ginsberg, *American Government: Freedom and Power*, 5th ed. (New York: Norton, 1998), 474.

22. Schattschneider, *Party Government*, 69.

23. For a discussion of various concepts of political parties, and an especially cogent statement of the dimensions across which the various conceptions of the political party can be distinguished, see Gerald M. Pomper, "Concepts of Political Parties," *Journal of Theoretical Politics* 4:2 (1992): 143–159.

24. Schattschneider, *Party Government* 35.

25. Ibid., 59.

26. This view is most famously propounded by Joseph Schumpeter, *Capitalism, Socialism, and Democracy* (New York: Harper, 1942). For a thorough account of its influence on United States political thought, and of critical reactions to this view, see David M. Ricci, "Democracy Attenuated: Schumpeter, the Process Theory, and American Democratic Thought," *Journal of Politics* 32 (1970): 239–267.

27. Schattschneider, *Party Government*, 60.

28. Ibid., 82.

29. R. M. MacIver, *The Web of Government* (New York: MacMillan, 1947), 213–214.

30. William Nisbet Chambers, *Political Parties in a New Nation: The American Experience, 1776–1809* (New York: Oxford UP, 1963), 112.

31. "Nader's Misguided Crusade," Editorial, *New York Times*, 30 June 2000: A24.

32. Douglas J. Amy, *Real Choices/New Voices* (New York: Columbia UP, 1993), 7.

33. Other states do require signature gathering but do not call for a statewide canvass. In others, a high-profile challenger like McCain, who had name recognition and a significant national following, could be listed on the ballot merely by paying a filing fee.

34. "Single-member plurality" means single-member districting, where only one seat is contested at a time, and plurality voting, where the win goes to the candidate with the most votes—the "first past the post." That the party with the biggest draw at the polls wins, regardless whether it is the biggest by a lot or by a little, produces coalition parties that tend to resemble one another over time.

35. Schattschneider, *Party Government*, 82.

36. David S. Broder, *The Party's Over: The Failure of Politics in America* (New York: Harper and Row, 1972), xxi.

37. Key, *Politics, Parties, and Pressure Groups*, 147.

38. See MacIver, *The Web of Government*; and Chambers, *Political Parties in a New Nation*.

39. Richard Hofstadter, *The Idea of a Party System* (Berkeley: U of California P, 1969).

40. James Q. Wilson, "Q," *Slate Magazine*, 3 November 2000, slate.msn.com

41. Jacqueline Rose, *Sexuality in the Field of Vision* (London: Verso, 1986), 86.

42. Leon D. Epstein recognizes the semiprotected status of United States political parties when he calls them "public utilities." Leon D. Epstein, *Political Parties in the American Mold* (Madison: U of Wisconsin P, 1986), 158. Protectionism is not the core of Epstein's argument, however. His claim is that to understand political parties "in the American mold" it is crucial to understand that the United States *regulates* its political parties more than any other nation and to explain this curiosity. Even while emphasizing the extraordinary phenomenon of state control, he recognizes that the "state's legal recognition of such duopolies [over elections and policy-making] might in at least limited respects solidify and perpetuate advantages for the existing parties. Established parties, it is true, could not be so fully protected against competition as were regulated electrical companies, but guaranteed ballot access was a privilege ordinarily denied minor or new parties. And though there is nothing in the history of party regulation like the industry-minded utility commission, state legislatures have not always been entirely unresponsive to the major parties they were regulating" (Epstein 158).

43. In common parlance, "discourse" is speaking. It can also mean speaking on a question of philosophy in an orderly way (as in Rousseau's *Discourse on the Origin of Inequality*). For contemporary social theorists working in many different theoretical traditions, *discourse* calls attention to the *politics* of speaking, to the ways that terms such as *gender* or *democracy* are contested and change over time, and to the *power* of speech to form the objects to which it seems only to refer. It is this

formative power of discourse and its effects on both the study and practice of electoral democracy that interests me most. In "The Order of Discourse" Michel Foucault lays out a way of thinking about this formative power, defining discourse as the historically specific rules that order the production of knowledge by delimiting a range of things that can be known, by defining positions from which to know and speak of those things with authority, and by accrediting schools and methods of investigation. Michel Foucault, "The Order of Discourse," *Untying the Text*, ed. Robert Young (Boston: Routledge and Kegan Paul, 1981), 48–78. Foucault emphasizes that the production of knowledge is not only a matter of excluding fantastical objects, disreputable methods, and the charlatans who claim to master them. It also has a positive or productive effect of forming the things that are to be known and the persons who are recognized for knowing them. Judith Butler explains that the power of discourse is that it dissimulates this formative aspect. That power is at work wherever the camouflage succeeds, so that a field of knowledge and its corresponding knowers "are taken for granted as prediscursive givens," in other words, as empirical facts of society, politics, or nature rather than as effects of our ways of knowing. Judith Butler, *Bodies that Matter* (New York: Routledge, 1993), 251 n12. For an alternative approach to the study of discourse that bears some affinities to this one, although it tends to center on texts and authors rather than institutions and to produce meticulous historical analyses of conceptual change (which is not what this book aims to do), see Terence Ball, *Transforming Political Discourse: Political Theory and Critical Conceptual History* (New York: Blackwell, 1988). For a comparison of aspects of these two approaches, see James Tully, "The Pen Is a Mighty Sword: Quentin Skinner's Analysis of Politics," *Meaning and Context: Quentin Skinner and His Critics*, ed. James Tully (Princeton: Princeton UP, 1988), 7–25.

44. Lawrence Goodwyn, *The Populist Moment: A Short History of the Agrarian Revolt in America* (New York: Oxford UP, 1978), x–xi.

45. Ibid., xi.

46. Ibid., xi.

47. In an excellent elucidation of the various meanings of Antonio Gramsci's often overused term, Geoff Eley cites Raymond Williams's argument that hegemony should not be understood in terms of consciously held ideas. Instead, hegemony is a process that affects the "whole substance of lived identities and relationships, to such a depth that *the pressures and limits of what can be seen as a specific economic, political, and cultural system seem to most of us the pressures and limits of common sense.* Hegemony is then . . . the whole body of practices and expectations, over the whole of living: our senses and assignments of energy, or shaping perceptions of ourselves and our world." Raymond Williams, *Marxism and Literature* (Oxford: Oxford UP, 1977), 109, as cited in Geoff Eley, "Nations, Publics, and Poltical Cultures: Placing Habermas in the Nineteenth Century," *Habermas and the Public Sphere*, ed. Craig Calhoun (Cambridge: MIT P, 1992), 322.

48. Goodwyn, *The Populist Moment*, xv.

49. "Shake It Up," Commentary, *Wall Street Journal*, 20 April 1999: A22.

50. Jane Perlez, "Poland Achieves Politics As Usual," *New York Times*, 28 September 1997: WK6; emphasis added.

51. *Timmons v. TCANP*, 137 L Ed 2d 589, at 603.

52. Fusion is not the same as cross-filing, a strategy that emerged later under the very different electoral conditions of the common ballot and direct primary. A California strategy that was first permitted in 1914 after the state adopted the direct primary, cross-filing takes place in the primary election when a candidate runs for the nomination of multiple parties. The goal of cross-filing is not, principally, to be listed in the general election on the ballot lines of several parties but to obviate the need for a general election campaign by making "it possible for candidates to achieve what amounted to election at the primaries" by winning the nominations of both dominant parties. Robert J. Pitchell, "The Electoral System and Voting Behavior: The Case of California's Cross-Filing," *Western Political Quarterly* 12 (1959): 484. Whereas fusion is a party-centered strategy that is negotiated between parties, and oriented toward the general election, cross-filing is a candidate-centered strategy that "tended to weaken partisanship appeals and partisan voting" because the successful cross-filing candidate would attempt to "obscure their party affiliation" in order to attract the voters of multiple parties. Pitchell, ibid., 473. As I will argue in chapter 2, fusion is a creature of the nineteenth-century party system in which parties both determined electoral processes and dominated them. By contrast, cross-filing became possible only under the system that succeeded it; it depends on primary nominations being decided by the electorate rather than by the party leadership.

53. Peter H. Argersinger, "The Value of the Vote: Political Representation in the Gilded Age," *Journal of American History* 76 (June 1989): 65.

54. Peter H. Argersinger, " 'A Place on the Ballot': Fusion Politics and Antifusion Laws," *American Historical Review* 85 (1980): 288–289.

55. Howard A. Scarrow, "Duverger's Law, Fusion and the Decline of American 'Third' Parties," *Western Political Quarterly* 39 (1986): 643.

56. Fusion is legal but not practiced in eight other states: Connecticut, Delaware, Idaho, Missouri, South Carolina, South Dakota, Utah, and Vermont. In New York some argue that fusion does not foster the kind of grassroots organizing that it made possible in the nineteenth century but rather perpetuates sham parties that function as patronage machines and "regard their line on the election ballot as so much real estate to be rented out to the highest bidder." "A Party for Hire," Editorial, *New York Times*, 24 February 1997: A14.

57. Scarrow, "Duverger's Law," 640.

58. *Timmons v. TCANP*, 137 L Ed 2d, 603.

59. Chief Justice Rhenquist wrote for the majority, joined by Justices O'Connor, Scalia, Kennedy, Thomas, and Breyer. Justice Stevens wrote a dissenting opinion, which was joined by Justice Ginsberg. Justice Souter filed a separate dissent.

60. *Timmons v. TCANP*, 137 L Ed 2d, 604.

61. Frank J. Sorauf and Paul Allen Beck, *Party Politics in America*, 6th ed. (Glenview, Ill.: Foresman/Little, Brown, 1988), 23, 34; John Aldrich, *Why Parties? The Origin and Transformation of Political Parties in America* (Chicago: U of Chicago P, 1995), 156; Steven J. Rosenstone, Roy L. Behr, and Edward H. Lazarus 10.

62. Dorothy Ross, *The Origins of American Social Science* (Cambridge: Cambridge UP, 1991), xv.

1. The Politics of Electoral Fusion, 1994–1997

1. The New Party was co-founded in 1992 by University of Wisconsin Political Science professor and activist Joel Rogers and Daniel Cantor, campaign manager for Jesse Jackson's 1988 presidential run. A coalition of labor, community groups, and other disaffected progressives, the organization counted ten thousand members at its peak. During its existence as a national organization, it mounted successful living-wage campaigns in Milwaukee, Wisconsin, St. Paul, Minnesota, and Chicago, Illinois (to name a few). It backed candidates for city council, school board, and state legislature in Arkansas, Illinois, Maryland, Minnesota, Missouri, Montana, New York, Washington, D.C., and Wisconsin. Beginning in 1997, prompted by the fusion decision, the national organization disbanded. State-level organizations are still pursuing these agendas in Arkansas, Minnesota, Montana, Wisconsin, and elsewhere. New Party organizers in New York used fusion to put a new third party on the ballot, the Working Families Party, which will confine its efforts to New York only, where fusion is legal.

2. E. E. Schattschneider, *The Semisovereign People: A Realist's View of Democracy in America* (New York: Holt, Rinehart and Winston, 1975 [1960]), 100; emphasis added.

3. 204B.04 subd. 2.

4. Although the Constitution makes no mention of political parties, the Court has construed these amendments to guarantee the right of a political party to identify members, to decide the processes of candidate selection, and, most important, to select the candidate that best represents its principles. By these rights, it is recognized that political parties engage in electoral activity to attract the interest and support of as broad a base of voters as possible. These protections are elaborated in *Eu v. San Francisco County Democratic Cent. Comm.*, 489 U.S. 214 (1989); *Tashjian v. Republican Party*, 479 U.S. 208 (1986); *Democratic Party v. Wisconsin ex rel. la Follette*, 450 U.S. 107 (1981). For a legal analysis of case law on fusion and the constitutional rights of third parties, see William R. Kirschner, "Fusion and the Associational Rights of Minor Political Parties," *Columbia Law Review* 95.5 (1995): 683–723.

5. *Twin Cities Area New Party v. McKenna*, 363 F. Supp. 988 (D. Minn. 1994).

6. The bill was co-sponsored by DFL senator Sandy Pappas, whose district overlaps that of Dawkins.

7. *Twin Cities Area New Party v. McKenna*, 73 F.3d 196, 200.

8. 73 F.3d 196, 199.

9. 73 F.3d 196, 198, 200.

10. There was Senator Sandy Pappas, co-sponsor of the New Democracy Act, whose constituency included Dawkins's district and several middle-class, progressive St. Paul neighborhoods. There was also Senator Ellen Anderson, whose territory abutted that of Dawkins (who was, incidentally, her spouse). In Minneapolis TCANP had ties to Karen Clark, who represented that city's lowest-income, lowest-turnout district and was the legislature's only out lesbian member.

11. The legislatures in Iowa, Missouri, North Dakota, and Nebraska could safely wait for the Supreme Court ruling, as there were no organized third parties

poised to implement fusion in the upcoming election. There was no change to the status quo in Arkansas and South Dakota, the two other states affected by the ruling, because they had no antifusion statutes on the books. Ironically, Arkansas moved quickly to *enact* a fusion ban once the Supreme Court ruled that they are constitutional.

12. He had helped to pass clean campaign legislation that maintains so strict a limit on gift giving that lobbyists cannot even buy a cup of cappuccino for a state employee who is inclined to order a biscotti with it.

13. In the House, DFL leadership assigned the bill to be drafted in the Ways and Means Committee, where it could be closely supervised, rather than to the elections committee, where it belonged. Ways and Means is highly susceptible to pressure from the party leadership because it is made up of committee chairs who are eager to please the speaker so as not to lose their posts. Throughout this period New Party organizers contacted Minnesota public radio and the major Twin Cities newspapers to persuade them to feature the issue in an editorial, opinion piece, or on one of MNPR's many local call-in shows. These organizations, which are exceptionally responsive toward local politics, let their characteristic suspicion toward third parties cloud their judgment about the newsworthiness of fusion. The legislative struggle, despite the cloak-and-dagger drama, and the despite an appellate ruling that made it likely that this Minnesota story would go all the way to the Supreme Court, passed almost without comment in print or on air.

14. For all their protests about voter confusion, every legislator at the conference committee owned up to being confused by the new law, which competed in mind-boggling ways with existing statutes on public campaign finance. The difficulty, which the conference committee devoted close to an hour of a three-hour meeting to sorting out, was that campaign finance law *did* prescribe criteria for being recognized as a minor party (although election law did not). There were three forms of public subsidy: party grants for electoral activity (provided through a tax check-off on the state income tax form that a party could earn by garnering 3 percent of the vote in a statewide contest), matching funds tied to contests for specific offices, and small donation rebates that could be used for both party building and campaigns. The program was a boon to qualified minor parties because they could receive public monies through the small donation program *whether they ran a candidate or not*, so long as they filed a petition signed by two thousand registered voters. The new fusion statute would compete (but not conflict) with the existing statute so that, for example, a party could be recognized as a minor party for the purposes of fusion but not for the purposes of the tax check-off (which required 3 percent of the vote in a statewide contest); at the same time, however, it could be a minor party for the purpose of access to rebate monies if it met the 1 percent threshold that qualified it for fusion status statewide. In effect, the state might recognize a minor party as such in one context but withhold that recognition in another.

15. It is worth noting that Minnesota uses an optically scanned ballot statewide. One of the more accurate ballot technologies to begin with, it also offers excellent protection against spoiled ballots because voters must pass their ballots through the scanner before they leave the polling place. The scanner can be programmed to

reject ballots that are spoiled either because citizens have failed to vote for an office or have voted more than once for the same office (undervotes and overvotes).

16. TCANP did devise an alternate ballot design that would have minimized the confusion. Fusion candidacies would list the candidate's name only once but list the different party lines underneath the name, with arrows corresponding to each party line. This design would make it clear that voters should mark their preference as always, by blacking in only *one* arrow; that arrow would indicate both a party and a candidate preference at once. The design was voted down in the House, with legislators justifying themselves by claiming that an election should not be a minor party "preference poll."

17. 73 F.3d 196, 199.

18. 73 F.3d 196, 199.

19. In New York, fusion candidacies do count toward ballot status; winning the ballot line is a principal motivation for cross-endorsing a dominant-party candidate.

20. 73 F.3d 196, 199.

21. S2720, lines 17–20, 21–25; emphasis added.

22. Although I have reached the end of the fusion story as it pertains to this chapter's analysis of the two-party doctrine, the New Party's grassroots effort to resurrect fusion in Minnesota did not end here. The Twin Cities Area New Party (newly renamed Progressive Minnesota), at its state convention in June 1996, voted to go forward with the four state-level fusion candidacies, in spite of the newly burdensome signature requirements. In a controversial move, the membership also decided to add U.S. Senator Paul Wellstone to its slate, although Wellstone never committed himself to consent to the fusion, and the leap into the national arena was a departure from what some members understood to be the party's commitment to build from the grass roots. With the financial support of the national New Party, a small team of paid signature gatherers (used primarily for the Wellstone nomination, which required almost twenty thousand signatures), and more than one hundred volunteers, the party managed to gather the twenty-five thousand signatures it needed to file the nominating petitions. The fusion candidacies never made it onto the ballot, however. At the last minute, DFL Party chair Mark Andrew declined to sign off on them, despite earlier assurances that he would do so.

23. Kirschner, "Fusion and the Associational Rights," 691.

24. "Fusion Candidacies, Disaggregation, and Freedom of Association," *Harvard Law Review* 109.6 (1996): 1303.

25. In a 1999 ballot initiative ruling, the Court spelled out a rule of thumb that carefully evaded the language of "scrutiny" and "burdens" in order not to invoke a more precise rule of law. The majority contended that "the First Amendment requires *vigilance* in making those judgments [regarding the distinction between valid ballot-access restrictions and invalid prohibitions], to guard against undue *hindrances* to political conversations and the exchange of ideas. *Buckley v. American Constitutional Law Foundation,* 1999 US Lexis 506, 2; emphasis added.

26. Kirschner, "Fusion and the Associational Rights," 686.

27. "Fusion Candidacies," 1317–1319.

28. Ibid.

29. *Timmons v. TCANP,* 137 L Ed 2d, 603–04.
30. 137 L Ed 2d, 600.
31. 137 L Ed 2d 599, 601.
32. Steven Rosenstone, Roy L. Behr, and Edward H. Lazarus, *Third Parties in America* (Princeton: Princeton UP, 1996), 40.
33. Ibid., 26.
34. Ibid., 3.
35. 137 L Ed 2d, 602, 603.
36. 137 L Ed 2d, 602, 609.
37. 137 L Ed 2d, 602.
38. 137 L Ed 2d, 603–4.
39. My thinking about legal double binds has benefited from Eve Kosofsky Sedgwick, *Epistemology of the Closet* (Berkeley: U of California P, 1990).
40. David Halperin, *Saint Foucault* (New York: Oxford UP, 1995), 34.
41. 137 L Ed 2d, 603.
42. 137 L Ed 2d, 604, citing *Davis v. Bandemer,* 478 US 109, 144–45; 92 L Ed 2d 85; 106 S Ct 2797 (1986), J. O'Connor concurring.
43. *Timmons v. TCANP,* 610.
44. *Timmons v. TCANP,* 613; emphasis added.
45. *Timmons v. TCANP,* 610.
46. E. E. Schattschneider, *Party Government* (New York: Holt, Rinehart and Winston, 1967 [1942]), 69.

2. The Politics of the Two-Party System

1. Peter H. Argersinger, "'A Place on the Ballot': Fusion Politics and Antifusion Laws." *American Historical Review* 85 (1980): 304, citing *Kalamazoo Weekly Telegraph* 20 March 1895; emphasis added.
2. E. E. Schattschneider, *Party Government* (New York: Holt, Rinehart and Winston, 1967 [1942]), 10.
3. Richard P. McCormick, *The Second American Party System: Party Formation in the Jacksonian Era* (Chapel Hill: U of North Carolina P, 1966), 19. Austin Ranney and Wilmoore Kendall note that there were "patriotic societies" in the legislative assemblies of the colonies but argue that these would scarcely qualify as parties because they had no channels of communication to constituents outside the legislature. Austin Ranney and Wilmoore Kendall, *Democracy and the American Party System* (New York: Harcourt Brace, 1956), 92–93. Internally, they were far from being republican institutions. Sustained by private allegiances, they were "secret, conspiratorial groupings" lacking formal mechanisms for nominating candidates and setting the party platform. Ibid., 116.
4. Henry Jones Ford, *The Rise and Growth of American Politics* (New York: Macmillan, 1898), 295.
5. James Madison, *Federalist* no. 10, *The Origins of the American Constitution,* ed. Michael Kammen (New York: Penguin, 1986), 149.

6. Ford, *The Rise and Growth of American Politics*, 90.

7. William Nisbet Chambers, *Political Parties in a New Nation: The American Experience, 1776–1809* (New York: Oxford UP, 1963), 127. Wilfred E. Binkley also implies that parties were a feature of the Federalist period, beginning his "natural history" of American political parties with *Federalist* no. 10. Wilfred E. Binkley, *American Political Parties: Their Natural History* (New York: Knopf, 1943).

8. Richard Hofstadter, *The Idea of a Party System* (Berkeley: University of California P, 1969), 127.

9. For this reason, Sorauf and Beck call them "congressional caucuses." Frank J. Sorauf and Paul Allen Beck, *Party Politics in America*, 6th ed. (Glenview, Ill.: Scott, Foresman, 1988), 20.

10. Ford, *The Rise and Growth of American Politics*, 91–92.

11. Ronald P. Formisano, "Deferential-Participant Politics: The Early Republic's Political Culture, 1789–1840," *American Political Science Review* 68 (1974): 474.

12. E. E. Schattschneider, *The Semisovereign People: A Realist's View of Democracy in America* (New York: Holt, Rinehart and Winston, 1975 [1960]), 101.

13. Steven J. Rosenstone, Roy L. Behr, and Edward H. Lazarus, *Third Parties in America* (Princeton: Princeton UP, 1996), 10. Cf. Paula Baker, "The Domestication of Politics: Women and American Political Society, 1780–1920," *American Historical Review* 89 (1984): 620–647; John Aldrich, *Why Parties? The Origin and Transformation of Political Parties in America* (Chicago: U of Chicago P, 1995), 97; Frank J. Sorauf, *Party Politics in America*, 4th ed. (Glenview, Ill.: Scott, Foresman, 1980).

14. Murray S. Stedman Jr. and Susan W. Stedman, *Discontent at the Polls: A Study of Farmer and Labor Parties, 1827–1948* (New York: Russell and Russell, 1967), 3. Similarly, James David Gillespie has noted that third-party intervention is "almost as ancient as [the] pattern of two major parties." J. David Gillespie, *Politics at the Periphery: Third Parties in Two-Party America* (Columbia: U of South Carolina P, 1993), 2.

15. Rosenstone, Behr, and Lazarus, *Third Parties in America*, 57.

16. Ibid., 4.

17. The Kansas-Nebraska Act of 1854 brought new energy to the abolitionist movement because it violated the 1820 Missouri Compromise, which had banned slavery from the territories acquired in the Louisiana Purchase north of the 36th parallel.

18. Rosenstone, Behr, and Lazarus, *Third Parties in America*, 55.

19. Mark Kornbluh, *Why America Stopped Voting: The Decline of Participatory Democracy and the Emergence of Modern American Politics* (New York: New York UP, 2000), 67.

20. Ibid., 69.

21. Ibid., 70.

22. Ibid., 70.

23. C. Vann Woodward, "The Promise of Populism," *New York Review of Books*, 28 October 1976: 28. The alliance first formed as a network of agricultural cooperatives through which farmers could buy equipment, seeds, foodstuffs, and sell their crops under less exploitative conditions than the crop lien system afforded them. In

1886 it formed the People's Party as a national farmer-labor coalition aspiring to far-reaching credit reform. For the classic account of the alliance movement and its ultimately lethal experiment with party politics, see Lawrence Goodwyn, *The Populist Moment: A Short History of the Agrarian Revolt in America* (New York: Oxford UP, 1978).

24. Rosenstone, Behr, and Lazarus, *Third Parties in America*, 70.

25. James L. Sundquist, *Dynamics of the Party System*, rev. ed. (Washington, D.C.: Brookings Institution, 1983), 137.

26. Baker, "The Domestication of Politics," 627.

27. Kornbluh, *Why America Stopped Voting*, 54. Of course it could be objected that the same holds today, as states deliberate over education vouchers, light rail, and the privatization of prisons. But today's deliberations, held in a context of an administrative infrastructure that delivers services (however imperfectly), lack the urgency they must have had when that administrative capacity was just coming to be.

28. Gillespie, *Politics at the Periphery*, 12.

29. Anthony Downs, *An Economic Theory of Democracy* (New York: Harper and Row, 1957), 28.

30. Samuel J. Eldersveld, *Political Parties: A Behavioral Analysis* (Chicago: Rand McNally, 1964), 6–7, citing phrases from Richard M. Cyert and James G. March, "A Behavioral Theory of Organizational Objectives," *Modern Organization Theory*, ed. Mason Haire (New York: Wiley, 1959), 76–89.

31. Frank J. Sorauf and Paul Allen Beck, *Party Politics in America*, 6th ed. (Glenview, Ill.: Scott, Foresman, 1988), 17; cf. Gerald M. Pomper, "Concepts of Political Parties," *Journal of Theoretical Politics* 4:2 (1992): 145.

32. Sorauf and Beck, *Party Politics in America*, 20.

33. Schattschneider, *Party Government*, 35; emphasis added.

34. Argersinger, " 'A Place on the Ballot,' " 289.

35. Argersinger has calculated that "minor parties regularly captured a significant share of the popular vote and received at least 20 percent in one or more elections from 1874 to 1892 in more than half of the non-Southern states. . . . Between 1878 and 1892 minor parties held the balance of power at least once in every state but Vermont, and from the mid-1880s they held that power in a majority of states in nearly every election, culminating in 1892 when neither major party secured a majority of the electorate in nearly three-quarters of the states." Ibid.

36. Richard Jensen, *The Winning of the Midwest: Social and Political Conflict: 1888–1896* (Chicago: U of Chicago P, 1971), 7.

37. Howard A. Scarrow, "Duverger's Law, Fusion and the Decline of American 'Third' Parties," *Western Political Quarterly* 39 (1986): 634.

38. Ibid., 637.

39. Ibid., 635.

40. There were probably even more fusion candidacies in local races but the documentary evidence is even more scarce at that level. Ibid., 635.

41. Ibid., 636.

42. Ibid., 635. The three presidential fusion candidates were Millard Fillmore, who ran in 1856 as the candidate of the Know Nothing and Whig parties; Horace

Greely, who was a Liberal Republican-Democratic candidate in 1872; William Jennings Bryan, who ran in 1896 on the Populist and Democratic tickets in many states.

43. Gillespie, *Politics at the Periphery*, 302.

44. Ibid., 302.

45. Argersinger, " 'A Place on the Ballot,' " 296–297. James L. Sundquist reports that the 1890 elections were devastating to the dominant parties in Kansas: "The Republicans succeeded in electing their governor, but only by 39% of the vote, as the People's candidate polled 36% and the Democrats finished a poor third. The fusion candidate for attorney general [formerly a Democrat, nominated by the Populists and then fusion-nominated by the Democrats] won with 58%. Only two Republican congressmen survived, and in each case only because the Democrats and the Populists split the opposition vote." *Dynamics of the Party System*, 130.

46. Argersinger, " 'A Place on the Ballot,' " 296–297.

47. Ibid., 289.

48. E. Pendleton Herring, *The Politics of Democracy: American Parties in Action* (New York: Norton, 1965 [1940]), 183.

49. Stephen Skowronek, *Building a New American State: The Expansion of National Administrative Capacities, 1877–1920* (Cambridge: Cambridge UP, 1982), 16, 25, 29, 165.

50. See Jensen, *The Winning of the Midwest*, 11.

51. I borrow here on the distinction that Eve Kosofsky Sedgwick has drawn between the homosexual and the "homosocial" in *Between Men: English Literature and Male Homosocial Desire* (New York: Columbia UP, 1985), 3.

52. With apologies to W. E. B. DuBois, who introduced the idea of a "public and psychological wage" to capture the intangible sense of superiority that keeps working-class white Americans invested in racist social relations, and to David R. Roedigier, who coined the term *wages of whiteness*. W. E. B. DuBois, *Black Reconstruction in the United States, 1860–1880* (New York: Atheneum, 1977 [1935]), 700–701, as cited in David Roediger, *The Wages of Whiteness: Race and the Making of the American Working Class* (London: Verso, 1991), 12.

53. Kornbluh, *Why America Stopped Voting*, 130.

54. Herbert Croly, *Progressive Democracy* (New York: Macmillan, 1914), 342.

55. Baker, "The Domestication of Politics," 628.

56. Elizabeth Clemens, *The People's Lobby: Organizational Innovation and the Rise of Interest Group Politics in the United States, 1890–1925* (Chicago: U of Chicago P, 1997), 4.

57. Skowronek, *Building a New American State*, 165.

58. Calvin Jillson, "Patterns and Periodicity in American National Politics," *The Dynamics of American Politics*, ed. Lawrence C. Dodd and Calvin Jillson (Boulder: Westview, 1994).

59. Jerrold G. Rusk, "Comment: The American Electoral Universe: Speculation and Evidence," *American Political Science Review* 68 (1974): 1040. Rusk even suggests that this unintended suppression of participation may have been all for the better insofar as it pruned "deadweight" from the electorate. Those voters who allowed simple registration laws to keep them from the polls (at least in the

North) may formerly have participated for the wrong reasons, "motivated more by the militaristic drilling of parties than by the issues." Ibid., 1041. By contrast, those who remained active were presumably an "issue-conscious core who had sufficient interest in politics to stay in the electorate despite the legal obstacles involved" and the independence of mind to abjure straight-ticket voting. Ibid., 1041. Piven and Cloward have challenged Rusk on his assumption that any citizen with a commitment to vote should have been able to surmount the obstacles posed by registration laws. They contend that these requirements "permitted the introduction of a series of informal barriers, having to do with the days and hours that voter registration was available, where the offices were located, how people were informed of where and when, and the manner in which they were treated by the officials who administered the procedures. Inevitably, over the long run, these informal barriers tended to exclude those who were less educated and less self-confident, *and in any case were often administered so as to secure that effect.*" Frances Fox Piven and Richard A. Cloward, *Why Americans Don't Vote* (New York: Pantheon, 1988), 93–94.

60. Kornbluh, *Why America Stopped Voting*, 130, 152; emphasis added at 152.

61. Schattschneider, *Party Government*, 79.

62. Walter Dean Burnham, "The Changing Shape of the American Voting Universe," *American Political Science Review* 59 (1965) 26.

63. Burnham, "The Changing Shape of the American Voting Universe," 23–26.

64. Rusk, "Comment," 1038.

65. Ibid., 1038.

66. Leon D. Epstein, *Political Parties in the American Mold* (Madison: U of Wisconsin P, 1986), chapter 6.

67. Peter H. Argersinger, *The Limits of Agrarian Radicalism: Western Populism and American Politics* (Lawrence: UP of Kansas, 1995), 136.

68. Kornbluh, *Why America Stopped Voting*, 124–125.

69. Argersinger, *The Limits of Agrarian Radicalism*, 136.

70. Argersinger, "'A Place on the Ballot,'" 303. It is not that third political parties disappeared entirely from the electoral landscape but rather that they were fewer and that their strategies and modes of organizing radically changed. From the turn of the century onward, few third parties would be built from the grass roots, exist in more than one state, successfully contest elections at the state and federal levels, or last beyond a single presidential campaign. There was Theodore Roosevelt's Bull Moose Party, for example, which did not grow as a third party but splintered off from the Republicans. The LaFollette Progressives contributed to a national farmer-labor coalition but, nonetheless, were principally concentrated in one state. This strategy was viable in the nineteenth century but became increasingly futile with the nationalization of politics in the twentieth. As for the Debsian Socialists, who made the most impressive third-party showing in that century by almost unseating the Democratic party as the second major party (in 1916), some historians credit their achievement at least in part to the Populists. Debs's party gave a home to the Populist constituency after that party disintegrated. See Murray S. Stedman Jr. and Susan W. Stedman, *Discontent at the Polls*, 8, 32–33.

71. James Ferguson, *The Anti-Politics Machine: "Development," Depoliticization, and Bureaucratic Power in Lesotho* (Minneapolis: U of Minnesota P, 1996), 19.

72. Goodwyn, *The Populist Moment*, xiii.

73. Piven and Cloward, *Why Americans Don't Vote*, 27; emphasis added.

74. I am grateful to Samuel A. Chambers for suggesting this analogy and helping me develop it.

75. The shorthanded team has a second advantage occasioned by an unwritten rule: the referee will rarely call a penalty against a team that is already down a man.

76. Certainly strategy continues to matter in football as well. There are no guarantees that a team will score just because it gets a "free" first down on a penalty; however, that set of downs is a quantifiable advantage regardless whether the team has the wherewithal to capitalize on it. In hockey the quantifiable advantage of the four-on-five situation is at least partially offset by the in-play advantage of being able to ice the puck. In addition, "killing" a penalty often leads to a momentum shift in favor of the shorthanded team.

77. Argersinger, *The Limits of Agrarian Radicalism*, 18.

78. Skowronek, *Building a New American State*, 287, 29.

79. Ibid., 27–28.

80. Ibid., 13.

81. Piven and Cloward, *Why Americans Don't Vote*, 27.

82. Skowronek, *Building a New American State*, 35.

83. The Progressive movement was a coalition that joined farmers, workers, suffragists, and integrationists with merchants and middle-class professionals under the mantle of good government. They first came together in the 1880s, with the passage of the Pendleton Act (1883), which was the start of civil service reform, and the first convention of the Farmers Alliance (1886), which was the grassroots movement that produced the People's Party in 1892.

84. Skowronek, *Building a New American State*, 35.

85. Like the much vaunted "third way" of fiscally conservative new Democrat Bill Clinton, or the Labor Party of Tony Blair, reform promised a politically painless integration of capitalism and democracy. At the turn of the previous century, however, reform meant state expansion; in the 1990s it has meant dismantling nationalized benefits and devolving responsibility from the federal government to the states.

86. Skowronek, *Building a New American State*, 165.

87. Jerrold Rusk has pointed out that voter registration was as significant a reform as the shift to the Australian or official ballot because "weak" registration—that poll books were infrequently purged of voters who had moved or died, and citizens could vote without providing written proof that they were who they claimed to be—helped create the possibility for corrupting party ticket voting. "Comment," 1033.

88. Piven and Cloward, *Why Americans Don't Vote*, 93–94.

89. Ibid., 70–78.

90. Rosenstone, Behr, and Lazarus found that the restrictions did not accompany the new ballot format as a matter of course. They were selectively adopted

only wherever the dominant parties needed to suppress third party activity, and where third parties could not prevent them from doing so. In eighteen states the new ballot was adopted *without* imposing a signature-gathering requirement on third parties. Of these states, six were "strongholds of Populist candidate James Weaver," which suggested that the People's Party had sufficient capacity to fend off access restrictions. The remaining twelve either "had no need for formal ballot access restrictions because they had strong party organizations that could deter third party voting . . . or were one-party states where third party activity would have been of little threat." Rosenstone, Behr, and Lazarus, *Third Parties in America*, 20n5.

91. Scarrow, "Duverger's Law," 639.

92. Argersinger, *The Limits of Agrarian Radicalism*, 137.

93. Argersinger, "A Place on the Ballot," 287–288; emphasis added.

94. Schattschneider, *Party Government*, 82.

95. Argersinger, " 'A Place on the Ballot,' " 290. Cf. Scarrow, "Duverger's Law," 642.

96. Argersinger, " 'A Place on the Ballot,' " 295.

97. As will be evident from citations, I am dependent on Argersinger (" 'A Place on the Ballot,' " and *The Limits of Agrarian Radicalism*) for the historical material of the next several pages.

98. The Democrats judged that their own candidate, Grover Cleveland, had no chance of taking the electoral college in that state, and that the Populist candidate might have a bigger draw. Thus, to prevent the Republicans from winning the electoral college in Oregon, the national party instructed Oregon Democrats to take their electors off the ballot and list the Populist nominees in their place. In the end, the state party removed only one of its four nominees to list one of the Populist electors.

99. In adopting the Australian ballot the year before, the Republican legislature had adopted a somewhat contradictory set of provisions. With one exception, the new ballot was to follow the office-bloc format, with the exception of electoral college nominees, which would continue to be grouped by party (approximating the old party ticket system).

100. Argersinger, " 'A Place on the Ballot,' " 294.

101. Ibid., 295.

102. Ibid., 295.

103. Argersinger has documented the measurable effect of vote splitting and voter disaffection on the outcome of the 1896 elections. Ibid., 299–303.

104. Ibid., 305, citing *State v. Anderson* (Wisc.), 76 N.W. Rep. 482.

105. Ibid., 297, 303, 306.

106. Argersinger, *The Limits of Agrarian Radicalism*, 105.

107. Ibid., 115.

108. Ibid., 32.

109. Goodwyn, *The Populist Moment*, 224. The most infamous instances of fusion backfiring came in 1897. That year Democrats in the Idaho legislature betrayed the Populist caucus by refusing to support their chosen candidate for the United States

Senate. In Kansas the Populists betrayed themselves. They failed to return their own United States senator William Peffer to Washington, voting instead for fusionist William A. Harris. Whereas Peffer was a movement Populist and opponent of fusion, Harris was a former Democrat who opposed significant planks of the Populist platform. Argersinger comments that "this election sharply indicated how the People's party had been transformed by interacting with the dynamics of the two-party system over the previous six years." Argersinger, *The Limits of Agrarian Radicalism*, 26.

110. Peter H. Argersinger, *Populism and Politics: William Alfred Peffer and the People's Party* (Lexington: UP of Kentucky, 1974), 46.

111. Le Roy Ashby, *William Jennings Bryan: Champion of Democracy* (Boston: Twayne, 1987), 57.

112. Watson had special reason to be disappointed by the Bryan fusion, as the Populists had tried to make it a condition of their ballot line that Watson supplant Arthur Sewall as Bryan's running mate. The Party went ahead with the fusion alliance *after* the Democratic ticket had been decided, even though Bryan had given every indication that he would not give up Sewall. Goodwyn, *The Populist Moment*, chapter 8.

113. Ibid., 285.

114. In 1924 Frederick E. Haynes characterized fusion as a seductive strategy that "often seems the open door to real political power" but has "probably been more often fatal to [third] parties than any other cause." Frederick E. Haynes, *Social Politics in the United States*, 2d ed. (New York: AMS, 1970 [1924]), 1955. Similarly, in 1933 historian John D. Hicks (who is otherwise sympathetic to the People's Party), called fusion one of "two fatal germs" that "gave the Populist party its death wounds" in 1896. John D. Hicks, "The Third Party Tradition in American Politics," *Mississippi Valley Historical Review* 20.1 (June 1933): 20. More recently, Murray S. Stedman and Susan W. Stedman have called fusion "one of the greatest menaces to farmer and labor parties." *Discontent at the Polls*, 110. And even Peter H. Argersinger, the leading historian of fusion, who initially emphasized how antifusion law impaired the People's Party along with third-party activity more generally, has come to denounce fusion (together with silver) as "the tangible death instruments of Populism [that] did not dominate the People's party until its leaders subordinated the early demands of the movement in a practical grasp for power." *The Limits of Agrarian Radicalism*, 135.

115. Kornbluh, *Why America Stopped Voting*, 125.

116. Robert F. Durden makes a strategic analysis of fusion in *The Climax of Populism: The Election of 1896* (Lexington: U of Kentucky P, 1965). His is by far the most detailed discussion of the fusion nomination of Bryan. In contrast to those who denounce that nomination as opportunistic, he paints the picture of a principled attempt by People's Party leaders to build (around the silver issue) a coalition against business that neither the Democrats nor the Populists could have achieved on their own.

117. In New York the Liberal Party taught Democrat David Dinkins about the power of exit by shifting its ballot line to Rudolph Giuliani in 1993 and thereby denying Dinkins reelection as mayor of New York.

118. Kornbluh, *Why America Stopped Voting*, 125. Cf. Scarrow, "Duverger's Law," 634.

119. Argersinger, *The Limits of Agrarian Radicalism*, 161; emphasis added.

120. Argersinger, " 'A Place on the Ballot,' " 304, citing the *Detroit Evening News*, 20 March 1895.

3. The Two-Party System: Genealogy of a Catchphrase

1. Ronald P. Formisano, "Deferential-Participant Politics: The Early Republic's Political Culture, 1789–1840," *American Political Science Review* 68.2 (1974): 473.

2. Ibid., 473.

3. Ibid., 473.

4. Frank J. Sorauf, *Political Parties in the American System* (Boston: Little, Brown, 1964), 27.

5. Ibid., 27.

6. Frank J. Sorauf, *Party Politics in America*, 4th ed. (Glenview, Ill.: Scott, Foresman, 1980), 419.

7. Austin Ranney and Wilmoore Kendall, *Democracy and the American Party System* (New York: Harcourt Brace, 1956), 161.

8. Ibid., 160.

9. Sorauf, *Political Parties in the American System*, 22. Competitiveness also varies within the states. Some states are "dual" party systems, dominated by a single party in presidential politics but sustaining two-party competition for the House, the Senate, and the statehouse. See Richard P. McCormick, *The Second American Party System: Party Formation in the Jacksonian Era* (Chapel Hill: U of North Carolina P, 1966), 10–11.

10. Giovanni Sartori, *Parties and Party Systems: A Framework for Analysis*, vol. 1 (Cambridge: Cambridge UP, 1976), 81.

11. Ibid., 186; emphasis added.

12. Ibid., 86; John F. Bibby, Cornelius P. Cotter, James L. Gibson, and Robert J. Huckshorn, "Parties in State Politics," *Politics in the American States*, 4th ed., ed. Virginia Gray, Herbert Jacob, and Kenneth Vines (Boston: Little, Brown, 1983).

13. E. E. Schattschneider, *Party Government* (New York: Holt, Rinehart and Winston, 1967 [1942]), 68; cf. James MacGregor Burns and J. W. Peltason, *Government by the People* (Englewood Cliffs, N.J.: Prentice-Hall, 1952), 348.

14. James MacGregor Burns, J. W. Peltason, and Thomas E. Cronin, *Government by the People*, 17th ed. (Englewood Cliffs, N.J.: Prentice-Hall, 1998), 248.

15. James Q. Wilson and John J. DiIulio Jr., *American Government*, 7th ed. (Boston: Houghton Mifflin, 1998), 183.

16. Ranney and Kendall, *Democracy and the American Party System*, 161.

17. Sorauf, *Party Politics in America*, 28.

18. Ibid., 29, 34.

19. Ibid., 29; emphasis added.

20. William Flanigan, personal communication, 1 October 1999.

21. Formisano, "Deferential-Participant Politics," 473.

22. Charles E. Merriam, *The American Party System: An Introduction to the Study of Political Parties in the United States* (New York: MacMillan, 1922).

23. Ibid., 370.

24. Ibid.

25. David M. Ricci, *The Tragedy of Political Science: Politics, Scholarship, and Democracy* (New Haven: Yale UP, 1984), 61.

26. Leon D. Epstein, *Political Parties in the American Mold* (Madison: U of Wisconsin P, 1986), 10. At this time, there was only one significant academic study of parties—see James Bryce, *The American Commonwealth*, abridged and rev. ed. (Philadelphia: John D. Morris, 1906 [1891]).

27. Among others, see Charles Beard (1919); E. M. Sait (1920); Charles Merriam (1922); James Albert Woodburn (1924); Arthur Holcombe (1924); R. M. MacIver (1926), as noted by Epstein, *Political Parties in the American Mold*, 14–25.

28. Merriam, *The American Party System*, 369–370.

29. Ibid., 373.

30. Edward Sait, *American Parties and Elections* (New York: Century, 1927), 177, 179.

31. Ibid., 174; emphasis added.

32. Merriam, *The American Party System*, 100–101.

33. Ibid., 380, 381, 387.

34. Political scientist William Riker quotes a use of this term as early as 1910, in a statement by American political scientist Arthur Holcombe, who held that the "tendency under the system of plurality elections toward the establishment of the two-party system is . . . almost irresistible," cited in William H. Riker, "The Two-Party System and Duverger's Law: An Essay on the History of Political Science," *American Political Science Review* 76 (1982): 757. Riker's article tracks the progression of Duverger's Law (the precept that winner-take-all voting systems tend to produce two-party systems) from common knowledge to a testable proposition of social science. Although Riker found other intimations of the law in the 1850s, dated its first "explicit" statement to 1881, and claimed that by 1901 it is a "commonplace," it appears that these early enunciations advanced the principle without recourse to the phrase *two-party system*. Ibid., 756. Riker seems to have introduced it himself into these early texts by the use of square brackets, as when he cites the views of Henry Droop (an advocate of proportional representation) in the following: "Droop's position in 1869 is ambiguous. But by 1881 he was prepared to argue 'these phenomena [i.e., two-party systems] I cannot explain by any theory of a natural division between opposing tendencies of thought, and the only explanation which seems to me to account for them is that the two opposing parties into which we find politicians divided in each of these countries [United Kingdom, United States, etc.] *have been formed and are kept together by majority voting*' [emphasis added; Droop means, of course, plurality voting]." Ibid.; all brackets and emphasis in Riker.

35. Bryce, *The American Commonwealth*, chapter 54.

36. Bryce attributed the pattern to the "centrifugal and centripetal tendencies" that found expression in both the conflict between the federalists and antifederal-

ists over the structure of the American system, and in the corresponding conflict that opposed the "love of liberty" in the political philosophy of the antifederalists against the federalist "love of Order." Ibid., 248–249.

37. Merriam, *The American Party System*, 406.

38. Ibid., 389.

39. Ibid., 419.

40. Ibid., 418–419.

41. Sait, *American Parties and Elections*, 205.

42. Ibid., 182.

43. Ibid., 183.

44. Ibid., 183. Quaint as his words may sound, Sait's perspective is far from old-fashioned. It persists today whenever journalists or politicians applaud the advent of two-party democracy in a formerly authoritarian regime. Was the *New York Times* so far off Sait's mark when it extolled the 1997 parliamentary elections in Poland (which showed signs of consolidating its multiparty system into a two-party pattern) as an indication that its political system was "fast approaching adulthood"? Jane Perlez, "Poland Achieves Politics As Usual," *New York Times*, 28 September 1997: WK6.

45. Charles E. Merriam and Harold F. Gosnell, *The American Party System: An Introduction to the Study of Political Parties in the United States*, 3d ed. (New York: MacMillan, 1940), 1.

46. Ibid., 1, 3.

47. Ibid., 11.

48. For example, Gosnell retained Merriam's discussion of third parties from the 1922 edition unchanged, except for minor historical updates. The attentive reader would notice a tension between the two-party patriotism of the 1940 introduction and Merriam's insistence, in the previous edition, on the influence and importance of third parties.

49. Epstein, *Political Parties in the American Mold*, 13.

50. Anthony King, "Political Parties in Western Democracies," *Polity* 2.12 (1969): 112.

51. Duverger, writing about the difficulty of producing a "general theory of parties" when the field tended to produce single-country studies, singled out the United States for criticism: "studies of political parties abound; they are based upon considerable and serious observation; they are often of great value; not one, however, throws any light upon problems like the evolution of party structures, the number and reciprocal relations of parties, the party they play in the State, for all these studies are conceived within the framework of America alone, they deal with problems that are specifically American and do not refer to general questions." Maurice Duverger, *Political Parties: Their Origins and Activity in the Modern State* (London: Methuen, 1954), xiii. One attempt to foster a comparative approach to the study of parties is a volume of single-country case studies edited by Neumann.

52. Riker, "The Two-Party System and Duverger's Law," 757.

53. Epstein, *Political Parties in the American Mold*, 29.

54. Schattschneider, *Party Government* 66; emphasis added.

55. Committee on Political Parties, American Political Science Association, *Toward a More Responsible Two-Party System* (New York: Rinehart, 1950), 18.

56. Burns and Peltason, *Government by the People*, 348.

57. Schattschneider, *Party Government*, 1.

58. Robert Dahl, "The Behavioral Approach in Political Science: Epitaph for a Monument to a Successful Protest," *Discipline and History: Political Science in the United States*, ed. James Farr and Raymond Seidelman (Ann Arbor: U of Michigan P, 1993), 258. Some might date behavioralism five or ten years later, or even twenty years earlier. The term *political behavior* came into currency in the 1920s and found its first institutional home at the University of Chicago in 1925, under the leadership of Charles Merriam in the department of political science. Ibid., 250. As an intellectual movement behavioralism gained momentum after the Second World War when funding institutions such as the Social Science Research Council and the Carnegie, Ford, and Rockefeller Foundations committed significant funds to the survey research on which its empirical claims depended. In the 1950s "the behavioral approach grew from the deviant and unpopular views of a minor sect into a major influence" within the discipline. Ibid., 254. The first glimpses of a behavioral orientation in party scholarship appear in the works of Herring (1940) and Key (1942). These texts both make an definitive break with the exclusively descriptive, historical approach to the study of parties by beginning to formulate theories of party organization. Key explicitly takes on the relationship between facts and values in the introduction to the 1947, 1952, and 1958 editions of his textbook. In an extensive discussion of "Politics and Ethics" he voices his reservations about the fact that the "study of politics is often approached with the hope, not so much of seeing and understanding what occurs, but of learning what 'ought to be.' " V. O. Key Jr., *Politics, Parties, and Pressure Groups* (New York: Crowell, 1947), 9; (1952), 17. Key counters that the "study of what people do in their political actions needs to be separated, at least for purposes of analysis, from the determination of what political behavior and ends are 'right.' " Ibid. (1952), 17.

59. Dahl, "The Behavioral Approach in Political Science," 254–255.

60. Farr and Seidelman contend that behavioralism was not a full-blown philosophy of science but some combination of methodology and ideolgy that "captured the appellative imagination of numerous political scientists (and their critics) who were wont to underscore (or to criticize) the *scientific* aspirations of the discipline." *Discipline and History*, 202–203.

61. David Easton, "Political Science in the United States: Past and Present," *Discipline and History: Political Science in the United States*, ed. James Farr and Raymond Seidelman (Ann Arbor: U of Michigan P, 1993), 294–295.

62. Ibid., 296.

63. Epstein, *Political Parties in the American Mold*, 10: cf. Sorauf, *Political Parties in the American System*, 173–175; Easton "Political Science in the United States," 292.

64. Duverger, *Political Parties*, xiii. The very term *party* proved to be especially elusive. In the 1952 edition of *Politics, Parties, and Pressure Groups*, V. O. Key elaborated the tripartite definition of party that remains influential today, proposing to

differentiate between the "party-in-the-electorate," the "professional party workers," and the "party-in-the-government." Whereas he acknowledged that these groups could "interact more or less closely and perhaps at times . . . as one," he contended that "analytically and operationally" it was important to have the vocabulary to differentiate between them. Key, *Politics, Parties, and Pressure Groups*, 181–182. For contemporary critics of this model, see Gerald M. Pomper, "Concepts of Political Parties," *Journal of Theoretical Politics* 4.2 (1992): 143–159; and John Aldrich, *Why Parties? The Origin and Transformation of Political Parties in America* (Chicago: U of Chicago P, 1995).

65. Sorauf, *Political Parties in the American System*, 175.

66. Ranney and Kendall, *Democracy and the American Party System*, 151–153.

67. Sorauf, *Political Parties in the American System*, 27; emphasis added.

68. David Easton, *The Political System: An Inquiry Into the State of Political Science* (New York: Knopf, 1953), 96, 60.

69. Ibid., 61

70. Frederick M. Dolan, *Allegories of America: Narratives, Metaphysics, Politics (Ithaca: Cornell U P, 1994), 97.*

71. *Burns and Peltason, Government by the People*, 348.

72. Schattschneider, *Party Government*, 67; emphasis added.

73. Ibid., 69.

74. Ibid., 69–75.

75. Ibid., 75.

76. Ibid., 68.

77. Ibid., 69.

78. Duverger's *Political Parties* was first published in France in 1951; 1954 is the publication date of its first translation into English.

79. Duverger, *Political Parties*, xv.

80. Ibid., 206.

81. Ibid., 206.

82. Key, *Politics, Parties, and Pressure Groups* (1952), 231.

83. Riker, "The Two-Party System and Duverger's Law," 753. In one respect, which typically passes unmentioned, Duverger's thinking about two-party systems actually resembled the cultural and essentialist theories his work is often credited with displacing. Duverger prefaced his law with an extensive discussion of "natural political dualism," an ontological theory that held the "two-party system . . . to correspond to the nature of things," which is for "political choice usually [to take] the form of a choice between two alternatives." Duverger, *Political Parties*, 215. Duverger formulated his law to "explain why nature should have flourished so freely in the Anglo-Saxon countries and their few imitators and why nature should have been thwarted on the continent of Europe." Ibid., 216.

84. Ibid., 217. For one refutation of Duverger's Law, see Douglas W. Rae, *The Political Consequences of Electoral Laws*, rev. ed. (New Haven: Yale UP, 1971). For a discussion of the debates, see Riker, "The Two-Party System and Duverger's Law," 758–761. On the contrary, even in the United States the law was easily falsified. This country had one of its most vigorous periods of *third* party activity in the mid-

nineteenth century, well after the conditions that Duverger would have expected to produce two-party competition were in place. I am grateful to Bill Flanigan for pointing this out to me.

85. Riker, "The Two-Party System and Duverger's Law," 754.

86. Riker found what he called "the earliest explicit statement of Duverger's Law" in 1881, in the work of Henry Droop, an English advocate of proportional voting, who wrote that "the two opposing parties into which we find politicians divided in each of these countries [United Kingdom, United States, etc.] have been formed and are kept together by majority voting," not by "a natural division between opposing tendencies of thought." Ibid., 756; square brackets in original, emphasis in original omitted. Riker noted that by contrast to barristers and members of parliament, theorists of politics were relatively slow to catch on. While John Stuart Mill possessed "some dim appreciation" for Duverger's companion hypothesis regarding the relationship of proportional representation to multi-partyism, he clearly did not grasp the "law," because he believed it would be possible to shift from a plurality to a cumulative voting scheme "without upsetting the two-party system." Ibid., 755.

87. Ibid., 56, 765.

88. Ibid., 755.

89. Ibid., 753.

90. Ibid., 754; emphasis added.

91. Ibid., 753–754.

92. Ibid., 753.

93. Ibid., 753.

94. Duverger, *Political Parties*, 215.

95. Ibid., 226. Because fusion offsets the predicted effect of plurality elections, Howard A. Scarrow has proposed that Duverger's Law should be amended to recognize the practice: it should be qualified to hold that plurality elections will tend to produce and maintain two-party competition except "where fusion candidacies are legally possible and other conditions, especially a competitive party environment, encourage their formation." Howard A. Scarrow, "Duverger's Law, Fusion and the Decline of American 'Third' Parties," *Western Political Quarterly* 39 (1986): 644. Insofar as it participates in the discourse of the two-party system, however, I contend that Duverger's Law resists amendment. We cannot simply add fusion to a theory that, because it perpetuates the belief in a two-party "system" that is historically constant, impervious to political challenge, and innocent of partisan content, renders every other aspect of fusion unintelligible.

96. This was, of course, not what motivated Downs to write. He aimed in part to defend the rationality of the voters against the mid-century studies that had so vilified them.

97. Anthony Downs, *An Economic Theory of Democracy* (New York: Harper and Row, 1957), 34.

98. Ibid., 38–39.

99. Ibid., 48; emphasis added.

100. Ibid., 36.

101. Ibid., 100.

102. Ibid., 136.

103. Ibid.

104. Burns and Peltason, *Government by the People*, 356.

105. Downs, *An Economic Theory of Democracy*, 146–154.

106. Dolan, *Allegories of America*, 98.

107. John Mowitt, *Text: The Geneology of an Antidisciplinary Object* (Durham: Duke UP, 1992), 33.

108. Michel Foucault, *Discipline and Punish: The Birth of the Prison*, trans. Alan Sheridan (New York: Vintage, 1979).

109. Michel Foucault, "The Order of Discourse," *Untying the Text*, ed. Robert Young (Boston: Routledge and Kegan Paul, 1981), 48–78.

110. Mowitt, *Text*, 35; emphasis added.

111. At the inception of professional political science at the turn of the twentieth century, its practitioners understood the state to furnish "the objective reality upon which political science can rest in the construction of a truly scientific political system." John W. Burgess, *Political Science and Comparative Constitutional Law*, vol. 1 (Boston: Ginn, 1890), 58, as cited in James Farr, "From Modern Republic to Administrative State: American Political Science in the Nineteenth Century," *Regime and Discipline: Democracy and the Development of Political Science*, ed. David Easton, John G. Gunnell, and Michael B. Stein (Ann Arbor: U of Michigan P), 131–167. I do not mean to suggest that the two-party system took primacy over the state in this regard but rather to call attention to the ways that it figured into the processes of both state and discipline formation.

112. Mowitt, *Text*, 35.

113. Ibid., 35.

114. Ibid., 27.

115. Ibid.

4. The Two-Party System and the Ideology of Process

1. Thomas E. Patterson, *The American Democracy* (Boston: McGraw-Hill, 1999), 221.

2. James MacGregor Burns, J. W. Peltason, and Thomas E. Cronin, *Government by the People*, 17th ed. (Englewood Cliffs, N.J.: Prentice-Hall, 1998), 258.

3. George C. Edwards II, Martin P. Wattenberg, and Robert L. Lineberry, *Government in America*, 8th ed. (New York: Longman, 1998), 188.

4. Theodore J. Lowi and Benjamin Ginsberg, *American Government: Freedom and Power*, 5th ed. (New York: Norton, 1998), 471.

5. Patterson, *The American Democracy*, 24.

6. Albert Stickney, *A True Republic* (New York: Harper, 1879), 146.

7. Ibid., 146–148.

8. Ibid., 148.

9. William H. Sewell, "Three Temporalities: Toward an Eventful Sociology,"

The Historic Turn in the Human Sciences, ed. Terrence J. McDonald (Ann Arbor: U of Michigan P, 1996), 247, 250–251.

10. William Nisbet Chambers, "Party Development and the American Mainstream," *The American Party Systems: Stages of Political Development*, ed. William Nisbet Chambers and Walter Dean Burnham (New York: Oxford U P, 1975), 4–5.

11. Theodore J. Lowi, "Party, Policy, and Constitution in America," *The American Party Systems: Stages of Political Development*, ed. William Nisbet Chambers and Walter Dean Burnham (New York: Oxford U P, 1975), 251.

12. Chambers, "Party Development and the American Mainstream," 22.

13. Ibid., 5.

14. Alex Keyssar, "Reform and an Evolving Electorate," *New York Times*, 5 August 2001: WK13.

15. Lawrence Goodwyn, *The Populist Moment: A Short History of the Agrarian Revolt in America* (New York: Oxford UP, 1978), xi.

16. Ibid., xiv.

17. Peter H. Argersinger, " 'A Place on the Ballot': Fusion Politics and Antifusion Laws," *American Historical Review* 85 (1980): 287.

18. Steven J. Rosenstone, Roy L. Behr, and Edward H. Lazarus, *Third Parties in America* (Princeton: Princeton UP, 1996), 72–74. These authors' omission of fusion is all the more noteworthy because the practice supports their central argument that structural barriers account for the futility of contemporary third-party organizing and that those barriers were intensified by turn-of-the-century reforms.

19. Leon D. Epstein, *Political Parties in Western Democracies* (New York: Praeger, 1967), 68n31.

20. Ruy A. Texeira, *The Disappearing American Voter* (Washington, D.C.: Brookings Institution, 1992), 19.

21. Frank Sorauf, *Party Politics in America*, 5th ed. (Glenview, Ill.: Scott, Foresman, 1984), 55.

22. Daniel A. Mazmanian, *Third Parties in Presidential Elections* (Washington, D.C.: Brookings Institution, 1974), 119.

23. Thomas Kuhn, *The Structure of Scientific Revolutions*, 3d ed. (Chicago: U of Chicago P, 1996 [1962]), 2.

24. Ibid., 6.

25. Ibid., 6.

26. Ibid., 150.

27. Ibid., 142, 138.

28. Ibid., 2.

29. Marshall Sahlins, "The Return of the Event, Again; with Reflections on the Beginnings of the Great Fijian War of 1843 to 1855 Between the Kingdoms of Bau and Rewa," *Clio in Oceania: Toward a Historical Anthropology*, ed. Aletta Biersach (Washington, D.C.: Smithsonian Institution Press, 1991), 43.

30. Ibid., 45.

31. Ibid., 45.

32. Ibid., 42; emphasis added.

33. Ibid., 78.

34. Herbert Croly, *The Promise of American Life* (New York: MacMillan, 1965 [1909]), 3.

35. Dorothy Ross, *The Origins of American Social Science* (Cambridge: Cambridge U, 1991), 150.

36. Ibid., 337.

37. Ibid., xiv.

38. Ibid., 36, 471.

39. Ibid., xvii.

40. Ibid., 26; emphasis added.

41. Ibid., 149.

42. Croly, *The Promise of American Life*, 22.

43. Ross, *The Origins of American Social Science*, 274.

44. Ibid., 149.

45. Ibid., 303.

46. Ibid., xv; emphasis added.

47. Ibid., 317.

48. It is only in her discussion of process that Ross makes the connection between exceptionalism and the notion of eventfulness that I have emphasized. Citing Hannah Arendt's "The Process of History," Ross contends that "the idea of process emerged within historicism from the increasing recognition of history as continuity, as a series not of discrete events but of means-ends relationships, each segment of history producing the next by an orderly series of changes." Ross, *The Origins of American Social Science*, 317. Ross connects process thinking to the production of uneventfulness, writing that by subsuming the "discrete event" in "pursuit of the deeper continuities of history," process thinking resulted "in events losing their meaningfulness in themselves to the process of history." Ibid., 317. Although I agree that process thinking renders events inconceivable, I would not frame this as a concern about losing the sense of events as "discrete" or meaningful "in themselves" because this suggests that events have an ontological presence or integrity apart from narration. As such, it undercuts my concern with the politics that goes into deciding what counts as an event and with the ways that uneventfulness participates in the production of common sense. See Hannah Arendt, *Between Past and Future* (New York: Penguin, 1954).

49. Russell L. Hanson, *The Democratic Imagination in America: Conversations with Our Past* (Princeton: Princeton UP, 1985), 4, 3.

50. Chambers, "Party Development and the American Mainstream," 22.

51. Burns, Peltason, and Cronin, *Government by the People*, 193.

52. Sorauf, *Party Politics in America*, 29.

53. Croly, *The Promise of American Life*, 150.

54. Frank Goodnow, *Politics and Administration: A Study in Government* (New York: Russell and Russell, 1967), 251, 149.

55. Croly, *The Promise of American Life*, 33.

56. James Woodburn, *American Politics: Political Parties and Party Problems in the United States* (New York: Putnam's, 1903), 134.

57. Croly, *The Promise of American Life*, 35. Croly's formulation of this vision was unique in concentrating power in an executive that would be linked to the people not by political parties but by a new form of initiative and referendum. Initiatives were to be put on the ballot by the executive rather than by popular petition. This would render policy making an executive prerogative and would virtually cut out the legislature, which Croly proposed to replace by a small elected body of "legal, administrative, and financial experts" charged with writing successful initiatives into proper statutes. Ibid., 329. Croly justified this astonishing concentration of executive power with an outlandish analogy: he imagined that the executive would function as "a veritable 'Boss,' " an elected official subject to recall who would be empowered to "destroy the sham 'Bosses' " and would command the administrative capacity to displace them as providers of public services. Ibid., 340.

58. Henry Jones Ford, *The Rise and Growth of American Politics* (New York: Macmillan, 1898), 214–215.

59. Goodnow, *Politics and Administration*, 3–4; emphasis added. Whereas Goodnow followed Ford in some respects, he did not share Ford's image of popular government unified by the parties' "powerful solvent influence" on America's diverse population. He understood elections and campaigns "to fuse [the population] into one mass of citizenship, pervaded by a common order of ideas and sentiments, and activated by the same class of motives." In his work the "solvent" of partisan fervor would substitute for the consensus that republican revisionists like Croly and Goodnow expected to be "a conscious social ideal." Thus, although Ross counts Ford's work as a "key document" for the early Progressives' recuperation of political parties, in this one respect Ford anticipated process exceptionalism and the process conception of democracy that would accompany it.

60. Woodburn, *American Politics*, 134.

61. Ibid., v.

62. Ibid., 134–35.

63. Charles E. Merriam, *The American Party System: An Introduction to the Study of Political Parties in the United States* (New York: MacMillan, 1922), 218; emphasis added.

64. Ibid., 92.

65. Ibid., 121, 218–219.

66. Edward Sait, *American Parties and Elections* (New York: Century, 1927), 198.

67. Ibid., 157–58.

68. Ibid., 144, quoting J. J. Murphy, "Non-partisanship in Municipal Affairs," *National Municipal Review* 6 (1917): 217–218. Downs would later formalize this view as the first premise of his "economic theory" of democracy: "Parties formulate policies in order to win elections, rather than win elections in order to formulate policies" Anthony Downs, *An Economic Theory of Democracy* (New York: Harper and Row, 1957), 27–28.

69. Moisei Ostrogorski, *Democracy and the Organization of Political Parties* (New York: Macmillan, 1902), 714. Ostrogorski is infamous today for advocating the abolition of parties, even though that was not the thrust of his argument. Ranney and Kendall are among those to have misread Ostrogorski in this way.

Austin Ranney and Wilmoore Kendall, *Democracy and the American Party System* (New York: Harcourt Brace, 1956). David Mayhew has suggested that his reception by contemporary scholars testifies to the "American political science community's firmly held belief that American parties somehow or other must be functional." David Mayhew, *Placing Parties in American Politics* (Princeton: Princeton UP, 1986), 310.

70. Ostrogorski, *Democracy and the Organization of Political Parties*, 758.

71. Ibid., 107.

72. Ibid., 106. Whereas he dismissed the Know Nothings as a failed party on account of the "fancifulness of its object," he praised the Republicans for having forced a "face to face" confrontation on slavery when the Whigs and Democrats had "organized a conspiracy of ambiguity and silence" to evade it. Ibid., 106, 110, 98. It is important to note that Ostrogorski was no friend of fusion. As one who believed that party conflict should be a rational confrontation based on opposed principles, he considered fusion an opportunistic strategy that muddied the lines of argument. In contrast to his praise for the Republicans, whom he recognized for forcing a decisive confrontation on slavery, Ostrogorski criticized the Populists and Greenbackers because they "neutralized" any "dissolvent action" they might have exerted by indiscriminately partnering with whichever of the dominant parties was the minority in a particular race. Ibid., 458.

73. For contemporary assessments of Ostrogorski's work, see Ranney and Kendall, *Democracy and the American Party System*, 150; Leon D. Epstein, *Political Parties in the American Mold* (Madison: U of Wisconsin P, 1986), 19; William H. Riker, "The Two-Party System and Duverger's Law: An Essay on the History of Political Science," *American Political Science Review* 76 (1982): 756.

74. Mayhew, *Placing Parties in American Politics*, 310.

75. Woodburn, *American Politics*, iv.

76. Merriam, *The American Party System*, 92.

77. James Bryce, *The American Commonwealth*, rev. ed. (New York: Macmillan, 1941), 2:49.

78. E. E. Schattschneider, *Party Government* (New York: Holt, Rinehart and Winston, 1967 [1942]), 1.

79. Ibid., 3.

80. R. M. MacIver, *The Web of Government* (New York: Macmillan, 1947), 209–210.

81. Ranney and Kendall, *Democracy and the American Party System*, 114. As I argued in the previous chapter, these scholars took it as understood that in speaking of "parties" generally they meant two-partyism in particular.

82. There are conflicting assessments of the influence of the report. Whereas Ranney and Kendall (who were critics of the committee) characterized it in 1956 as the "most widely held position on political parties" by "professional political scientists today" (ibid., 151), David Ricci has contended that the report "was so much at odds with scientific research findings as to be more ignored than explicitly criticized in the heyday of behavioralism," observing that its findings "found no prominent place in [political scientists'] teaching during the behavioral era." David Ricci, *The*

Tragedy of Political Science: Politics, Scholarship, and Democracy (New Haven: Yale UP, 1984), 167, 165. Epstein cuts a balance between these two extremes, arguing that "for a time [the responsible party position] had less prestige among political scientists than those of pluralist defenders of existing parties, but they were never disregarded and their popularity revived in the late 1960s and 1970s." Epstein, *Political Parties in the American Mold*, 32. One such revival is Gerald M. Pomper, "Toward a More Responsible Two-Party System? What, Again?" *Journal of Politics* 33 (1971): 916–940.

83. Committee on Political Parties, American Political Science Association, *Toward a More Responsible Two-Party System* (New York: Rinehart, 1950), 14. They proposed these reforms to make them so: reducing obstacles to voter registration, declaring election day a national holiday, combating literacy tests and poll taxes, and turning the national party convention in to a "grand assembly" where the party would deliberate over the details of its platform.

84. Ricci, *The Tragedy of Political Science*, 167. Despite the affinities to those Progressive-era ideals, the report differed from that tradition in two significant respects. First, responsible popular government as someone like Frank J. Goodnow had defined it primarily meant accountability, which he understood to call for reforming the "autocratic party organization[s]" whose oligarchic structures were at odds with democratic representation (*Politics and Administration*, 28). By contrast, the committee wanted the kind of programmatic responsibility that comes with parliamentary forms of government, with the major parties serving "as the mechanisms through which American voters could choose between competing programs, and through which the winning majority of voters could be assured of the enactment of its choice." Frank J. Sorauf, *Party Politics in America*, 4th ed. (Glenview, Ill.: Scott, Foresman, 1980), 326. This departed so much from "responsibility" in its earlier incarnation as to constitute a "difference in kind and not merely in degree" (Epstein, *Political Parties in the American Mold*, 31). Methodologically, it was actually a violation of the historical realism that Progressive-era scholars observed because the committee did not derive its model from the empirical world but proposed to remake American parties after what they imagined the contemporary British parties to be: doctrinal and disciplined. Ricci, *The Tragedy of Political Science*, 167.

85. The phrase is from David M. Ricci, "Democracy Attenuated: Schumpeter, the Process Theory, and American Democratic Thought," *Journal of Politics* 32 (1970): 239. Ricci traces this conception of democracy to Joseph Schumpeter's theory of competing elites. Robert Dahl modified Schumpeter's work at mid-century to emphasize the importance of the social context within which elites operate. In contrast to the responsible party advocates, who called for beliefs to be fully articulated as party doctrine, Dahl maintained that it is enough for the competitive process to operate within the constraints of an unstated "underlying consensus" that is derived from constitutional procedure and economic practice. Robert Dahl, *A Preface to Democratic Theory* (Chicago: U of Chicago P, 1956), 132.

86. E. Pendleton Herring, *The Politics of Democracy: American Parties in Action* (New York: Norton, 1965 [1940]), 55. Although it preceded the committee's report,

Herring's work was crucial to the responsible parties debate because it inspired the responses that Austin Ranney, Robert Dahl, and others made to the committee. Herring derived his own analysis from Arthur Bentley's classic, *The Process of Government* (Evanston, Ill.: Principia Press of Illinois, 1949 [1908]), 269, 370–371, which he adapted to model political parties.

87. Committee on Political Parties, *Toward a More Responsible Two-Party System*, 13.

88. Herring, *The Politics of Democracy*, 55.

89. For example, Ervon M. Kirkpatrick put science on the side of the critics of the Responsible Parties doctrine when he criticized the Report for "a pervasive imprecision of language combined with a total failure to distinguish between normative and empirical statements" (967). Evron M. Kirkpatrick, " 'Toward a More Responsible Two-Party System': Political Science, Policy Science, or Pseudo-Science?" *American Political Science Review* 65 (1971): 965–90. Ricci has contended that the report "was so much at odds with scientific research findings as to be more ignored than explicitly criticized in the heyday of behavioralism." Ricci, *The Tragedy of Political Science*, 167. Gerald M. Pomper turned this charge back against its source. Noting that time has proven the accuracy of many of the committee's concerns, he contended that "a review of criticisms of the Report reveals as much about the state of political science in 1950 as it demonstrates about the failings of the Committee. Particularly notable among the critics was their relative satisfaction with the state of the nation, a satisfaction derived from their pluralist bias." Pomper, "Toward a More Responsible Two-Party System?" 917.

90. Jeffrey Isaac, *Democracy in Dark Times* (Ithaca: Cornell UP, 1998), 32.

91. Ibid., 32.

92. Committee on Political Parties, *Toward a More Responsible Two-Party System*, 18.

93. Ibid., 1, 14–18, 37, 84, 92, 95–96.

94. Ibid., 18.

95. Ibid., 10.

96. Herring, *The Politics of Democracy*, 179.

97. Ibid., 179. For his own part, Herring did seem to frown on third-party movements of "recent decades," which he characterized as "aspects of a continuous rebellion against big business" and charged with inclining "strongly to the devil theory of history . . . [insisting that] plutocracy . . . is the cause of all evil." Ibid., 182.

98. Ranney and Kendall, *Democracy and the American Party System*, 511.

99. Richard Hofstadter, *The Age of Reform* (New York: Knopf, 1955), 97.

100. V. O. Key, "A Theory of Critical Elections," *Journal of Politics* 17 (1955): 3–18.

101. Ibid., 4, 11.

102. See Paul Allen Beck, "The Electoral Cycle and Patterns of American Politics," *British Journal of Political Science* 9 (1979): 129–156; Walter Burnham, *Critical Elections and the Mainsprings of American Politics* (New York: Norton, 1970), 3; Richard P. McCormick, *The Second American Party System: Party Formation in the Jacksonian Era* (Chapel Hill: U of North Carolina P, 1966), 6; Steven J. Rosenstone, Roy L. Behr, and Edward H. Lazarus, *Third Parties in America* (Princeton: Princeton

UP, 1996), 144. James L. Sundquist has significantly refined the notion of realignment by enumerating the various elements that must be present for the rise of a new issue to effect a system transformation. James Sundquist, *Dynamics of the Party System*, rev. ed. (Washington, D.C.: Brookings Institution, 1983). Contrary to the insistence of Key and Burnham on the suddenness of realignments, Sundquist argues that realignment is a protracted process that may reach a climax in a critical election but probably also "extend[s] over a considerable period before and after" that moment (317; emphasis in original omitted). Sundquist specifies a distinction between "critical election" and "realignment" that Burnham did not make in his earlier work but began to anticipate in later elaborations of his argument. See Walter Dean Burnham, "Theory and Voting Research: Some Reflections on Converse's 'Change in the American Electorate,' " *American Political Science Review* 68 (1974):1002–1023.

103. See Paul Kleppner, *The Third Electoral System, 1853–1892* (Chapel Hill: U of North Carolina P, 1979), 19; Burnham, *Critical Elections and the Mainsprings of American Politics*, 69. Scholars typically argue that, beginning in 1800, there have been five party systems with realignments occurring approximately every thirty years: 1828 (second), 1860 (third), 1896 (fourth), 1932 (fifth). Some argue that 1968 was a sixth realignment.

104. Burnham, *Critical Elections and the Mainsprings of American Politics*, 11, 66; emphasis added.

105. In contrast to the work of Key and Burnham, a more recent realignment scholar, James L. Sundquist, emphasizes the "extraordinary degree of institutional continuity" despite these periodic realignments, contending that the "basic two-party system has prevailed with only occasional brief interruptions for fifteen decades" (48). Sundquist's interpretive choice to emphasize continuity over breaks makes sense within the context of his project, which is to construct a theory of realignment that can be generalized across disparate historical periods.

106. Burnham, *Critical Elections and the Mainsprings of American Politics*, 10.

107. Key, *Politics, Parties, and Pressure Groups* (1958), 282.

108. Ibid., 282.

109. Ibid., 286; (1964), 259.

110. Ibid. (1958), 307; (1964), 279.

111. Key did not take third parties so seriously in the first editions of his textbook. Initially, he introduced them under a subheading, "Deviations: Third Parties," that subsumed them within a chapter on the "Nature and Function of Party." His disposition toward them is as evident from that subheading as from his dismissive opening claim: "The relative insignificance of minor parties in recent years makes it pointless to devote extended attention to their activities, yet these parties possess sufficient historical interest to merit brief notice." Ibid. (1947), 235–236. It is noteworthy that Key grew more convinced of the significance of third parties at a time when most of his colleagues moved in the opposite direction; likely, his views changed as he developed his critical elections theory.

112. Ibid. (1947), 243.

113. Ibid. (1952), 296.

114. Ibid., 299; (1964), 277.

115. Ibid.; (1964), 277.

116. Samuel J. Eldersveld, *Political Parties: A Behavioral Analysis* (Chicago: Rand McNally 1964), 14; cf. Sorauf, *Political Parties in the American System* (Boston: Little, Brown, 1964), 172.

117. Eldersveld, *Political Parties: A Behavioral Analysis*, 21.

118. Sorauf, *Party Politics in America*, 4th ed. (Glenview, Ill.: Scott, Foresman, 1980), 5.

119. Sheldon Wolin, "Foreword," Sorauf, *Political Parties in the American System*; ibid., viii.

120. Ibid., 172; emphasis added.

121. Ibid., 174–175.

122. Ibid., 172.

5. Oppositional Democracy and the Promise of Electoral Fusion

1. E. E. Schattschneider, *Party Government* (New York: Holt, Rinehart and Winston, 1967 [1942]), 15–16.

2. James S. Fishkin, *Democracy and Deliberation: New Directions for Democratic Reform* (New Haven: Yale UP), 1981.

3. Robert A. Dahl, *Democracy and Its Critics* (New Haven: Yale UP, 1989), 340.

4. Benjamin R. Barber, *Strong Democracy* (Berkeley: U of California P, 1984), chapter 10, especially 275–279.

5. Amitai Etzioni, "Minerva: An Electronic Town Hall," *Policy Sciences* 3 (1972): 457–474.

6. Schattschneider, *Party Government*, 3.

7. Hannah Arendt, *On Revolution*, rev. ed. (New York: Penguin, 1984), 271.

8. Benjamin Barber, "The Undemocratic Party System: Citizenship in an Elite/Mass Society," *Political Parties in the Eighties*, ed. Robert A. Goldwin (Washington, D.C.: American Enterprise Institute, 1980), 34.

9. Ibid., 188.

10. Walter Dean Burnham, *Critical Elections and the Mainsprings of American Politics* (New York: Norton, 1970), 133.

11. E. E. Schattschneider, *The Semisovereign People: A Realist's View of Democracy in America* (New York: Holt, Rinehart and Winston, 1975 [1960]), 126.

12. Schattschneider famously identified the "flaw in the pluralist heaven" as being "that the heavenly chorus sings with a strong upper-class accent." Ibid., 35.

13. Ibid., 69.

14. Ibid., 69.

15. Ibid., 108.

16. Ibid., 126.

17. Ibid., 70.

18. Ibid., 3.

19. Ibid., 3.

20. Ibid., 107.

21. Ibid., 102.

22. National Public Radio, "Talk of the Nation: Voter Turnout," featuring Ray Suarez, host, and Curtis Gans, guest, 14 April 1998.

23. Schattschneider, *The Semisovereign People,* 5.

24. Ibid., 5, 3.

25. Ibid., 3.

26. Ibid., 1–3; emphasis added.

27. Robert Dahl, *A Preface to Democratic Theory* (Chicago: U of Chicago P, 1956), 13.

28. Schattschneider, *The Semisovereign People,* 2. Today the notion that power both prohibits and produces is a commonplace. In its time, however, Schattschneider's "revolution" transformed the way that political scientists conceived of power. See Bachrach and Baratz, "The Two Faces of Power"; Lukes, *Power*; Digeser, "The Fourth Face of Power." Peter Mair has also argued that Schattschneider anticipated central debates in critical social theory, in particular, he credits him with advancing the "then more novel, and now more acceptable notion of the autonomy of the political." Peter Mair, "E. E. Schattschneider's *The Semisovereign People,*" *Political Studies* 45 (1997): 950. Mair is certainly correct to emphasize Schattschneider's corrective to reductionist views of power and conflict but it may be misleading to praise him for promoting the "*autonomy* of the political," because that phrase can play into a way of thinking about politics as spontaneous and unconstrained that is utterly at odds with Schattschneider's emphasis on the systematic biases of the conflict system. What makes Schattschneider interesting to me is that he checked the autonomy of politics against his own "realist" perspective on the politics of institutional frameworks.

29. Schattschneider, *The Semisovereign People,* 100.

30. Ibid., 4; emphasis added. Although these terms *scope* and *bias* bear the burden of Schattschneider's realist democratic theory, he never precisely spells them out. In fact, he defines bias in terms of scope, as the tendency of an organization toward either enlarging or narrowing the scope of conflict, and establishes the meaning of scope largely by example. It is synonymous with scale. Ibid., 12. How many people joined the fight? How much damage resulted? Scope is not a purely quantitative measure, however. It is also a matter of the principles that open the very definition of politics to political contestation. Schattschneider contends that "ideas concerning equality, consistency, equal protection of the laws, justice, liberty, freedom of movement, freedom of speech and association, and civil rights tend to socialize conflict[, or . . .] make conflict contagious; they invite outside intervention in conflict and form the basis of appeals to public authority for redress of private grievances." Ibid., 7. Whereas principles such as individualism and laissez-faire, coordination mechanisms such as the market, and such voluntarist forms of organizing as pressure groups tended to privatize conflict, Schattschneider contended that principles such as universal suffrage and equality, coordination by government regulation, and organizational forms such as the two-party system, unions, and social movements would enlarge its scope. Ibid., 7–12.

31. This is, of course, to put Schattschneider's concept to what *he* would have considered a perverse conclusion. He juxtaposed the party system (meaning the two-party system) against the pluralist system of interest group conflict, holding the former to open the scope of conflict and the latter to narrow it.

32. Thomas Byrne Edsall, "The Changing Shape of Power: A Realignment in Public Policy." *The Rise and Fall of the New Deal Order, 1930–1980*, ed. Steve Fraser and Gary Gerstle (Princeton: Princeton UP, 1989), 279.

33. Steven J. Rosenstone and John Mark Hansen, *Mobilization, Participation, and Democracy in America* (New York: Macmillan, 1993), 33.

34. Margaret Weir and Marshall Ganz, "Reconnecting People and Politics," *The New Majority: Toward a Popular Progressive Politics*, ed. Stanley B. Greenberg and Theda Skocpol (New Haven: Yale UP, 1997), 170.

35. John Harwood, "Apathetic Voters in Middle Lose Out," *St. Paul Pioneer Press*, 14 July 1998, http://www.pioneerpress.com.

36. Whereas citizens who live at or below the poverty level are less than half as likely to go to the polls as are voters in households with incomes of $50,000 or more, voting rates are highest among the college educated, whites, and the middle-aged.

37. It is not surprising that turnout disparities parallel disparities in mobilization. Whereas, like turnout, mobilization has declined generally, with only one-quarter of the population reporting contacts from parties and candidates, in 1992 citizens were almost twice as likely to receive a solicitation for support if they lived in households earning $50,000 or more than if they lived at or below the poverty level. Michael X. Delli Carpini and Scott Keeter, *What Americans Know About Politics and Why It Matters* (New Haven: Yale UP, 1996), 214. Similarly, parties and candidates focus their voter registration efforts on the populations that are most likely to *vote* rather than on those who are most likely to need to be registered.

38. Stephen Skowronek, *Building a New American State: the Expansion of National Administrative Capacities, 1877–1920* (Cambridge: Cambridge UP, 1982), 290.

39. Elizabeth Clemens, *The People's Lobby: Organizational Innovation and the Rise of Interest Group Politics in the United States, 1890–1925* (Chicago: U of Chicago P, 1997), 11.

40. Mark Kornbluh, *Why America Stopped Voting: The Decline of Participatory Democracy and the Emergence of Modern American Politics* (New York: NYU P, 2000), 160.

41. Benjamin Ginsberg, "Money and Power: The New Political Economy of American Elections," *The Political Economy*, ed. Thomas Ferguson and Joel Rogers (Armonk, N.Y.: Sharpe, 1984), 163–179.

42. Party reform began as a Democratic initiative in 1968 with the McGovern Commission and was revised several times over the next two decades. Campaign finance reform began in 1972 and 1974 with disclosure rules, limits on campaign contributions, and regulations of PACs.

43. Edsall, "The Changing Shape of Power," 277–278.

44. Burdett A. Loomis and Allan J. Cigler, "Introduction: The Changing Nature of Interest Group Politics," *Interest Group Politics*, 3d ed., ed. Allan J. Cigler and Burdett A. Loomis (Washington, D.C.: Congressional Quarterly, 1991).

45. M. Margaret Conway, "PAC's in the Political Process," *Interest Group Politics*, 202.

46. John Aldrich, *Why Parties? The Origin and Transformation of Political Parties in America* (Chicago: U of Chicago P, 1995), 168, 7.

47. Bob Herbert, "In America: The Donor Class," *New York Times*, 19 July 1998: WK15. At the same time, according to a 1998 study by the Joyce Foundation of Chicago, reported in the *New York Times*, individual donations come from an increasingly elite, unrepresentative sector of society. Ninety-five percent of those who contributed $200 or more to Congressional candidates in 1996 were white, 80 percent were men. Whereas most donors lived in households with annual incomes of $100,000 or higher, 20 percent claimed annual household incomes in excess of half a million dollars. However, soft money is *not* the principal source of campaign finance; on the contrary, as the costs of running for office skyrocket, political action committees account for an ever greater percentage of monies spent. For this reason, analysts who have argued that the 2001 campaign finance reform bill will destroy the party system are not far from wrong. The parties turned to soft money to combat PAC influence over candidates. By regulating so-called independent expenditures by the parties (i.e., soft money) without restricting independent expenditures by PACs, reform will only redirect the flow of money into elections; it will do little to curtail its influence.

48. Walter Dean Burnham, "The System of 1896: An Analysis," *The Evolution of American Electoral Systems*, ed. Paul Kleppner, Walter Dean Burnham, Ronald P. Formisano, Samuel P. Hays, Richard Jensen, and William G. Shade (Westport, Conn.: Greenwood, 1981), 168.

49. Skowronek, *Building a New American State*, 165.

50. Ibid., 18; emphasis added.

51. Jürgen Habermas, *Toward a Rational Society*, chapter 5; James A. Morone, *The Democratic Wish* (New York: Basic, 1990). Habermas argued that the Weberian model compromised the balance it meant to strike between politics and administration by the very distinction it drew between them and by the accompanying separation of fact and value. This epistemological divide proved to privilege techniques of rational administration, such as demography, epidemiology, actuarial analysis, and even survey research, so that these quantitative methods turned out to be not a tool of administration but, rather, a practice that came to "rationalize *choice as such*" by discrediting any reasoning that did not proceed "by means of calculated strategies and automatic decision procedures." Ibid., 63–64; emphasis added. By consigning politics, together with "values" to the domain of irrationality, this conception of rationalization identified "the rational" with a narrowly instrumental calculus. This definition persists today, underwriting the investiture of political authority in technocrats—single-issue specialists who are neither intellectually equipped nor temperamentally inclined to mobilize a broad public in support of a policy initiative—and discrediting public opinion as a source of political value. See Hugh Heclo, "Issue Networks and the Executive Establishment," *The New American Political System*, ed. Anthony King (Washington: American Enterprise Institute, 1978), 87–124.

52. Frank Goodnow, *Politics and Administration: a Study in Government* (New York: Russell and Russell, 1967), 251.

53. Jürgen Habermas, *Toward a Rational Society: Student Protest, Science, and Politics*, trans. Jeremy J. Shapiro (Boston: Beacon, 1970), 63; emphasis added.

54. James A. Morone, *The Democratic Wish* (New York: Basic, 1990), 11, 7.

55. James A. Morone, "The Health Care Bureaucracy: Small Changes, Big Consequences," *Journal of Health Politics, Policy, and Law* 18.3 (1993): 731, 737.

56. Skowronek, *Building a New American State*, 165.

57. Hannah Arendt, *The Human Condition* (Chicago: U of Chicago P, 1958); Jürgen Habermas, *The Structural Transformation of the Public Sphere*, trans. T. Burger and F. Lawrence (Cambridge: MIT P, 1989 [1962]).

58. Nancy Fraser emphasizes debate oriented toward issues; Seyla Benhabib emphasizes debate oriented toward norms and procedures of adjudication. See Nancy Fraser, "Rethinking the Public Sphere: A Contribution to the Critique of Actually Existing Democracy," 109–142, and Seyla Benhabib, "Models of Public Space: Hannah Arendt, the Liberal Tradition, and Jürgen Habermas," 73–98, both in *Habermas and the Public Sphere*, ed. Craig Calhoun (Cambridge: MIT P, 1992).

59. Arendt, *The Human Condition* 244.

60. Ibid., 50.

61. Ibid., *The Human Condition* 201.

62. Jeffrey Isaac, *Democracy in Dark Times* (Ithaca: Cornell UP, 1998), chapter 5.

63. George Yudice, "For a Practical Aesthetics," *The Phantom Public Sphere*, ed. Bruce Robbins (Minneapolis: U of Minnesota P, 1993).

64. For example, Tipper Gore's infamous crusade against sexually explicit rock lyrics *did* strike a chord but with conflicting publics: she pitted those who were incensed by what they saw as obscenity against those who were incensed by what they regarded as censorship.

65. Jürgen Habermas, *Between Facts and Norms: Contributions to a Discourse Theory of Law and Democracy*, trans. William Rehg (Cambridge: MIT Press, 1998), 327, 371.

66. Ibid., 368.

67. Ibid., 381.

68. Isaac, *Democracy in Dark Times*, 121.

69. For two different vantage points on this dynamic, see Nancy Fraser's "Struggle Over Needs: Outline of a Socialist-Feminist Critical Theory of Late Capitalist Political Culture," *Unruly Practices: Power, Discourse, and Gender in Contemporary Social Theory* (Minneapolis: U of Minnesota P, 1989), 161–187; and Wendy Brown's "Wounded Attachments," *States of Injury: Power and Freedom in Late Modernity* (Princeton: Princeton UP, 1995), 52–76. Fraser offers an account of the domestic violence movement that details how municipal funding for battered women's shelters transformed the shelters from sites of feminist consciousness-raising and activism to sites for individualized therapy. Brown charts how identity-based claims upon the liberal pluralist state found a politics of supplication rather than empowerment. Note that I do not dispute the validity or value of either account; rather, I suggest

that the two-party system in its present incarnation has helped to produce the dynamic they describe.

70. Isaac, *Democracy in Dark Times*, 121–122; emphasis added.

71. Schattschneider, *The Semisovereign People*, 71; emphasis in original removed.

72. Habermas, *Between Facts and Norms*, 330.

73. Ian Shapiro, *Democracy's Place* (Ithaca: Cornell UP, 1996), 126. Shapiro contends that empirical theorists preoccupy themselves with self-government as a formal impossibility, by virtue of voting cycles (which invalidate the Rousseauean ideal of a general will). By contrast, it is for normative theorists a public imperative to be realized by innovative participatory and/or deliberative design. See chapter 2.

74. Ibid., 126.

75. Ibid., 260.

76. Ibid., 238.

77. Ibid., 182. He does acknowledge that they are limited where representation is concerned.

78. William E. Connolly, *The Ethos of Pluralization* (Minneapolis: U of Minnesota P, 1995), 100.

79. Burnham, *Critical Elections and the Mainsprings of American Politics*, 30.

80. It has been argued, for example, that Ross Perot's 1992 totals had exactly this effect. Perot did not "spoil" the election for Bush (as many feared he would); he did render Clinton vulnerable, however, and softened him up for the Gingrich revolution in 1994.

81. James Madison, *Federalist* no. 10, *The Origins of the American Constitution*, ed. Michael Kammen (New York: Penguin, 1986), 149.

82. Anthony Downs, *An Economic Theory of Democracy* (New York: Harper and Row, 1957), 140.

83. Ibid., 140, 93.

84. Ibid., 95.

85. Ibid., 257.

86. Iris Marion Young, "Polity and Group Difference: A Critique of the Ideal of Universal Citizenship," *Ethics* 99 (Jan 1989): 257.

87. I should note here a subtle but significant difference between my argument about the "tyranny" of the two-party system, the Progressive-era perspective on two-partyism, and Burnham's position. Whereas the Progressives (and I) contend that two-party competition *itself* tends toward inertia, Schattschneider, Key, and Burnham were concerned about *one-party* rule, which they regarded as a pathology of the two-party system for which healthy two-party competition was a corrective. These theorists took the measure of two-party contests during a time when American party scholars were alternately haunted by the specter of fascism in the multiparty regimes of Europe, encouraged by the New Deal coalition, and appalled at the one-party rule of the Dixiecrats in the Jim Crow South. Because they viewed the South as an *anomaly* within the two-party system, they could take these phenomena to confirm that so long as there was healthy competition between the dominant parties the United States need not risk a proportional voting system to

ensure minority representation. Piven and Cloward pose a counterargument, based on a contrary reading of Jim Crow as "the model for a new kind of polity that left formal voting rights intact but stripped poorer and less-educated people of the ability to exercise those rights." Frances Fox Piven and Richard A. Cloward, *Why Americans Don't Vote* (New York: Pantheon, 1988), 78. In other words, Piven and Cloward read the South not as an anomaly of the twentieth-century electoral system but as exemplary of the ways that voter registration, ballot, and civil service reform did insidious damage to electoral democracy.

88. Burnham, *Critical Elections and the Mainsprings of American Politics*, 27. Burnham worked within a framework defined by V. O. Key's pathbreaking essay "A Theory of Critical Elections," *Journal of Politics* 17 (1955): 3–18.

Conclusion: Against the Tyranny of the Two-Party System

1. Theodore J. Lowi, "The Party Crasher," *New York Times Magazine*, 23 August 1992: 28.

2. Although there is a "None of these candidates" ballot option for all statewide offices in Nevada, it is not, strictly speaking, a protest vote that counts. As the "None of these candidates" vote is not binding, it neither figures into the calculation of total votes cast nor affects calculations of the candidates' share of the electorate. Because voters who choose this option are prohibited from voting in addition for a candidate, they have effectively thrown their vote away by casting a ballot that has no impact on the outcome of the election. Nevada "None of the Above" Statute, Nevada Revised Statutes, Title 24. Elections. Chapter 293.269. In contrast, in Israel white ballots are tallied and included in the final vote count; consequently, they are more than a symbolic protest. By raising the total votes cast, they effectively make it more difficult for any candidate to win office by raising the number of votes it takes to make the threshold for a seat in parliament. In short, the "white" ballot expresses organized opposition in a way that cannot be discounted as apathy, or construed as consent.

3. It is difficult to say whether either of these candidacies "spoiled" the election, however. Public perception to the contrary, Ralph Nader did not cost Vice President Gore the White House. A state-by-state analysis of close votes revealed only two states, Florida and New Hampshire, where Nader votes cost Gore the victory, denying him twenty electoral college votes. On the other side, however, the Buchanan vote took four close states (Iowa, New Mexico, Oregon, Wisconsin) from Bush. These states, which combine for an electoral college total of thirty votes, would have given Bush the White House *without* either Florida or New Hampshire. Thus, Buchanan, who received less than 450,000 popular votes, may have effected the outcome of the election more severely than Ralph Nader did, with 2.8 million popular votes. See David Leonhardt, "The Election: Was Buchanan the Real Nader?" *New York Times*, 10 December 2000, "Week in Review," www.newyorktimes.com.

4. Douglas J. Amy, *Real Choices/New Voices* (New York: Columbia UP, 1993), 9.

5. Ibid., 33.

6. E. E. Schattschneider, *Party Government* (New York: Holt, Rinehart and Winston, 1967 [1942]), 84.

7. Amy, *Real Choices/New Voices*, 38.

8. Edward Sait, *American Parties and Elections* (New York: Century, 1927), 157–158.

9. Ibid., 158.

10. Daniel A. Smith reports that "in 1996 alone, voters in twenty-two states were asked to decide a total of ninety statewide initiatives, the most ballot questions proposed nationally by citizens in over eighty years." Daniel A. Smith. *Tax Crusaders and the Politics of Direct Democracy* (New York: Routledge, 1998), 158.

11. Ibid., 159.

12. Ibid., 167.

13. Smith calls this "*faux* populism," because it is interest-group politics in the guise of direct democracy that substitutes money, technology, and "a populist-sounding message . . . [for] the political mobilization of 'the people,' " 48.

14. E. E. Schattschneider, *The Semisovereign People: A Realist's View of Democracy in America* (New York: Holt, Rinehart and Winston, 1975 [1960]), 100.

15. Lani Guinier, *The Tyranny of the Majority: Fundamental Fairness in Representative Democracy* (New York: Free, 1994), 122.

16. Ibid., 140.

17. Ibid.

18. Susan Bickford, "Reconfiguring Pluralism: Identity and Institutions in the Inegalitarian Polity," *American Journal of Political Science* 43 (January 1999): 102; emphasis added.

19. In 1996 more than 60 percent of United States House races were landslides. In 1998 four in ten state legislative candidates ran unopposed, which means that in these years there was little or nothing at all "to do" with the vote. Center for Voting and Democracy, "Electing the People's House: 1998," Washington, D.C., www.fairvote.org.

20. Guinier herself acknowledges this when she remarks that for cumulative voting to produce genuine interest representation it must be paired with such "organizational alternatives" to the existing media-intensive, candidate-centered electoral apparatus as community groups, churches, and "minority political parties." *The Tyranny of the Majority*, 255.

21. Amy, *Real Choices/New Voices*, 186.

22. Schattschneider, *The Semisovereign People*, 69.

23. Alexander Bickel, *Reform and Continuity: The Electoral College, the Convention, and the Party System* (New York: Harper and Row, 1971), 80, as cited in *Timmons v. TCNP*, Stevens dissenting, 612 n10.

24. Steven J. Rosenstone, Roy L. Behr, and Edward H. Lazarus argue that Perot prevailed because he had the financial resources to "break through many of the constraints that had impeded independent challengers before him. The $73 million that Perot pumped into his first crusade, his extensive and relatively positive media

coverage, and his participation in the presidential debates all boosted his vote total way beyond what it would have been had Perot been just an ordinary third party challenger." Steven J. Rosenstone, Roy L. Behr, and Edward H. Lazarus, *Third Parties in America*, 2d ed. (Princeton: Princeton UP, 1996), x.

25. J. David Gillespie made this point on National Public Radio's *Morning Edition* immediately prior to the election, characterizing this position as the "militant center," 23 October 2000.

26. Bickel, *Reform and Continuity*, 80, as cited in *Timmons v. TCNP*, Stevens dissenting, 612 n10.

27. Other strategies that would work as well or better include the alternative vote, also called instant run-off vote (IRV), which third-party advocates in some states have promoted in the wake of the 2000 election. Like fusion, IRV does not require a wholesale change to proportional victories by using the instant run-off to redistribute votes from last-place candidates to the top finishers until a majority result is achieved. In an IRV system, voters rank their choices. If there is no majority winner on the first count, the votes are automatically redistributed from the lowest vote-getter (thereby activating the second-choice—i.e., the "alternative" votes—of those who had ranked that candidate first). In the 2000 presidential election a Green Party voter who designated Ralph Nader first and Al Gore second would have had nothing to regret because *both* votes would have counted. Like fusion, the run-off offsets the greatest disincentive to casting a third-party vote: there is no risk of spoiling or sending a candidate into office whom a majority of the electorate may have opposed. Also like fusion, third parties can use the run-off as leverage over the established parties by pledging to deliver their alternative votes in return for concessions on policy and appointments. The instant run-off vote may even be superior to fusion in that it does not force third parties to run establishment party candidates on their ballot lines (as fusion does) but preserves the option of an independent candidacy and, with it, the possibility for an uncompromising vote on the first round.

28. Peter H. Argersinger, " 'A Place on the Ballot': Fusion Politics and Antifusion Laws." *American Historical Review* 85 (1980): 304, citing *Kalamazoo Weekly Telegraph*, 20 March 1895; emphasis added.

Works Cited

Aldrich, John. *Why Parties? The Origin and Transformation of Political Parties in America.* Chicago: U of Chicago P, 1995.

Amy, Douglas J. *Real Choices/New Voices.* New York: Columbia UP, 1993.

Arendt, Hannah. *Between Past and Future.* New York: Penguin, 1954.

—— *The Human Condition.* Chicago: U of Chicago P, 1958.

—— *On Revolution.* Rev. ed. New York: Penguin, 1984.

Argersinger, Peter H. *The Limits of Agrarian Radicalism: Western Populism and American Politics.* Lawrence: UP of Kansas, 1995.

—— "'A Place on the Ballot': Fusion Politics and Antifusion Laws." *American Historical Review* 85 (1980): 287–306.

—— "The Value of the Vote: Political Representation in the Gilded Age." *Journal of American History* 76 (June 1989): 59–90.

Ashby, Le Roy. *William Jennings Bryan: Champion of Democracy.* Boston: Twayne, 1987.

Bachrach, Peter and Morton S. Baratz. "The Two Faces of Power." *American Political Science Review* 56 (1962): 947–952.

Baker, Paula. "The Domestication of Politics: Women and American Political Society, 1780–1920." *American Historical Review* 89 (1984): 620–647.

Ball, Terence. *Transforming Political Discourse: Political Theory and Critical Conceptual History.* New York: Blackwell, 1988.

Barber, Benjamin R. *Strong Democracy.* Berkeley: U of California P, 1984.

—— "The Undemocratic Party System: Citizenship in an Elite/Mass Society." *Political Parties in the Eighties.* Ed. Robert A. Goldwin. Washington, D.C.: American Enterprise Institute, 1980. 34–49.

Beck, Paul Allen. "The Electoral Cycle and Patterns of American Politics." *British Journal of Political Science* 9 (1979): 129–156.

Belluck, Pam. "A 'Bad Boy' Wrestler's Unscripted Upset." *New York Times,* 5 November 1998: B10.

Benhabib, Seyla. "Models of Public Space: Hannah Arendt, the Liberal Tradition, and Jürgen Habermas." *Habermas and the Public Sphere.* Ed. Craig Calhoun. Cambridge: MIT P, 1992. 73–98.

Bentley, Arthur. *The Process of Government.* Evanston, Ill.: Principia Press of Illinois, 1949 [1908].

Bibby, John F., Cornelius P. Cotter, James L. Gibson, and Robert J. Huckshorn. "Parties in State Politics." *Politics in the American States.* 4th ed. Ed. Virginia Gray, Herbert Jacob, and Kenneth Vines. Boston: Little, Brown, 1983. 85–112.

Bickford, Susan. “Reconfiguring Pluralism: Identity and Institutions in the Inegalitarian Polity.” *American Journal of Political Science* 43 (January 1999): 86–108.

Binkley, Wilfred E. *American Political Parties: Their Natural History.* New York: Knopf, 1943.

Bohman, James. *Public Deliberation.* Cambridge: MIT P, 1996.

Brown, Wendy. *States of Injury: Power and Freedom in Late Modernity.* Princeton: Princeton UP, 1995.

Bryce, James. *The American Commonwealth.* 1891. Rev. and abridged ed. Philadelphia: John D. Morris, 1906.

—— *The American Commonwealth.* 1891. Vol. 2. Rev. ed. New York: Macmillan, 1941.

Burnham, Walter Dean. “The Changing Shape of the American Voting Universe.” *American Political Science Review* 59 (1965): 7–28.

—— *Critical Elections and the Mainsprings of American Politics.* New York: Norton, 1970.

—— “The System of 1896: An Analysis.” *The Evolution of American Electoral Systems.* Ed. Paul Kleppner, Walter Dean Burnham, Ronald P. Formisano, Samuel P. Hays, Richard Jensen, and William G. Shade. Westport, Conn.: Greenwood, 1981. 147–202.

—— “Theory and Voting Research: Some Reflections on Converse’s ‘Change in the American Electorate.’ ” *American Political Science Review* 68 (1974): 1002–1023.

Burns, James MacGregor and J. W. Peltason. *Government by the People.* Englewood Cliffs, N.J.: Prentice-Hall, 1952.

Burns, James MacGregor, J. W. Peltason, and Thomas E. Cronin. *Government by the People.* 17th ed. Englewood Cliffs, N.J.: Prentice-Hall, 1998.

Butler, Judith. *Bodies That Matter.* New York: Routledge, 1993.

Center for Voting and Democracy. “Electing the People’s House: 1998.” Washington, D.C. http://www.fairvote.org

Chambers, William Nisbet. “Party Development and the American Mainstream.” *The American Party Systems: Stages of Political Development.* Ed. William Nisbet Chambers and Walter Dean Burnham. New York: Oxford U P, 1975.

—— *Political Parties in a New Nation: The American Experience, 1776–1809.* New York: Oxford UP, 1963.

Clemens, Elizabeth. *The People’s Lobby: Organizational Innovation and the Rise of Interest Group Politics in the United States, 1890–1925.* Chicago: U of Chicago P, 1997.

Committee on Political Parties, American Political Science Association. *Toward a More Responsible Two-Party System.* New York: Rinehart, 1950.

Connolly, William E. *The Ethos of Pluralization.* Minneapolis: U of Minnesota P, 1995.

—— *The Terms of Political Discourse.* 2d ed. Princeton: Princeton UP, 1983.

Conway, M. Margaret. “PAC’s in the Political Process.” *Interest Group Politics.* 3d ed. Ed. Allan J. Cigler and Burdett A. Loomis. Washington, D.C.: Congressional Quarterly, 1991.

Croly, Herbert. *Progressive Democracy.* New York: Macmillan, 1914.

—— *The Promise of American Life*. New York: MacMillan, 1965 [1909].
Cyert, Richard M. and James G. March. "A Behavioral Theory of Organizational Objectives." *Modern Organization Theory*. Ed. Mason Haire. New York: Wiley, 1959. 76–89.
Dahl, Robert A. "The Behavioral Approach in Political Science: Epitaph for a Monument to a Successful Protest." *Discipline and History: Political Science in the United States*. Ed. James Farr and Raymond Seidelman. Ann Arbor: U of Michigan P, 1993 [1961]. 249–265.
—— *Democracy and Its Critics*. New Haven: Yale UP, 1989.
—— *Pluralist Democracy in the United States*. Chicago: Rand, McNally, 1967.
—— *A Preface to Democratic Theory*. Chicago: U of Chicago P, 1956.
Delli Carpini, Michael X. and Scott Keeter. *What Americans Know About Politics and Why It Matters*. New Haven: Yale UP, 1996.
Digeser, Peter. "The Fourth Face of Power." *Journal of Politics* 54 (November 1992): 977–1007.
Dolan, Frederick M. *Allegories of America: Narratives, Metaphysics, Politics*. New York: Cornell UP, 1994.
Dornfeld, Steven. "Jesse's Election Not a Victory for Reform, But a Triumph for Trivialization of Politics." *St. Paul Pioneer Press* 9 November 1998: 10A.
Downs, Anthony. *An Economic Theory of Democracy*. New York: Harper and Row, 1957.
Durden, Robert F. *The Climax of Populism: The Election of 1896*. Lexington: U of Kentucky P, 1965.
Duverger, Maurice. *Political Parties: Their Origins and Activity in the Modern State*. London: Methuen, 1954.
Easton, David. "Political Science in the United States: Past and Present." *Discipline and History: Political Science in the United States*. Ed. James Farr and Raymond Seidelman. Ann Arbor: U of Michigan P, 1993 [1984]. 291–309.
—— *The Political System: An Inquiry Into the State of Political Science*. New York: Knopf, 1953.
Edsall, Thomas Byrne. "The Changing Shape of Power: A Realignment in Public Policy." *The Rise and Fall of the New Deal Order, 1930–1980*. Ed. Steve Fraser and Gary Gerstle. Princeton: Princeton UP, 1989.
Edwards, George C., II, Martin P. Wattenberg, and Robert L. Lineberry. *Government in America*. 8th ed. New York: Longman, 1998.
Eldersveld, Samuel J. *Political Parties: A Behavioral Analysis*. Chicago: Rand McNally, 1964.
Eley, Geoff. "Nations, Publics, and Political Cultures: Placing Habermas in the Nineteenth Century." *Habermas and the Public Sphere*. Ed. Craig Calhoun. Cambridge: MIT P, 1992. 289–339.
Epstein, Leon D. *Political Parties in the American Mold*. Madison: U of Wisconsin P, 1986.
—— *Political Parties in Western Democracies*. New York: Praeger, 1967.
Etzioni, Amitai. "Minerva: An Electronic Town Hall." *Policy Sciences* 3 (1972): 457–474.

Farr, James. "From Modern Republic to Administrative State: American Political Science in the Nineteenth Century." *Regime and Discipline: Democracy and the Development of Political Science.* Ed David Easton, John G. Gunnell, and Michael Stein. Ann Arbor: U of Michigan P, 1995. 131–167.

Farr, James and Raymond Seidelman. *Discipline and History: Political Science in the United States.* Ann Arbor: U of Michigan P, 1993.

Ferguson, James. *The Anti-Politics Machine: "Development," Depoliticization, and Bureaucratic Power in Lesotho.* Minneapolis: U of Minnesota P, 1996.

Fisher, Marc. "Minnesota's Surprise: 'Governor Body.' " *Washington Post,* 4 November 1998: A1.

Fishkin, James S. *Democracy and Deliberation: New Directions for Democratic Reform.* New Haven: Yale UP, 1981.

Ford, Henry Jones. *The Rise and Growth of American Politics.* New York: Macmillan, 1898.

Formisano, Ronald P. "Deferential-Participant Politics: The Early Republic's Political Culture, 1789–1840." *American Political Science Review* 68 (1974): 473–487.

Foucault, Michel. *Discipline and Punish: The Birth of the Prison.* Trans. Alan Sheridan. New York: Vintage, 1979.

—— "The Order of Discourse." *Untying the Text.* Ed. Robert Young. Boston: Routledge and Kegan Paul, 1981. 48–78.

Fraser, Nancy. "Rethinking the Public Sphere: A Contribution to the Critique of Actually Existing Democracy." *Habermas and the Public Sphere.* Ed. Craig Calhoun Cambridge: MIT P, 1992. 109–142.

—— *Unruly Practices: Power, Discourse, and Gender in Contemporary Social Theory.* Minneapolis: U of Minnesota P, 1989.

"Fusion Candidacies, Disaggregation, and Freedom of Association." *Harvard Law Review* 109.6 (1996): 1,302–1,337.

Gillespie, J. David. *Politics at the Periphery: Third Parties in Two-Party America.* Columbia: U of South Carolina P, 1993.

Ginsberg, Benjamin. "Money and Power: The New Political Economy of American Elections." *The Political Economy.* Ed. Thomas Ferguson and Joel Rogers. Armonk, N.Y.: Sharpe, 1984. 163–179.

Goodnow, Frank. *Politics and Administration: A Study in Government.* New York: Russell and Russell, 1967.

Goodwyn, Lawrence. *The Populist Moment: A Short History of the Agrarian Revolt in America.* New York: Oxford UP, 1978.

Grimes, William. "After You. No, After You. Ouch!" *New York Times,* 29 November 1998: WK2.

Guinier, Lani. *The Tyranny of the Majority: Fundamental Fairness in Representative Democracy.* New York: Free, 1994.

Habermas, Jürgen. *Between Facts and Norms: Contributions to a Discourse Theory of Law and Democracy.* Trans. William Rehg. Cambridge: MIT Press, 1998.

—— *Legitimation Crisis.* Trans. Thomas McCarthy. Boston: Beacon, 1975.

—— *The Structural Transformation of the Public Sphere.* Trans. T. Burger and F. Lawrence. 1962. Cambridge: MIT P, 1989.

—— *Toward a Rational Society: Student Protest, Science, and Politics.* Trans. Jeremy J. Shapiro. Boston: Beacon, 1970.
Halperin, David. *Saint Foucault.* New York: Oxford UP, 1995.
Hanson, Russell L. *The Democratic Imagination in America: Conversations with Our Past.* Princeton: Princeton UP, 1985.
Harwood, John. "Apathetic Voters in Middle Lose Out." *St. Paul Pioneer Press,* 14 July 1998: 1A+. http://www.pioneerpress.com
Haynes, Frederick E. *Social Politics in the United States.* 2d ed. 1924. New York: AMS, 1970.
Heclo, Hugh. "Issue Networks and the Executive Establishment." *The New American Political System.* Ed. Anthony King. Washington: American Enterprise Institute, 1978. 87–124.
Herbert, Bob. "In America: The Donor Class." *New York Times,* 19 July 1998: WK15.
Herring, E. Pendleton. *The Politics of Democracy: American Parties in Action.* 1940. New York: Norton, 1965.
Hicks, John D. "The Third Party Tradition in American Politics." *Mississippi Valley Historical Review* 20.1 (June 1933): 3–28.
Hofstadter, Richard. *The Age of Reform.* New York: Knopf, 1955.
—— *The Idea of a Party System.* Berkeley: U of California P, 1969.
Hallonquist, Sarah. "Exit Polling Indicates That Many People Would Not Have Bothered If Ventura Had Not Been Among Their Choices for Governor." *Star Tribune,* 5 November 1998: A24.
Ionescu, Ghita and Ernest Gellner. *Populism: Its Meanings and National Characteristics.* London: Weidenfeld and Nicolson, 1969.
Isaac, Jeffrey. *Democracy in Dark Times.* Ithaca: Cornell UP, 1998.
Jensen, Richard. *The Winning of the Midwest: Social and Political Conflict, 1888–1896.* Chicago: U of Chicago P, 1971.
Jillson, Calvin. "Patterns and Periodicity in American National Politics." *The Dynamics of American Politics.* Ed. Lawrence C. Dodd and Calvin Jillson. Boulder: Westview, 1994.
Key, V. O., Jr. *Politics, Parties, and Pressure Groups.* New York: Crowell, 1947.
—— *Politics, Parties, and Pressure Groups.* Rev. ed. New York: Crowell, 1952.
—— *Politics, Parties, and Pressure Groups.* Rev. ed. New York: Crowell, 1958.
—— *Politics, Parties, and Pressure Groups.* Rev. ed. New York: Crowell, 1964.
—— "A Theory of Critical Elections." *Journal of Politics* 17 (1955): 3–18.
Keyssar, Alex. "Reform and an Evolving Electorate." *New York Times,* 5 August 2001: WK13.
King, Anthony. "Political Parties in Western Democracies." *Polity* 2.12 (Winter 1969): 111–141.
Kirkpatrick, Evron M. " 'Toward a More Responsible Two-Party System': Political Science, Policy Science, or Pseudo-Science?" *American Political Science Review* 65 (1971): 965–990.
Kirschner, William R. "Fusion and the Associational Rights of Minor Political Parties." *Columbia Law Review* 95.5 (1995): 683–723.

Kleppner, Paul. *The Third Electoral System, 1853–1892*. Chapel Hill: U of North Carolina P, 1979.

Kornbluh, Mark. *Why America Stopped Voting: The Decline of Participatory Democracy and the Emergence of Modern American Politics*. New York: New York UP, 2000.

Kuhn, Thomas. *The Structure of Scientific Revolutions*. 3d ed. Chicago: U of Chicago P, 1996 [1962].

Leonhardt, David. "The Election: Was Buchanan the Real Nader?" *New York Times*, 10 December 2000: WK.

Loomis, Burdett A. and Allan J. Cigler. "Introduction: The Changing Nature of Interest Group Politics." *Interest Group Politics*. 3d ed. Ed. Allan J. Cigler and Burdett A. Loomis. Washington, D.C.: Congressional Quarterly, 1991. 1–30.

Lowi, Theodore J. "Party, Policy, and Constitution in America." *The American Party Systems: Stages of Political Development*. Ed. William Nisbet Chambers and Walter Dean Burnham. New York: Oxford U P, 1975.

—— "The Party Crasher." *New York Times Magazine*, 23 August 1992: 28+.

Lowi, Theodore J. and Benjamin Ginsberg. *American Government: Freedom and Power*. 5th ed. New York: Norton, 1998.

Lukes, Steven. *Power: A Radical View*. London: Macmillan, 1974.

McCormick, Richard P. *The Second American Party System: Party Formation in the Jacksonian Era*. Chapel Hill: U of North Carolina P, 1966.

MacIver, R. M. *The Web of Government*. New York: Macmillan, 1947.

Madison, James. *Federalist* no. 10. *The Origins of the American Constitution*. Ed. Michael Kammen. New York: Penguin, 1986.

Mair, Peter. "E. E. Schattschneider's *The Semisovereign People*." *Political Studies* 45 (1997): 947–954.

Mayhew, David. *Placing Parties in American Politics*. Princeton: Princeton UP, 1986.

Mazmanian, Daniel A. *Third Parties in Presidential Elections*. Washington, D.C.: Brookings Institution, 1974.

Merriam, Charles E. *The American Party System: An Introduction to the Study of Political Parties in the United States*. New York: Macmillan, 1922.

Merriam, Charles E. and Harold F. Gosnell. *The American Party System: An Introduction to the Study of Political Parties in the United States*. 3d ed. New York: Macmillan, 1940.

Morone, James A. *The Democratic Wish*. New York: Basic, 1990.

—— "The Health Care Bureaucracy: Small Changes, Big Consequences." *Journal of Health Politics, Policy, and Law* 18.3 (1993): 723–739.

Mowitt, John. *Text: The Genealogy of an Antidisciplinary Object*. Durham: Duke UP, 1992.

"Nader's Misguided Crusade." Editorial. *New York Times*, 30 June 2000: A24.

National Public Radio. "Talk of the Nation: Voter Turnout." Featuring Ray Suarez, host, and Curtis Gans, guest, 14 April 1998.

Ostrogorski, Moisei. *Democracy and the Organization of Political Parties*. New York: Macmillan, 1902.

"Our Perspective: The Ventura Vote." Editorial. *Minneapolis Star Tribune*, 8 November 1998: A26.

"A Party for Hire." Editorial. *New York Times*, 24 February 1997: A14.

Patterson, Thomas E. *The American Democracy*. Boston: McGraw-Hill, 1999.

Perlez, Jane. "Poland Achieves Politics As Usual." *New York Times*, 28 September 1997: WK6.

Pitchell, Robert J. "The Electoral System and Voting Behavior: The Case of California's Cross-Filing." *Western Political Quarterly* 12 (1959): 484.

Piven, Frances Fox, and Richard A. Cloward. *Why Americans Don't Vote*. New York: Pantheon, 1988.

Pomper, Gerald M. "Concepts of Political Parties." *Journal of Theoretical Politics* 4.2 (1992): 143–159.

—— *Elections in America*. New York: Dodd, Mead, 1968.

—— "Toward a More Responsible Two-Party System? What, Again?" *Journal of Politics* 33 (1971): 916–940.

Rae, Douglas W. *The Political Consequences of Electoral Laws*. Rev. ed. New Haven: Yale UP, 1971.

Ranney, Austin and Wilmoore Kendall. *Democracy and the American Party System*. New York: Harcourt Brace, 1956.

Ricci, David M. "Democracy Attenuated: Schumpeter, the Process Theory, and American Democratic Thought." *Journal of Politics* 32 (1970): 239–267.

—— *The Tragedy of Political Science: Politics, Scholarship, and Democracy*. New Haven: Yale UP, 1984.

Riker, William H. "The Two-Party System and Duverger's Law: An Essay on the History of Political Science." *American Political Science Review* 76 (1982): 753–766.

Roediger, David. *The Wages of Whiteness: Race and the Making of the American Working Class*. London: Verso, 1991.

Rose, Jacqueline. *Sexuality in the Field of Vision*. London: Verso, 1986.

Rosenstone, Steven J. and John Mark Hansen. *Mobilization, Participation, and Democracy in America*. New York: Macmillan, 1993.

Rosenstone, Steven J., Roy L. Behr, and Edward H. Lazarus. *Third Parties in America*. 2d ed. Princeton: Princeton UP, 1996.

Ross, Dorothy. *The Origins of American Social Science*. Cambridge: Cambridge UP, 1991.

Rusk, Jerrold G. "Comment: The American Electoral Universe: Speculation and Evidence." *American Political Science Review* 68 (1974): 1028–1049.

Sahlins, Marshall. "The Return of the Event, Again; with Reflections on the Beginnings of the Great Fijian War of 1843 to 1855 Between the Kingdoms of Bau and Rewa." *Clio in Oceania: Toward a Historical Anthropology*. Ed. Aletta Biersach. Washington, D.C.: Smithsonian Institution Press, 1991. 37–99.

Sait, Edward. *American Parties and Elections*. New York: Century, 1927.

Sartori, Giovanni. *Parties and Party Systems: A Framework for Analysis*. Vol. 1. Cambridge: Cambridge UP, 1976.

Scarrow, Howard A. "Duverger's Law, Fusion and the Decline of American 'Third' Parties." *Western Political Quarterly* 39.4 (1986): 634–647.

Schattschneider, E. E. *Party Government.* 1942. New York: Holt, Rinehart and Winston, 1967.
—— *The Semisovereign People: A Realist's View of Democracy in America.* 1960. New York: Holt, Rinehart and Winston, 1975.
Schumpeter, Joseph. *Capitalism, Socialism, and Democracy.* New York: Harper and Brothers, 1942.
Sedgwick, Eve Kosofsky. *Between Men: English Literature and Male Homosocial Desire.* New York: Columbia UP, 1985.
—— *Epistemology of the Closet.* Berkeley: U of California P, 1990.
Seidelman, Raymond. "Political Scientists, Disenchanted Realists, and Disappearing Democrats." *Discipline and History: Political Science in the United States.* Ed. James Farr and Raymond Seidelman. Ann Arbor: U of Michigan P, 1993. 311–325.
Sewell, William H. "Three Temporalities: Toward an Eventful Sociology." *The Historic Turn in the Human Sciences.* Ed. Terrence J. McDonald. Ann Arbor: U of Michigan P, 1996. 245–280.
"Shake It Up." Commentary. *Wall Street Journal,* 20 April 1999: A22.
Shklar, Judith N. *American Citizenship: The Quest for Inclusion.* Cambridge: Harvard UP, 1991.
Shapiro, Ian. *Democracy's Place.* Ithaca: Cornell UP, 1996.
Skowronek, Stephen. *Building a New American State: The Expansion of National Administrative Capacities, 1877–1920.* Cambridge: Cambridge UP, 1982.
Smith, Daniel A. *Tax Crusaders and the Politics of Direct Democracy.* New York: Routledge, 1998.
Sorauf, Frank J. *Party Politics in America.* 4th ed. Glenview, Ill.: Scott, Foresman, 1980.
—— *Party Politics in America.* 5th ed. Glenview, Ill.: Scott, Foresman, 1984.
—— *Party Politics in America.* Boston: Little, Brown, 1968
—— *Political Parties in the American System.* Boston: Little, Brown, 1964.
Sorauf, Frank J. and Paul Allen Beck. *Party Politics in America.* 6th ed. Glenview, Ill.: Scott, Foresman, 1988.
Stedman, Murray S., Jr. and Susan W. Stedman. *Discontent at the Polls: A Study of Farmer and Labor Parties, 1827–1948.* New York: Russell and Russell, 1967.
Stickney, Albert. *Democratic Government.* New York: Harper, 1885.
—— *A True Republic.* New York: Harper, 1879.
Sundquist, James L. *Dynamics of the Party System.* Rev. ed. Washington, D.C.: Brookings Institution, 1983.
Sunstein, Cass R. *Democracy and the Problem of Free Speech.* New York: Free, 1995.
Teixeira, Ruy A. *The Disappearing American Voter.* Washington, D.C.: Brookings Institution, 1992.
Truman, David. *The Governmental Process.* New York: Knopf, 1951.
Tully, James. "The Pen Is a Mighty Sword: Quentin Skinner's Analysis of Politics." *Meaning and Context: Quentin Skinner and His Critics.* Ed. James Tully. Princeton: Princeton UP, 1988. 7–25.

Weir, Margaret, and Marshall Ganz. "Reconnecting People and Politics." *The New Majority: Toward a Popular Progressive Politics*. Ed. Stanley B. Greenberg and Theda Skocpol. New Haven: Yale UP, 1997. 149–171.

Williams, Raymond. *Marxism and Literature*. Oxford: Oxford UP, 1977.

Wills, Garry. "The People's Choice." *New York Review of Books*, 12 August 1999. http://www.nybooks.com/nyrev

Wilson, James Q. *American Government*. 3d ed. Lexington, Mass.: Heath, 1986.

—— "Q." *Slate Magazine*, 3 November 2000. http://www.slate.msn.com

Wilson, James Q. and John J. DiIulio Jr. *American Government*. 7th ed. Boston: Houghton Mifflin, 1998.

Wolin, Sheldon. Foreword. *Political Parties in the American System*. Frank J. Sorauf. Boston: Little, Brown, 1964.

Woodburn, James. *American Politics: Political Parties and Party Problems in the United States*. New York: Putnam's, 1903.

Woodward, C. Vann. "The Populist Heritage and the Intellectual." *American Scholar* 29.1 (1959–1960): 55–72.

Young, Iris Marion. "Polity and Group Difference: A Critique of the Ideal of Universal Citizenship." *Ethics* 99 (January 1989): 250–274.

Yudice, George. "For a Practical Aesthetics." *The Phantom Public Sphere*. Ed. Bruce Robbins. Minneapolis: U of Minnesota P, 1993.

Index

POWER, CONFLICT, AND DEMOCRACY:
AMERICAN POLITICS INTO THE TWENTY-FIRST CENTURY
ROBERT Y. SHAPIRO, EDITOR

John G. Geer, *From Tea Leaves to Opinion Polls: A Theory of Democratic Leadership*
Kim Fridkin Kahn, *The Political Consequences of Being a Woman: How Stereotypes Influence the Conduct and Consequences of Political Campaigns*
Kelly D. Patterson, *Political Parties and the Maintenance of Liberal Democracy*
Dona Cooper Hamilton and Charles V. Hamilton, *The Dual Agenda: Race and Social Welfare Policies of Civil Rights Organizations*
Hanes Walton Jr., *African-American Power and Politics: The Political Context Variable*
Amy Fried, *Muffled Echoes: Oliver North and the Politics of Public Opinion*
Russell D. Riley, *The Presidency and the Politics of Racial Inequality: Nation-Keeping from 1831 to 1965*
Robert W. Bailey, *Gay Politics, Urban Politics: Identity and Economics in the Urban Setting*
Ronald T. Libby, *ECO-WARS: Political Campaigns and Social Movements*
Donald Grier Stephenson Jr., *Campaigns and the Court: The U.S. Supreme Court in Presidential Elections*
Kenneth Dautrich and Thomas H. Hartley, *How the News Media Fail American Voters: Causes, Consequences, and Remedies*
Douglas C. Foyle, *Counting the Public In: Presidents, Public Opinion, and Foreign Policy*
Ronald G. Shaiko, *Voices and Echoes for the Environment: Public Interest Representation in the 1990s and Beyond*
Hanes Walton Jr., *Reelection: William Jefferson Clinton as a Native-Son Presidential Candidate*
Demetrios James Caraley, editor, *The New American Interventionism: Lessons from Successes and Failures—Essays from* Political Science Quarterly
Ellen D. B. Riggle and Barry L. Tadlock, editors, *Gays and Lesbians in the Democratic Process: Public Policy, Public Opinion, and Political Representation*
Robert Y. Shapiro, Martha Joynt Kumar, Lawrence R. Jacobs, Editors, *Presidential Power: Forging the Presidency for the Twenty-First Century*
Kerry L. Haynie, *African American Legislators in the American States*
Marissa Martino Golden, *What Motivates Bureaucrats? Politics and Administration During the Reagan Years*
Geoffrey Layman, *The Great Divide: Religious and Cultural Conflict in American Party Politics*
Sally S. Cohen, *Championing Child Care*